WILDER SHORES

Robin Lucas was born in country Victoria in 1947, and often travelled by steam train to visit her Melbourne grandparents. She has also covered most of Australia in light aircraft and was navigator on many flights to Central Australia. She has been a literary columnist for the *Australian*, and is the author of *The Good Reading Guide*. She currently writes a weekly paperback review column for the *Sydney Morning Herald* from her home in the Glasshouse Mountains. Her favourite travel destination these days is Indonesia, where one of her daughters is living.

Clare Forster was born in Geelong in 1965 to an Irish mother and English father who came to Australia in the 1950s. The family later moved to Melbourne, although as a child she spent a year on tiny Ocean Island in the Gilbert and Ellice group (now Kiribati and Tuvalu). In the 1970s she moved to Townsville and later studied at the University of Queensland. She currently works in book publishing and has travelled in Canada, Ireland and Italy.

WILDER SHORES

WOMEN'S TRAVEL STORIES OF AUSTRALIA & BEYOND

EDITED BY ROBIN LUCAS & CLARE FORSTER

University of Queensland Press

First published 1992 by University of Queensland Press
Box 42, St Lucia, Queensland 4067 Australia

Typeset by University of Queensland Press
Printed in Australia by The Book Printer, Victoria

Publication of this title was
assisted by the Australia Council,
the Federal Government's arts
funding and advisory body

Cataloguing in Publication Data
National Library of Australia

Wilder shores: women's travel stories of Australia & beyond.

Bibliography.

1. Women — Travel. 2. Women travelers — Australia. I. Lucas,
Robin, 1947-   . II. Forster, Clare, 1965-   .

910.4082

ISBN 0 7022 2477 4

CONTENTS

JOURNEYS WITHIN

PREFACE

We always travel, travel, travel, travel to other places. We leave the camels, have a spell, help the camels up, let go the camels, you know, the bell ringing . . . . Take a lot of blankets and all, everything, water. There was my old man, my uncle and auntie, big mob, lot of them . . . . Everyone travel around.

Lorna Grantham[1]

My travels began in Sydney, in the suburb of Strathfield, where at the age of three I left home alone to go and see the turkey gobblers at a house a mile away . . . . Restlessness and moving around is certainly an Australian tradition. In all families whose forebears arrived on the continent since 1788 are those who had to make that enormous move to Australia in the first place.

Glenda Adams[2]

The diverse journeys gathered together in this first collection of Australian women's travel stories go far beyond the nineteenth-century cliche of good-hearted adventure stories by unusual spinsters.

Journeys and quests have played an important part in the formation of Australian society, as Glenda Adams comments above, and also in the establishment of national identity.[3] Sue Rowley, in her discussion of bush mythology, points out that it is largely men — ''explorers, immigrants, pioneers, drovers, shearers, gold-seekers, bushrangers and swagmen'' — who have traditionally embarked upon important Australian journeys.[4] Epics of such colonial exploration and exploitation mark out one version of this nation's origins. But the intricate wanderings described above by Lorna Grantham suggest that, for many thousands of years, journeys have provided other ways of understanding the land.

The narratives of such quests — real or imaginary — provide rich comment on our political, social and spiritual views of ourselves and others. Notions of place, of "home" and "away", have always influenced our personal and national identities.[5] The journey, often a potent metaphor for a psychological voyage, offers unique opportunities for myth-making.

When it is women who are the questers in a genre and mode which has been primarily male terrain, narratives of travel can start to shift and change in a number of ways. Unlike many of their male predecessors in literature, most of these journeyers do not travel a straight path of progress to the greater glory of their nation, or even to smaller personal epiphanies; these are voyages with ambiguous outcomes, multiple meanings, uncertain motives. Travel writing comments on the place and space women occupy in society, their own and others'; on the presentation of our private and public "selves"; and the ways in which we seek to define our identities. As illustrated in Kate Grenville's story, "The Space Between", gender becomes an intriguing complication in the role of being "foreign".[6]

The reasons for these journeys are as varied as the stories themselves — from political activism, family holidays, and escape from a stifling suburban marriage, to the search for an unknown mother, pilgrimage to a spiritual site, careers abroad, and return to the homeland. It is interesting to compare such motives to the romantic ones frequently presumed to be the "real story" behind women's travels. The collection's title, *Wilder Shores*, is souvenired from Lesley Blanch's study, *The Wilder Shores of Love*,[7] which explores the lives of four British women in the East at the close of the nineteenth century. We have appropriated the first half only of the phrase, to break away from the idea of women travelling "for love alone" — an idea which ultimately keeps them indoors, in the domestic, emotional sphere — and to make room for the consideration of other desires which might be operating in these journeys.

A map of this collection, and how we compiled it, may be helpful to the reader. It is only our own map, and we hope readers will feel free to deviate from its highways, and to make their own tracks through it.

We began with an enormous and tantalising amount of material: pilgrimages by each generation of non-Aboriginal Australians to "mother countries" (mostly European), and also encounters with Asia; journeys to Australia by pioneer and settler women, and refugees and migrants after World War II; journeys within Australia by Aboriginal women and others, in the outback, between country towns, and to the great seaboard cities.

We decided to arrange this material in three sections: "Arrivals" — journeys to Australia; "Away" — journeys abroad; and "Journeys Within" — travel within Australia. By grouping the material in these categories, we wanted to encourage new ways of thinking about travel, and about the connections between these stories. It was important, also, to avoid a narrow chronological approach, or showing preferences for some sorts of journey — and journeyers — above others.

"Arrivals" includes stories of postwar migrants like Rosa Cappiello's factory worker alongside the writing of early settlers like Ada Cambridge and the goldfields-bound visitor Ellen Clacy. "Away" has Jessica Anderson's Nora tracing the traditional route to London in her escape from an unsatisfactory marriage and disapproving family, Drusilla Modjeska's powerful, separate journeys to Crete by a mother and daughter, and writer and political activist Nettie Palmer in Barcelona in 1939. In "Journeys Within", Robyn Davidson treks the desert with a dog and her camels, Ruby Langford visits Uluru for the first time with a group of urban Aboriginal women, and Thea Astley remembers some bus and train journeys which led her to write the short story "Diesel Epiphany".

We aimed for an entertaining collection in which the journeys themselves would emerge; this meant that most of the narrators and characters would be on the move, in transit, rather than simply being somewhere new or exotic. These journeys are not necessarily long ones (Leanne Hollingsworth is on her way to Brisbane from Ipswich) but many share a sense of change, adventure, risk and curiosity (even those which are return journeys, like Charmian Clift's reflections on Australia after fifteen years abroad).

In view of the paths traced and retraced across the world between non-English speaking countries and Australia, we sought to represent writers from some of these places. The work of Aboriginal writers had a pressing claim, particularly in the section "Journeys Within". And realigning our axis in order to consider our much-discussed place in Asia meant that we frequently chose the Asian journey over the European one.

We drew on short stories and excerpts from novels, and a variety of nonfiction material — letters, diary entries, autobiography, journalism and essays, as well as the sort of "straight" travel account which has been traditionally classified as travel writing. Our choice of the term "stories" in the subtitle reflects the belief that all travel writing is fictionalised to some degree.

There are many modes of travel and many moods of travel in this collection. Louise Mack's 1901 voyage to London is wholly exuberant. Emma Ciccotosto is both excited and sad as she makes her way to Australia in the 1930s, while Eve Langley's quirky young woman is full of bravado as she and her sister, dressed as men, travel by train to Gippsland for seasonal work.

Wilder Shores contains trips by sailing ship, cutter, mule-powered litter, elephant, outrigger canoe, aeroplane, camel, car, wagon, buckboard, horseback and foot. Mabel Edmund is almost defeated by the London Underground, but struggles on with skinned knees and wounded dignity. Yasmine Gooneratne's Navaranjini (who renames herself Jean after living in Sydney for some time) imbues a simple cab ride with visions, and a solemn self-dedication to the task ahead. Another Jean, Jeannie Gunn, is slung across a river on a flying fox of wire, sitting uncomfortably in a surcingle borrowed from a pack-horse.

We hope these entertaining and varied stories will send readers eager for more to the original sources. Meanwhile, we invite you to set off, without delay, on these journeys of the imagination.

Robin Lucas
Clare Forster

Notes

1   Lorna Grantham in *Women of the Centre*, ed. Adele Pring (Apollo Bay: Pascoe Publishing, 1990), p. 83.

2   Glenda Adams, ''Beyond the Turkey Gobblers'' in *Inner Cities: Australian Women's Memory of Place*, ed. Drusilla Modjeska (Ringwood: Penguin, 1989), p. 17.

3   Scholarly discussions of Australian travel writing may be found in dissertations by John Borthwick and Margriet Bonnin; also in Laurie Hergenhan and Irmtraud Petersen's forthcoming collection of Australian travel writings on Europe between 1960 and 1990. An annotated bibliography of Australian travel writing, funded by the Australian Research Council, is currently being prepared by Ros Pesman, David Walker and Richard White with Terri McCormack.

4   Sue Rowley, ''The Journey's End: Women's Mobility and Confinement'', *Australian Cultural History*, ''Travellers, Journeys, Tourists'', vol. 10, 1991.

5   An issue explored in the travel collection *Home and Away*, ed. Rosemary Creswell (Ringwood: Penguin, 1985).

6   Further collections of women's travel writing include *Indiscreet Journeys: Stories of Women on the Road*, edited by Lisa St Aubin de Teran (London: Virago, 1989; Sceptre, 1991); and *The House on Via Gombito: Writing by North American Women Abroad*, edited by Madelon Sprengnether and C.W. Truesdale (Canada: New Rivers, 1991).

7   Lesley Blanch, *The Wilder Shores of Love* (J. Murray, 1954; London: Abacus, 1984).

ACKNOWLEDGMENTS

We would like to acknowledge Nicola Evans, Craig Munro, and Judy MacDonald for their encouragement and advice.

My thanks are due to Edit Daws, Geoffrey Dutton, Elaine McKay, and Ailsa Zainuddin.

— Robin Lucas

Thanks to those who've travelled with me, especially Craig, Sarah, and Rosemary.

— Clare Forster

For permission to reproduce the following material acknowledgment is made to Aboriginal Studies Press for Marnie Kennedy, "Hit the Road", from *Born a Half-Caste* (Canberra: Aboriginal Studies Press, 1985); to Allen & Unwin Australia for Nancy Keesing, "Once I Rode an Elephant", from *Riding the Elephant* (Sydney: Allen & Unwin, 1988); to Australian Literary Management for Elizabeth Jolley, "A Sort of Gift", from "A Sort of Gift: Images of Perth" in *Inner Cities: Australian Women's Memory of Place*, ed. Drusilla Modjeska (Ringwood: Penguin, 1989); to Cape UK for Robyn Davidson, "The Desert", from *Tracks* (London: Cape Books UK, 1980); to Collins Angus & Robertson Publishers for Mena Abdullah and Ray Mathew, "Because of the Rusilla", from *The Time of the Peacock* (Sydney: Angus & Robertson, 1965); Charmian Clift, "On Being a Home-Grown Migrant", from *Trouble in Lotus Land*, ed. Nadia Wheatley (Sydney: Collins Angus & Robertson); Eve Langley, "A Woman in

Man's Clothes", from *The Peapickers* (Sydney: Angus & Robertson, 1942); and Betty Roland, "Smuggling", from *Caviar for Breakfast* (Sydney: Collins Angus & Robertson, 1989); to Fremantle Arts Centre Press for Emma Ciccotosto, "The New World", from *Emma — A Translated Life*, with Michal Bosworth (Fremantle: Fremantle Arts Centre Press, 1990); and Vasso Kalamaras, "The Anchorage Was Not Blue", from *The Same Light* (Fremantle: Fremantle Arts Centre Press, 1989); to Rosemary Goldie for Dulcie Deamer, "India's Alleyways", from "The Golden Decade" (unpublished ML MSS 3173); to Methuen London Ltd for Henry Handel Richardson, "To School", from *The Getting of Wisdom* (London: Heinemann, 1910); to Hickson Associates Ltd for Thea Astley, "Why I Wrote a Story Called 'Diesel Epiphany' "; Janette Turner Hospital, "Changes and the Things that Don't Change: India 1977 and 1990", from "The Secret of India", in *Whig Standard Magazine*; and Georgia Savage, "Vietnam", from "Color Me Vietnam", in *Millenium: Time Pieces by Australian Writers*, hosted by Helen Daniel (Ringwood: Penguin, 1991); to Margaret Jones for "Sweet-and-Sour", from "Travels with Myself", in *Inner Cities: Australian Women's Memory of Place*, ed. Drusilla Modjeska (Ringwood: Penguin, 1989); to McPhee Gribble Publishers for Drusilla Modjeska, "To Crete", from *Poppy* (Ringwood: McPhee Gribble Publishers, 1990); to New South Wales University Press for Agnes Hodgson, "Granen", from *The Last Mile to Huesca: An Australian Army Nurse in the Spanish Civil War*, ed. J. Keene (Sydney: New South Wales University Press, 1988); to Pan Macmillan Publishers Australia for Jessica Anderson, "Reckless, Cynical and Frivolous", from *Tirra Lirra by the River* (Sydney: Pan Macmillan, 1978); Yasmine Gooneratne, "Navaranjini Takes Note of Signs and Visions", from *A Change of Skies* (Sydney: Pan Macmillan, 1991); to Pascoe Publishing for Lorna Grantham, "Every Rockhole a Story", from *Women of the Centre*, ed. Adele Pring (Apollo Bay: Pascoe Publishing, 1990); to Penguin Books Australia Ltd for Christina Stead, "The Flying Village", from "Another View of the Homestead", in *Ocean of Story*, ed. R.G. Geering (Ringwood: Penguin, 1985); Blanche d'Alpuget, "Chaos and Confusion", from *Turtle Beach* (Ringwood: Penguin, 1986); Kate Jennings, "Aunt Dot's Camel", from *Save Me, Joe Louis* (Ringwood: Penguin, 1988); and Ruby Langford, "Uluru", from *Don't Take Your Love to Town* (Ringwood: Penguin, 1988); to Penguin Books UK Ltd for Shirley

Hazzard, "Observing the Conventions", from *The Bay of Noon* (Harmondsworth: Penguin, 1973); to Random House UK Ltd for Joan Colebrook, "A World of Water", from *A House of Trees* (London: Chatto & Windus, 1988); to University of Queensland Press for joanne burns, "out of order", first published in *Meanjin*, 3/1990, reprinted in a slightly different form in *on a clear day* (St Lucia: University of Queensland Press, 1992); Rosa Cappiello, "The Migrant's Inferno", from *Oh Lucky Country* (St Lucia: University of Queensland Press, 1984); Margaret Coombs, "Regards to the Czar", from *Regards to the Czar* (St Lucia: University of Queensland Press, 1988); Jean Devanny, "Inland", from *Point of Departure*, ed. Carole Ferrier (St Lucia: University of Queensland Press, 1986); Mabel Edmund, "The Only Black Woman at Ealing Station", from *No Regrets* (St Lucia: University of Queensland Press, 1992); Marian Eldridge, "A Sense of Place", from *The Woman at the Window* (St Lucia: University of Queensland Press, 1989); Kate Grenville, "The Space Between", from *Bearded Ladies* (University of Queensland Press, 1985); Marion Halligan, "Hard Sausage", from *The Living Hothouse* (St Lucia: University of Queensland Press, 1988); Barbara Hanrahan, "Some Girls", from *Michael and Me and the Sun* (St Lucia: University of Queensland Press, 1992); Lolo Houbein, "Pacific Sidetracks", from *Wrong Face in the Mirror* (St Lucia: University of Queensland Press, 1989); Olga Masters, "The Getting Away", from *Amy's Children* (St Lucia: University of Queensland Press, 1987); Gillian Mears, "Aeroplane Jelly", from *Fineflour* (St Lucia, University of Queensland Press, 1990); Nettie Palmer, "Barcelona", from *Fourteen Years* reprinted in *Nettie Palmer: Her private journal* Fourteen Years, *poems, reviews and literary essays*, ed. Vivian Smith (St Lucia: University of Queensland Press, 1988); and Nancy Phelan, "Escape", from *The Romantic Lives of Louise Mack* (St Lucia: University of Queensland Press, 1991).

Acknowledgment is also made to Verdon Morcom for permission to reprint the pen drawings that accompanied the first edition of Nettie Palmer's *Fourteen Years* (Melbourne: Meanjin Press, 1948).

ARRIVALS

❧ *Christina Stead* ❧

The Flying Village

All night the sleeper sleeps close to a board, irons rattle, a violin played aft vibrates along the side, the body of the ship rises and falls, the engines beat on through seven hundred sleeps. The first day, yellow cliffs, blue coasts, next day, the steep green island south; a new world. Homeward bound on that ship in 1938, a Lithuanian woman in grey knitted skullcap, fifty-five, short, sour, salty; a tall English woman, eighty-four in black, small hat and scarf, who stands for hours by the lounge wall waiting for the Great Bear to rise; a missionary woman, thirty-nine, invalided home, worn by tropical disease, her soft dark skin like old chamois; she is going back to the town, street, church she left eighteen years before, because of a painful love-affair with the pastor: his wife now dead, he has just married a girl from the choir, "Just as I was then," she says. There's an Australian girl, lively, thin, black hair flying, doing tricks with a glass of water, by the big hold aft, and around her her new nation, Sicilians, her husband one — they are playing the fiddle. There's a redgold girlish mother from the Northern Rivers, scurrying, chattering, collecting cronies. Three times she booked for England, twice cancelled; the third time, her youngest daughter brought her to the boat in Sydney. Three unmarried daughters, "Oh, but we are not like other families; we cannot bear to part." Before Hobart, she telegraphs that she will land at Melbourne, go home by train; but they telegraph, "Go on, Mother, please." "They don't say how they are!" She is faded, sleepless. "What are they doing now?" At Melbourne, the women dissuade her and she goes on. Across the surly Bight they make her laugh at herself; she laughs and turns away, aggrieved. As we approach Fremantle, she is dreadfully disturbed; the ship may dock in the night and leave before morning. She sends a message to the Captain. At Fremantle, she telegraphs, disembarks, her rose color all back. "I'm going home! They'll be getting ready! Oh, what a party we'll have!" What about the presents? "I'll give them back; I did before."

There's a country minister and his wife, two dusty black bundles who conduct services in the cabin before a number of meek, coloured bundles in Sydney hats. The couple gain in stature the farther they travel, until in the Red Sea, having lost all provincial glumness, the minister shouldering tall against the railing, arm and finger stretched, explains the texts, the riddle of the Pyramids, the meaning of Revelations.

For years, I thought lazily about returning; and like that, it would be, in just such a varied society, myself unhampered, landing unknown, "Poor amongst the poor" (a line of Kate Brown's I always liked) and would see for myself. After I had looked round lower Sydney where I walked every morning and evening of my highschool college and work life, I would go out and stand in front of Lydham Hill, the cold sandstone cottage on a ridge which, from a distance looks east over Botany Bay, straight between Cape Banks and Cape Solander, to the Pacific; and the other way, due west, over a grass patch and the yellow road to Stoney Creek, to the Blue Mountains. That is how it was when my cousin and I lived there with other little ones and played in the long grass and under the old pines.

I knew all that was gone; they had driven surveyors' pegs into the gardens, the neglected orchard, before we left for Watson's Bay; and a friend in the Mitchell Library archives some years ago sent me coloured slides of the house that is. But still I would go and look at the homestead.

The other place — "Watson's"? By a magic that I came by by accident, I was able to transport Watson's noiselessly and as if it were an emulsion or a streak of mist to the Chesapeake; and truly, the other place is not there for me anymore; the magician must believe in himself. And then for long years I had a nightmare, that I was back at Watson's, without a penny saved for my trip abroad, my heart like a stone. It was otherwise. I came by air, the sailor dropped by a roc, Ulysses home without all that reconnoitering of coasts, a temporary citizen of a flying village with fiery windows, creaking and crashing across the star-splattered dark; and looking down on the horizontal rainbows which lie at dawn around Athens, around Darwin.

Unlike the ship, though close-packed as a crate of eggs, we travel with people we may hear but never see. There is only one street in the flying village and in it you mainly see children conducted up and down. Beside me, is a Greek-born mother with her Australian-born son, aged seven, she talking across the alley in English to her Greek-born neighbours, about the good life in Australia, the peace, the prospects, the education. What you hear in her tones is the good news, the rich boast delivered somewhere outside Athens to the grandparents; it is a wonderful country, we are lucky to be there, no social struggle, plenty of work, success ahead, money everywhere, no coloured people. (It turns out she thinks this.) Standing now in the alley stretching, a tall Italian proud that he has been in the country forty-two years (a year longer than my absence). There are fourteen children of all ages, three high-stomached young women hurrying out to give birth in the lucky place. Few get much sleep but all are goodtempered, it does not matter; their urge and hope is on, on. "Are you an Australian?" "Yes." I am looked at with consideration.

We are a day late, mysteriously stalled at Bangkok: and the talk is of husbands, friends waiting. It is a neighbourly climate — our friendships are nearly three days old; but there is no time for histories and secrets to come out. They will be met soon, go off by plane, train and car, I will never know them . . .

Under the soft spotted skies of the countries round the North Sea I had forgotten the Australian splendour, the marvellous light; the "other country" which I always had in me, to which I wrote letters and meant one day to return, it had softened, even the hills outlined in bushfire (which we used to see over Clovelly from Watson's Bay) were paler. The most exquisite thing in my recent life was a giant eucalypt on the North Shore as we turned downhill, the downward leaves so clear, the bark rags, so precise, the patched trunk, so bright. "Look at that tree!" It was outlined in light. It was scarcely spring, but the lawn outside the house was crowded with camellias, magnolias in bloom, even falling; at both dawn and dusk the kookaburras thrilling high in the trees, the magpies — I had quite forgotten those musicians and their audacity — and there was even a scary fiendish cry in the bush early; it came nearer, but remained distant. It was just a bantam cockerel — I had one myself years ago in Santa Fe and had forgotten the little dawn-demon with his one-string violin. Too long in London! Everything was like ringing and bright fire and all sharpness.

∾ *Ada Cambridge* ∾

On the Ship

We reached Plymouth at a ghastly hour before anybody was up. At the hotel recommended to us by our latest friend we were shown into a room where the dirty glasses and tobacco ashes of the night before still defiled the air and the tablecloth. Here we sat until a bedroom was ready for us, when we went to bed — which seemed a most useless proceeding — until there was a fair chance of getting breakfast. A bath and a good meal pulled us together, and then we went out for our last walk on English ground. A charming walk it was, exploring that old town — I would give something to be able to repeat it — and a sweet conclusion to our home life. We returned to our hotel for a bite of lunch, hired an old man and a barrow to trundle our few things (the heavy baggage having been put on board in London) to the waterside, and after him a waterman and a boat, and got out to our ship lying in the Sound — the first we saw of her — at a little before noon, which was her advertised sailing hour . . ..

We had one of the only large two cabins on the ship; the other was the captain's; the rudder clanked between us and him, behind the bulkhead at the end of our wide curved sofa, where the pillow, tucked into a bright rug, was a full-sized feather bed, a wedding present that at first we did not know what to do with, but which soon proved the most valuable of them all, as it still is, in the form of plenty of soft, fat cushions all over the house. I spent a large part of my days at sea reclining upon this downy mass, which began below my shoulderblades and sloped upward nearly to the ceiling; as I lay I could look out of and down from the row of stern windows that made one side of my couch, and watch the following birds and fishes — sometimes a shark be-

guiled with a piece of pork — without lifting my head. It was an
envied place in the tropics, when the air swept free to the main
deck through open doors; but in rough weather — and it was
nearly all rough weather — the swing of the seasaw was killing.
It used to fling me out of bed over a high bunk board until I was
black and blue . . .

I forget the hard-bottomed and treacherous bunks, the soon-
carpetless, soaked floors, the dancing table that shot fowls and
legs of mutton into our laps out of dish and fiddle, the cold that
one could find no shelter from except in bed, the terrible gales,
the incurable sea-sickness, the petty feuds of the lady passengers;
that is, I think of them as not worth thinking of, with the feeling
that it was finer to rough it a bit as we did than to be pampered at
every turn as sea-travellers are now, and in recognition of the fact
that my sufferings brought me many pleasures that otherwise I
should have been deprived of. The captain wanted to — only I
would not let him — give me his own swinging cot. The head
steward used to smuggle in mysterious parcels, which, when un-
wrapped, disclosed little dainties, specially prepared and hot
from the cooking-stove, to tempt her who was said to be "the
most sea-sick lady they had ever carried". The other ladies,
when not immersed in their social broils, from which my physical
state and geographical position detached me, were kindness itself. One of them gave me that nearly extinct article, a hair net —
it was the day of chignons, the manufacture of which was beyond
me — and seldom have I received a more useful gift. With my
hair tucked into this bag, dressing-gowned and shawled, I used to
go up after nightfall to a couch on the skylight; there I would
enjoy myself, feeling fairly well until I moved to go down again
— amused with the little comedies going on around me, and en-
raptured with the picture of the winged vessel as I looked up
through her labyrinth of rigging to the mastheads and the sky,
and then down and around at the sea and the night through
which she moved so majestically. Pictures of her sweeping
through a dream-like world of moonlight and mystery are indel-
ible in my mind. Sometimes the moonlight was so bright that we
played chess and card games by it on the skylight and about the
deck. At other times we lay becalmed, and I had my chance to
dress myself and enjoy the evening dance or concert, or whatever
was going on. But at the worst of times — even in the tremendous
storms, when the ship lay poop-rail under, all but flat on her
beam ends (drowning the fowls and pigs on that side), or plunged

and wallowed under swamping cross-seas that pounded down through smashed skylights upon us tumbling about helplessly in the dark — even in these crises of known danger and physical misery there was something exhilarating and uplifting — a sense of finely-lived if not heroic life, that may come to the coddled steamer passenger when the machinery breaks down, but which I cannot associate with him and his "floating hotel" under any circumstances short of impending shipwreck.

❦ *Gillian Mears* ❦

Aeroplane Jelly

The rinsed summer sky. The rich stained-glass red of a coiling river as the plane groans over the first clouds. The clouds are soft and fat. They cast shadows that Nadia can see floating in the water below. *What river?* She tries to think of the name of one major Victorian river. No name springs immediately from memory. It is years since she has flown over a country that sprawls into her mind like this, as Australia does, obliterating the need for names. *My country of birth*, she stretches to switch off the air conditioning vent. *My home.* It sounds like the title of a primary school essay. *Could the river be the Murray? The Murrumbidgee? The Myrtle?* Names from hot, listless geography lessons. The school clock creeping, the whole class waiting for the last bell which would mean release from the heat, permission to head for the river. The Fineflour River. *My childhood river.* Nadia can think fondly of it now. It is pretty to say and blue and wide in her mind.

Out of the distorting round window there are no obvious borders to be seen, no soldiers, no towns, no wars real or imagined. Just the river below that she can't name for certain and its tributary creeks growing leaner and leaner.

A few dams and farmhouses appear. The dams are shaped like small, crooked hearts. The sort Judy used to draw neatly in the back of their schoolbooks and then fill with the initials of all the boys who'd never even look their way.

The land looks empty. Too high now to make out if there are people below but Nadia can imagine the empty stretches of river, the kilometres of rivers with no-one swimming, the clear water, the cool secret gorges. Whereas in Israel on such a hot day, any river near a town would be a crazy place. The ocean the same and terribly polluted: toilet paper sodden in the waves. Once, somewhere near one of the territories, Nadia had pulled over, intending to give the children a quick dip in a river. It was one of those terrible days. August weather and no respite from the eighty per cent humidity. The heat had turned the unsealed roads into sand-dunes. The dust hung in the throats of her children and made them weep with anger. But that day there was no hope of a real swim. There was a small, dying park above the swimming hole. Around the roots of sick trees you could see the barest traces of dark, wet soil. The water boiled with life and small, dark bodies. Davey held her hand like a limp puppet and whimpered when she tried to take his shorts off. When a thin, white-haired girl entered the water she was nearly drowned in the rush to touch, stoke, tug at her white skin and hair. Her mother was in a bikini at one end of the small beach. She was so pregnant her belly touched the sand between her legs. She had to go swaying out into the river to rescue her girl. The Arab women put their hands to their mouths and cried out loudly to their own children. Nadia remembers how it all looked vaguely biblical. The parting of the waters. The dark-skinned children falling back, falling back until there was a distinct channel of clear river.

༄

The two air hostesses wear bright, ugly uniforms. Nadia giggles at the terrible koala and flower motifs. As the air hostesses wheel the drinks trolley, their mouths set into tough, thin, lipstick positions. The burgundy ribbons in their elaborate coiffures match their high burgundy heels. They approach Nadia as if she's foreign, deaf or delinquent. ''Tea? You'd like tea?'' The tall hostess with red hair leans across to pour tea into a plastic teacup. Nadia grins to see the elaborate plait and ribbon are falling out. By Albury-Wodonga where there's a change of plane to Sydney, the immaculate, unfriendly hair could be totally awry.

Everyone is crackling open their cellophane three-pack of Jatz crackers. Across the aisle the handsome boy with blond hair helps the dark-eyed four-year-old open his biscuits. *My sons.* Nadia watches them, leaning forward to see past the two men who have the aisle seats on her side of the plane. Her children are intent on each other. Rupert the bear sits between them. ''Rupy want some?'' Her smaller boy puts a fragment of cracker up to the teddybear.

''Davey, don't let Dufey be messy.'' David sucks in his cheeks. He is trying to be so good. Even after the tiring flight from London he can think of being good. He is concentrating on not spilling his milk tea or juice. The juice is in a sealed plastic cup. Neatly, he arranges the paper doily left by the air hostess. He positions the doily in the middle of the drinks tray and then takes a series of delicate sips. So neat. So immaculate, so like his real father who hasn't seen him since he was a toddler in nappies. So unlike Etai, his Israeli stepfather who loves and adores both the boys but who likes to live in wild disorder. Little Dufek is copying Davey, dabbing his lips with the paper napkin. They wriggle with laughter. Nadia whispers at them to be quiet without wanting them to be. The man next to Nadia asks would she like to swap seats to be near the children. She shakes her head and gestures at the window. "I want to watch Australia from the air."

The men next to her must be — agricultural scientists? They are talking about wilted silage and sewage sludge. Perhaps they are on their way home from a Melbourne conference? Their shirts are white and yellow, horizontal, wash'n'wear stripes. Fat pink nipples are easy to see. Sturdy, long socks are pulled up to their knees. David's father hated all public servants but the Department of Agriculture most of all. He hated the Department of Agriculture for not testing the acidity of the rose-sick-soil in his garden the day after he made the request. He was a selfish, impatient man with strange obsessions. Each morning after David's difficult birth, he'd visit his cacti: touching the bristles in the fond way he would never touch her again. And treating them — extra nitrogenous fertilisers to make the cacti grow weird little knobs and warty eyes that glowed in the dark. Even after he'd stopped loving her, he liked to surprise and shock. For Davey's first birthday, he organised a party. He invited people she barely knew and ordered the Aeroplane Jelly factory in Sydney to manufacture special blue and white crystals. They arrived by air freight express post, fifteen hours before January 26th, Australia Day, David's date of birth. She was to assemble a jelly cake, in the shape of the flag. He bought the appropriate star-shaped moulds back from his shop and left them for her with the jelly crystals on the kitchen table.

The Aeroplane Jelly cake, in the shape and colours of the Australian flag, was the centrepiece of the table decorations. It sat in a tray of ice to stop it from melting. The guests brought lavish gifts and picked at smoked salmon roulades and delicately assembled vol-au-vents. The jelly cake quivered. It shook and trembled like her heart beating through her milk into David's mouth. He sucked in her heartbeat. He bit her with his sharp, new teeth but she kept feeding him so as not to go outside. From behind the darkened glass of the baby room she could see out into the garden. Under the coloured fairy lights, bunches of children ran in and out of the azalea grove in secretive mobs. They clutched the small packets of sweets she'd assembled the night before and grew restless for the cutting of the cake. Instead of a birthday candle, there was a single, beautifully stitched linen flag. The blue jelly shone like the glassy, chemical blue waters of the swimming pool. But it was a big hit with all the children. They interrupted "Happy Birthday To You" to sing the Aeroplane Jelly jingle instead. Their parents didn't seem to care for their children. They kept their expensive frocks and suits away from sticky fingers, they shooed their children away and flirted delicately with one another.

From the baby room, Nadia watched the flight of the children back into the old azaleas. The darting glimpses of their bright party clothes caught Davey's eyes so that he chuckled fatly and playfully grabbed at her swinging breasts with his small hands. She shivered to see David's father eddy past the window with a thin, beautiful woman clinging to his arm. His aged face was full of charm and animation. Nadia went into the kitchen to stop watching the party. The empty packets of jelly sat on the kitchen bench. She sat on a stool rocking David to sleep while with one free hand she crunkled the jelly packets. "Above all" said the Aeroplane Jelly logo around a red graphic of a jumbo jet. "Above all!" It had a triumphant ring that made the tears roll uncontrollably down her face and onto David's sweet smelling scalp. In the morning the flag cake, what was left of it, had maintained some shape. The red jelly was full of child-sized finger marks: the bored exploratory holes of the last children to leave the party.

༜

As the plane descends for Albury-Wodonga, Nadia calls out in Hebrew to make David do up his and Dufek's seatbelts. The use of another language makes the two agricultural scientists look vaguely alarmed. They rearrange their groins, have a bit of a scratch and stop telling anti-women, anti-affirmative action jokes.

Durfek and David race across the tarmac. They run on strong, sturdy legs towards the tiny, tin-roofed airport building.

One of the scientists helps her with her hand luggage. He blushes. "There you go, kiddo," he says and the blush travels right across his baldness. Nadia hears the other one, who is also balding, teasing him about his embarrassment and lack of hair.

"It's all that testosterone surging through you."

"It's knowing a good-looking bird when you see one."

When Nadia glances back at them, they're both fiddling what remains of their hair across the bare bits. Their large freckled boof heads remind her of Australian men she thought she had long forgotten.

"Look! Look at that man in the white dress. Maybe he's from Israel too. Do you think, Mummy?" Dufek calls out in loud English at the sight of an immaculate priest hurrying through the airport door. The priest holds the door open for an old woman and then is caught by his own politeness into keeping the door open for the surge of other passengers.

David and Dufek have seated themselves next to two small girls. The girls have arms covered in thick, blond hair. There are blond hairs on their fingers and both wear rings, trinkets and bluebird earrings. The smell of sunstan cream oozes from their white-gold skin. They're eating candy from inside green, plastic skulls. They carry Donald Duck comics in a possessive way.

"You ever been on a jet?" one of the girls nudges David. She is bossy and the freckles burst across her face. "Have you?" Under the fluorescence, her freckles are luminous and green.

"We've been on a jumbo," David stares straight ahead. "From Israel. We're on holiday."

"You've got a funny voice. Want a skeleton jube?"

"No, thank you," he sucks in his cheeks. Dufek is singing to himself and staring in a fixed way at the skeleton jubes.

"Gee whizz. A jumbo jet. Hear that, Jacinta!"

"He's got a funny voice," says Jacinta and goes back to Donald Duck.

Dufek peers under his chair. "Mummy," he says. "Spidernets."

Jacinta and her sister clutch their sides and roll their eyes. "Spider*webs*, we call them here."

Going across the tarmac to the Sydney plane, David stays close to Nadia. He is full of relief when the two blond girls are seated right away. Nadia knows how he feels. The agricultural scientists are also at the other end of the plane.

The connecting plane to Sydney is smaller than the one

they've just been on. They're all sitting together this time, next to the left wing exit sign. The flimsy walls of the plane rattle as they lift off. Dufek crows as the wheels fold and disappear. David follows through the safety procedures of the card provided. Dufek begins to whine. He wants to get out his wooden duck on a stick. He wants a sweetie. He wants a drink. He wants Daddy Etai. "I want my duck and I want it NOW." His voice has taken on a particularly dangerous note. Nadia notices the steward has a sweet, boyish face too. Undeniably gay. Undeniably kind. He kneels down next to Dufek and offers him a peppermint from his own pocket. Close up, the steward's face is incredibly, beautifully perfect. It takes her breath away. Already she feels full of lust for Etai who is impossibly far off; full of longing for the warm, close touch of someone who loves unconditionally. Something — some look — must pass across her face because the steward squeezes her shoulder and asks if she's all right.

"Yeah. Thank you. Thanks very much for the peppermint. Dufey. Say thank you to the man."

"Alfred."

"Say thank you to Alfred."

He leaves half the peppermint pack with David and half with Dufek. He winks to make them smile.

Nadia watches the steward's lean walk and is surprised by the sharpness of lewd images filling her mind. It would never happen in Tel Aviv. Such desire. Such freedom. Such a conscious flaunting of a good bum!

Sydney is not far away. Dufek falls asleep. His small lips pant the smell of mint. Outside the sky is incredibly blue. Approaching Sydney, Nadia feels her heart turning bumpy with emotion. Judy has promised to be there to meet them.

"We'll sweep through the southern suburbs and head for Neilsen Park!" During the phone conversation from Melbourne Judy's voice was high with excitement.

What was Neilsen Park, Nadia wonders as the plane touches down. Botany Bay bobs with pleasure craft. "Wake him up. Wake Dufey up." Davey shakes his little brother's round head.

"See. See. It is Sydney, Dufek. Dear old Sydney where our mate Judy lives. Where Davey and I lived for just a bit. Before you were born, huh? Long time ago. We'll have to look hard to not miss Judy. Have to keep eyes peeled, okay?"

Gravely, Dufek and David turn their faces to the window.

"Be *happy*, you little bastards."

They grin uneasily, staring out towards the fleet of Qantas jumbos in the distance.

"But how will we know? How do we *know* which one?" David wrinkles his nose.

"You'll know."

"But how?"

"Because she'll be striding our way. She'll be the prettiest one with the pretty hair. You'll see. Don't worry."

Above All. Nadia thinks of the Aeroplane Jelly logo and tries to stay calm. *Above All*. She hopes she won't cry. Now the moment of reunion is almost upon them, she feels a mixture of pride and emotion. She brushes the hair of the children hastily, breathing deeply. She breathes deeply the way she was taught when pregnant with Dufek.

"Dufey and Davey. Ready?"

"Call us by our proper names," says David. He hangs his head with shyness and temper. He kicks her ankle.

Above All.

Struggling towards the terminal, Nadia gets out Dufek's wood duck. *Above All*. She hopes Davey isn't going to sulk. The rubber feet of the duck slap the cement in a steady, happy rhythm. *Above All*. She repeats the words like a favourite, soothing mantra that will not fail, and hums the jingle so loudly that David tugs at her hand.

"Everyone will look . . . Mum," he is pleading.

Above All. "Don't worry mate. I'll shut up now," she holds his sweaty little hand and together they follow Dufek and his duck inside the terminal.

There seems to be an excess of short men in stretch denim jeans. She scans the arrival lounge. She notices a man — little and old and skin-cancered — looking just as panicky as she feels. He is all dressed up. His tie flaps the wrong way; *100% Polyester* says the little label. Nadia would straighten it up for him, only at that moment, there is Jude, she thinks, and begins to run as if the speed of a collision will wipe out any clumsiness of greeting.

✤ *Emma Ciccotosto* ✤

The New World

The day we left the farm everything looked just as it always had. I trotted beside the donkey that my mother was riding while my brother-in-law walked with us into town. We left my sister in charge of everything. She stood by the road waving and was so upset to see us go that she fainted away. There was nothing we could do. My mother began to cry and she cried all the way into Casalbordino, where we picked up a lift to Vasto and the train station. Her sisters took care of my sister, but nothing ever replaced that bond between my mother and her eldest child. At Vasto we met another mother who was in tears. She was farewelling her daughter, Anna, who was travelling to Australia in the same boat as us to meet her husband whom she had married by proxy. The mother said to my mother, "Look after her for me, she is so young". She was only twenty, and it was a long way to be going to meet a new husband. I have never forgotten the pain of those goodbyes.

✤

It was at Vasto that I first saw a train, and I was so excited when we actually boarded it. In spite of all the sadness of saying goodbye there was something bubbling along inside me — so many new things were happening. I couldn't wait to see the sea, but I did not see it until we reached Naples. Our train trip started at night, and although we went along the coast I couldn't see a thing. We sat upright on hard wooden seats which didn't make my mother any happier. She was worried about travelling, because we had never done it before. I was too excited to worry.

Naples was the biggest city we had ever seen and it was to be some years before I saw anything bigger. It was noisy and confusing when we arrived, but we did eventually find our way to the port and our ship, the *Remo*, and I saw the sea. The Bay of Naples was as blue as could be, and the sea was huge.

Before we could board we had to pass a medical examination, and all I can remember of that now is the nit comb. My hair was long and it was agony to have a fine-toothed nit comb dragged through it, and worse when the nurse actually found a couple of nit eggs. My hair had been carefully washed and cleaned by my aunts before we left home so I was upset at this. Nits were common in those days, for no one bathed as much as we do today. When my father came back from the First World War, my mother had to throw away his clothes, which were crawling with lice, and scrub him back and front to get rid of them from his body. Things were never that bad again, but without a supply of running water or a bathroom, people like us washed daily, but bathed once a week.

When we were finally allowed on the ship we made our way down many stairs to find our beds in the *camerone*. This was a dormitory which we shared with twenty-eight other women and girls. It was the cheapest way to travel to Australia. There was a row of fifteen double bunks along one side of the cabin. I had the top one and my mother took the bottom, and we stowed our case beneath it. There were portholes to let in the fresh air, but I can still remember the smell of that part of the ship, so I don't think they were open very often. Attached to this room was a bathroom with a toilet and shower. It was the first time I had seen a shower and I enjoyed finding out how it worked.

Because of the smell downstairs I stayed on deck as much as I could for most of the trip. I liked watching the sea and I also liked playing the deck games that were provided for us. Travelling that way we quickly became friendly with the other passengers in the *camerone*. There were other girls my age to talk to and get to know. We explored the ship as much as we could, although we were forbidden to go into the first-class areas. Yet one day we managed to do that too. We stole away one mealtime and got as far as the first-class dining room where we could see what the others were eating. Our food wasn't marvellous. We ate a lot of soup, and I remember filling myself up on bread rolls which I loved, but the first-class passengers had much more elaborate dishes. They sat at small tables, too, while we sat at long, big ones. It looked so nice to me that I decided straight away that if I ever travelled again I would go first class.

This boat trip was full of new experiences for me. It was part of a shedding of an old way of life in preparation for the new, for it was on the boat that I began to see that our busy life on the farm was one which not everyone had shared. Some girls even had short hair! One of my new friends persuaded me to have my hair cut and to have a perm. I took a couple of weeks to be brave enough to ask my mother for permission, because she had never had her hair cut, but in the end she allowed me. I couldn't believe how different I looked.

Yet despite all this newness of understanding, underneath I remained anxious. I was worried about leaving home and I missed my sister and her son and my aunt Zia Ermilia quite intensely. That was when I looked back, which I couldn't help doing. When I looked forward to what was coming to us, I was even more uncertain. I worried about meeting my father. I could not remember him at all. I don't remember any photograph of him from those early years, so I don't think I had any idea of what he looked like apart from what my mother said, and she was a bit vague, because she too was nervous about meeting him again. I could not imagine what it was going to be like living in a house with a father as well as a mother.

We sailed from Naples in 1939, just before the Second World War broke out. It started while we were at sea and our captain decided that he could not take the risk of continuing to Australia with what might be a boatload of unwanted migrants so, despite the fact that Italy was still neutral, he waited near Singapore until he was informed by the Australian authorities that he could proceed. He hid the boat beside a small island for about six days. After two or three days we noticed that we were being given less bread at each meal. Rumours sped around the ship, that we would all be sent back, or put into concentration camps on our arrival. We were not supposed to call in at Singapore, but we had to after this delay because we needed more supplies. We stayed there for about ten hours, and were allowed off the ship to visit the town, which in those days was a little way from the docks. We didn't go in, although we did get off the boat to walk along the dock, and I still remember the surprise of seeing women dressed in saris. But some of our friends did make the trip into the town. We had all been told that we had to be back on board by a certain time or else the ship would sail without us. The time went very quickly and eleven passengers did not get back to the ship in time. The *Remo* sailed and they were left in Singapore without their clothes, their papers or their money. They had a very bad time for a while, but they did get to Australia in the end.

On the morning we were to dock at Fremantle we were up early waiting to see land. When we could see it I thought it looked very strange because all we could see were some trees. Where were the houses, the towns? On the ship, the transit passengers, the ones who were planning to get off and sightsee and then continue with the boat, had their papers processed first. Those of us who were landing and staying came second, so it took ages and ages to get off the ship. When we docked we stood at the rail, looking at the crowd gathered there to greet us. My mother was wearing a special dress she had saved for this occasion, it was navy blue with tiny white spots, and I was wearing my winter coat. The first person we recognised was my brother, who was waving at us, and then my mother said, "There is your father". I looked at him, he had a moustache, and I felt very strange. I said to myself, "I can't call him papa".

Eventually we got through all the formalities and we met. When my father kissed me I could feel the stiffness of his moustache and I didn't like it. I didn't know what to say to him. My brother was very pleased to see us again. He had just bought himself a utility truck which he was very proud of, and we all sat together in the front of this truck as he drove us into Perth where we stayed our first night in Australia in a boarding-house. We spent that night at a wedding celebration in North Perth given by Anna and her new husband. We were the only friends she had and she wanted us there. I could see immediately, even in North Perth with its old houses, that people in Australia had more things than we had ever had in Casalbordino, yet I was unsure of how to react.

The following day we saw a bit of Perth, although I cannot remember very clearly where we were taken, and then we drove out to my father's farm. It was at Waroona, near Harvey. He and my brother had bought it after two hard years of digging potatoes for other farmers in that area. During this trip I had to sit on my father's lap, as there was no other way of transporting the four of us in the cab of the ute. I was so shy of my father. He was a complete stranger to me and I didn't know whether I liked him or not. I could not call him "Papa". It took me months to be able to do this and even then I was not easy about it. My brother told me he had been the same. "I call him Papa", he said, "but still it doesn't feel right".

The farm was about three kilometres beyond Waroona. We left the good road and turned on to a sand track which wound up-hill through the bush. The sand was so deep that the utility began to sway from side to side and my stomach began to feel upset and nervous. We saw some cows in a clearing and my father said they were his. I looked around and I could see nothing but bush and sand, and I said to myself, "We are in a desert here".

When we reached the house it was getting dark, so we couldn't see a great deal outside. The house itself was bigger than the one we had left, but it was old and made of weatherboard which I thought looked funny after the mud brick houses I was used to seeing in Italy. But here I had a room of my own with a window that opened out to the verandah and — luxury of luxuries — there was an outside dunny that my father emptied each week. Water came from a tank outside the kitchen and from a well when the tank ran dry. The kerosene lamps where much brighter than the oil ones back home and my mother had a cooking range rather than an open fire.

The next morning when I woke up I was surprised to look out of the windows in the house and see only bush. Where were the other people, I wondered? My mother had the same feeling. Even breakfast was strange. My father told us there was plenty of meat in the cooler and eggs and butter to cook with. "What is butter?" I asked him. He showed me and told me that I should spread it on toast and have it with coffee for breakfast. I had never seen butter before. Butter, combined with the strange un-familiar landscape outside, made me realise I was in a different country. When we asked my father where our neighbours were he said, "Down there", waving in the direction of the hillside covered with scrub, before he stumped out to do the milking. My mother and I flung our arms about each other and cried and cried. It was my first realisation of the distance we had come and of the impossibility of return.

Elizabeth Jolley

A Sort of Gift

Perhaps there is something invisible which a person is given early in life, a sort of gift, but the giver of it, not expecting any thanks, is never given it.

My father liked what he called a splendid view. He would dismount from his high bicycle and, parting the hedge, he would exclaim on the loveliness of what he could see. We would have to lean our bicycles up against a fence or a gate, scramble across the wet ditch and peer through the rain-soaked hedge at a sodden field or a dismal hill hardly visible through the rain mist. But first something about his bicycle. This may seem irrelevant but perhaps it is necessary to say that the bicycle was enormous; twenty-eight inch wheels and a correspondingly large frame. He collected the parts and made it himself, and once, when it was stolen he went round the barrows and stalls in the Bullring market place in Birmingham and bought back all the parts as he recognised them and rebuilt it. I mention this because it shows something of the kind of man he was.

We had to ride bicycles too. When I was six I had a twenty-four inch wheel with hand brakes, left and right, back and front respectively.

"Never use the right hand brake before you use the left," my father said. Excellent advice of course but my problem then was that I was not sure about my left hand and my right. The back mudguard had small holes in it for strings which were meant to keep a lady's skirt from getting caught in the spokes. I was terribly ashamed of these small holes and wished I could fill them in with thick paint or something . . .

The reason that I mention all this is because I believe that my own love of what my father called *scenery* or a *splendid view* comes in part from the bicycle rides he insisted upon. We had to go with him. The bicycle rides through the rural edges of the Black Country in England were his relaxation and pleasure. We stopped frequently while he studied gravestones in small over-grown cemeteries and explained about lychgates. He told us about turnpike houses and about towing paths and locks — those mysterious sluice gates so powerful in altering the water levels in the canals. My own love of the quality of the air comes too, I re-alise, from my father who often simply stood at the roadside en-joying what he declared was fresh air, *unbreathed air*. He marvelled at the beech trees in the fenced parklands of the wealthy. He paused before fields and meadows explaining about the rotation of crops and about fallow fields. He was inclined to make a lesson out of everything. To him health and learning were the means to a particular form of freedom and the bicycle was the way in which to achieve these.

I developed the habit in my letters to my father of describing in detail the places where I lived and through which I journeyed. Wherever I went to I was always composing, in my head, my next letter to him . . ..

Is it possible to hear an image? Something unforgettable is the screaming and complaining of a flock of black cockatoos as they fly over waters changed by gale and heavy rain. One of the ques-tions I am asked from time to time is, has it made a difference to my writing coming to live in Western Australia? And what would my writing be like if I had stayed in Britain. There is no answer to the second question, I am unable to answer it. To the first, of coruse, there *is* a difference. Until I came to Western Australia I had never seen or heard a flock of cockatoos. These marauding birds, heralding a mysteriousness unfathomable to us, fly low, al-most breasting the choppy waves of the river swollen with rain-storm and purple brown with top soil washed down from the vineyards in the Swan valley. As the cockatoos disappear the rain bird calls, little phrases of bird notes climbing up in among the flame tree flowers brilliant against the dark clouds. Drops of water quiver on the fencing wire and the thin narrow leaves of the eucalypts tremble. To come to this country is to come to foreign land.

How can I be the same person after the flight of the cockatoos? The images of Western Australia on arrival made and continue to make an impact. They serve, too, to sharpen the images from the places where I was before.

Can air be described as an image? Can it really be as my father used to think it was? Fresh and unbreathed?

It seemed, on my first visit to the vineyards in the wide sand plain through which the Swan River flows (close to Perth) that the air there was light and clean and softly refreshing. The sweet fragrance I discovered came from the flowers of the beans growing between the vines. Later, I was told, the stalks would be ploughed back into the earth. The road through the vineyards was crossed then by sandy tracks and there was a fig tree standing in a sandy patch just back off the road. A rough trestle table stood under the tree and some scales hung in one of the lower branches. Behind the golden tranquillity which seemed to drop from the heart of the fig tree there was a small shabby weatherboard and iron house. The wooden planks of the table were piled with melons and the sweet muscat grapes.

This place, after a great many years, is still there. Whenever I pass the place now, though I am unable to see it as I saw it the first time (it is always hard to recapture something exactly), I never fail to feel again a deep excitement. I *gave* the place, on my first visit, to my character *Uncle Bernard*. I caused him to think it would be his.

There was a time when writers, some writers, felt they had to deny their regions. But it is in the very places where you live and walk and carry out the small things of living that the imagination, from some small half-seen or half-remembered awareness, springs to life and goes on living.

I never thanked my father for giving me the gift of looking. I was never able to show him the places which he would have liked very much. I could only describe them for him first in my letters and later in some of my fiction. I do not regret that I never thanked him because he understood that some things do not come back to the parent from the child.

⊸ *Mrs Charles Clacy* ⊸

Camping Up

*Ellen Clacy arrived in Australia in 1852, a year after gold was
discovered.*

The anxiously-expected morning at length commenced, and
a dismal-looking morning it was — hazy and damp, with a
small drizzling rain, which, from the gloomy aspect above,
seemed likely to last. It was not, however, sufficient to damp our
spirits, and the appointed hour found us all assembled to attack
the last meal that we anticipated to make for some time to come
beneath the shelter of a ceiling. At eight o'clock our united party
was to start from the "Duke of York" hotel, and as that hour
drew nigh, the unmistakable signs of "something up," attracted
a few idlers to witness our departure . . . .

In every belt was stuck either a large knife or a tomahawk; two
shouldered their guns (by the bye, rather imprudent, as the sight
of fire-arms often brings down an attack); some had thick sticks,
fit to fell a bullock; altogether, we seemed well prepared to encounter an entire army of bushrangers. I felt tolerably comfortable perched upon our dray, amid a mass of other soft lumber; a
bag of flour formed an easy support to lean against; on either side
I was well walled in by the canvas and poles of our tent; a large
cheese made a convenient footstool. My attire, although well
suited for the business on hand, would hardly have passed muster
in any other situation. A dress of commonly dark blue serge, a
felt wide-awake, and a waterproof coat drapped around me,
made a ludicrous assortment.

Going along at a foot-pace we descended Great Bourke Street,
and made our first halt opposite the Post-office, where one of our

party made a last effort to obtain a letter from his lady-love, which was, alas! unsuccessful. But we move on again — pass the Horse Bazaar — turn into Queen Street — up we go towards Flemington, leaving the Melbourne cemetery on our right, and the flag-staff a little to the left; and now our journey may be considered fairly begun . . ..

Saturday, 18. — Fine day; we now approached Bendigo. The timber here is very large. Here we first beheld the majestic iron bark, *Eucalypti*, the trunks of which are fluted with the exquisitive regularity of a Doric column; they are in truth the noblest ornaments of these mighty forests. A few miles further, and the diggings themselves burst upon our view. Never shall I forget that scene, it well repaid a journey even of sixteen thousand miles. The trees had been all cut down; it looked like a sandy plain, or one vast unbroken succession of countless gravel pits — the earth was everywhere turned up — men's heads in every direction were popping up and down from their holes. Well might an Australian writer, in speaking of Bendigo, term it "The Carthage of the Tyre of Forest Creek." The rattle of the cradle, as it swayed to and fro, the sounds of the pick and shovel, the busy hum of so many thousands, the innumerable tents, the stores with large flags hoisted above them, flags of every shape, colour, and nation, from the lion and unicorn of England to the Russian eagle, the strange yet picturesque costume of the diggers themselves, all contributed to render the scene novel in the extreme.

We hurried through this exciting locality as quickly as possible; and, after five miles travelling, reached the Eagle Hawk Gully, where we pitched our tents, supped, and retired to rest — though, for myself at least, not to sleep. The excitement of the day was sufficient cure for drowsiness.

Let us take a stroll round Forest Creek — what a novel scene! — thousands of human beings engaged in digging, wheeling, carrying, and washing, intermingled with no little grumbling, scolding and swearing. We approach first the old Post-office Square; next our eye glances down Adelaide Gully, and over the Montgomery and White Hills, all pretty well dug up; now we pass the Private Escort Station, and Little Bendigo. At the junction of Forest, Barker, and Campbell Creeks we find the Commissioners' quarters — this is nearly five miles from our starting point. We must now return to Adelaide Gully, and keep alongside Adelaide Creek, till we come to a high range of rocks, which we cross, and then find ourselves near the head-waters of

Fryer's Creek. Following that stream towards the Loddon, we pass the interesting neighbourhood of Golden Gully, Moonlight Flat, Windless and Red Hill; this latter which covers about two acres of ground is so called from the colour of the soil, it was the first found, and is still considered as the richest auriferous spot near Mount Alexander. In the wet season, it was reckoned that on Moonlight Flat one man was daily buried alive from the earth falling into his hole. Proceeding north-east in the direction of Campbell's Creek, we again reach the Commisioners' tent.

The principal gullies about Bendigo are Sailor's, Napoleon, Pennyweight, Peg Leg, Growler's, White Horse, Eagle Hawk, Californian, American, Derwent, Long, Piccaninny, Iron Bark, Black Man's, Poor Man's, Dusty, Jim Crow, Spring, and Golden — also Sydney Flat, and Specimen Hill — Haverton Gully, and the Sheep-wash. Most of these places are well-ransacked and tunnelled, but thorough good wages may always be procured by tin dish washing in deserted holes, or surface washing.

It is not only the diggers, however, who make money at the Gold Fields. Carters, carpenters, storemen, wheelwrights, butchers, shoemakers, &c., usually in the long run make a fortune quicker than the diggers themselves, and certainly with less hard work or risk of life. They can always get from £1 to £2 a day without rations, whereas they may dig for weeks and get nothing. Living is not more expensive than in Melbourne: meat is generally from 4*d.* to 6*d.* a pound, flour about 1*s.* 6*d.* a pound, (this is the most expensive article in housekeeping there,) butter must be dispensed with, as that is seldom less than 4*s.* a pound, and only successful diggers can indulge in such articles as cheese, pickles, ham, sardines, pickled salmon, or spirits, as all these things, though easily procured if you have gold to throw away, are expensive, the last-named article (diluted with water or something less innoxious) is only to be obtained for 30*s.* a bottle.

The stores, which are distinguished by a flag, are numerous and well stocked. A new style of lodging and boarding house is in great vogue. It is a tent fitted up with stringy bark couches, ranged down each side the tent, leaving a narrow passage up the middle. The lodgers are supplied with mutton, damper, and tea, three times a day, for the charge of 5*s.* a meal, and 5*s.* for the bed; this is by the week, a casual guest must pay double, and as 18 inches is on an average considered ample width to sleep in, a tent 24 feet long will bring in a good return to the owner.

The stores at the diggings are large tents generally square or oblong, and everything required by a digger can be obtained for money, from sugar-candy to potted anchovies; from East India pickles to Bass's pale ale; from ankle jack boots to a pair of stays; from a baby's cap to a cradle; and every apparatus for mining, from a pick to a needle. But the confusion — the din — the medley — what a scene for a shop walker! Here lies a pair of herrings dripping into a bag of sugar, or a box of raisins; there a gay-looking bundle of ribbons beneath two tumblers, and a half-finished bottle of ale. Cheese and butter, bread and yellow soap, pork and currants, saddles and frocks, wide-awakes and blue serge shirts, green veils and shovels, baby linen and tallow candles, are all heaped indiscriminately together; added to which, there are children bawling, men swearing, store-keeper sulky, and last, not *least*, women's tongues going nineteen to the dozen.

∽ *Rosa Cappiello* ∾

The Migrant's Inferno

The sky here compensates for solitude. Blue-clouded. Cloudy blue. Intensely blue. It's not the promised land. Maybe in the distant future it'll be the last one on earth — the basis is here for the much-vaunted lucky country — but for the moment it's neither the realisation of one's dreams nor the land of milk and honey. It's a kaleidoscope of dances: gigs, gavottes, minuets, boogiewoogies, twists, madisons, rhumbas, often of burps and farts which catch you full in the face at the pictures or at a party.

Over-exasperated thoughts. Not produced by a rigorous process of logic but by the rhythm of personal and impersonal emotions. Well-sifted on the migrant bus and then refined at the hostel or in the streets. Right at the start I felt like saying to hell with it all and commented ironically on, of all things, the subject of public toilets! This land we had to conquer did not seem to stimulate our sense of the ridiculous or the poetic but rather our hope, the unforeseen and the unforeseeable. What struck me was the unforeseeable. Oh, to discern a time-worn grey-stone urinal in some corner of a public square! What sort of people were these Australians? Where did they answer the call of nature? In the little square asymmetric red brick houses as arid and depersonalised as their souls. In my most intimate being a stone urinal in the shade of a gum tree was all I wanted as a background monument to my long-awaited celebration-initiation. It was a decidedly negative impact. How could I be so hard-boiled at the very moment that the city was welcoming me with open arms? Where I longed for the human touch expressed in the architectural lines of a public toilet, the other girls missed their mothers, a terminated love affair, the national anthem, the promenades in the main street, the display of elegance, human understanding. My travelling companions were better than I, more sensitive, more refined. They took in their surroundings by degrees, reaching ill-defined conclusions which, later on, they would have to take back with a curse. It would come to them while they were awake. Mysteriously and inhumanly wronged, they would lower their heads and cry. For years they felt shattered because they had got all mixed up about brotherhood, manners and togetherness. They had a very high price to pay.

In the space of a few hours I took in so many strange things that the brain could hardly register them. The novelty of Christmas in summer held me spellbound. We got off the boat at Sydney on 24 December, an iridescent sun-soaked day which abruptly separated me from another time, another culture, another life, and projected me towards a dualistic conception. Discontinuous eurhythmy, I think it was, because excitement, fear, and the remains of the euphoria which were stuck on me like a label on boarding ship combined to strangle my adenoids.

When we arrived at the hostel a few witless old women took us in charge. We soon got the hang of the inhabitants of this particular zoo: lesbians, expectant mothers, delirious old women, dole bludgers, drug addicts, sluts, misfits, divorcees. The stench of the poorhouse, cockroaches, worn carpets, cats, orders in an incomprehensible language. Then the first, second and third floors, dark and damned with the sleeping cells all boxed in one inside the other. A prison. You go to prison to be punished. We must have made some mistake. Maybe in our choosing.

The doghouse assigned to me didn't have windows. A bed, a beside table, a chair, a small wardrobe, a dresser with a mirror. The wooden partitions were raised some twenty centimetres from the floor and by standing on a chair you could spy on your neighbours in their most intimate moments. Draughts all over the place. I caught cold, dyspepsia, constipation, found it difficult to breathe in bed, had diphtheria, nausea. I attributed my cretinous behaviour to the food and to disappointment. I raved. I had to give vent to the raging frenzy churning inside me. I begged for strength. Only the walls heard me. I felt so empty and disgusted I took to having temper tantrums. I was falling ill because of emigration rejection. I plugged the gaps in the floor and the keyhole with crumpled up newspaper. I bought fresh fruit and vegetables which the cockroaches ended up eating. I developed a terror of finding myself atrophied in bed with no one to look after me. Then, very gradually, I returned to normal. I began to appreciate the good side of the situation and to evaluate the results. Nearly all the factories were closed for the Christmas holidays. It was a bit hard to find work. They told us to be patient. I bided my time. In any case I didn't want to take up anything without first settling down. I discovered the marvellous beaches. Young people barefoot in various states of casual undress. Men in shorts and long socks walking in a grotesque and tired sort of way as if they'd had a little too much to drink. I couldn't think of a funnier sight than this latest male fashion juxtaposed with the women's long gaudy dresses. Then there was the plain ordinary Australian housewife, condor profile and sundried skin, driving her car or doing the shopping with curlers in her hair. I discovered the huge parks, cream-laden milk, indifference, the diverse nationalities of my fellow lodgers, the same defeated melancholy. I found out there were different hells: one for single girls, one for single guys, one for married women, one for children. Together they added up to a single prefabricated hell — the migrant's inferno.

∾ *Charmian Clift* ∾

On Being a Home-grown Migrant

It is now all of sixteen months ago — on a wild winter night, with the lights of Sydney Harbour blazing away like a festival of coloured candles — that I struggled off a migrant ship with my three children and onto home territory for the first time in nearly fifteen years.

There were more than a thousand of us on that ship, including families of English migrants, Greek proxy brides, be-shawled and bemused grandmothers shrouded in shapeless black and already wailing ritually, and young Greek labourers with the sturdiness and aggressiveness of Cretan bulls. Individually and all together we shoved and jostled and pushed and heaved, and finally hurtled down the gangways like a herd of Gadarene swine into the shrieks and explosions and turbulence and tears of arrival and/or reunion.

For us it was arrival and reunion, my husband George Johnston having come ahead six months before us from Greece, where we had been living for the last ten years, to launch a new novel and scout out the land (fifteen years is a long time to be away from one's country, even if exile has been self-imposed, and we were both dubious about returning to it: we hadn't liked it much at the time we had left it).

It is quite interesting that we did return to Australia quite literally as migrants, subsidised by the government, whose policy is to encourage its own nationals to return (I know that most cultural expatriates will challenge this, but I am not talking about cultural encouragement, only passage money) as well as to welcome the two million odd British, Austrian, German, Greek, Hungarian, Italian, Dutch, Polish, Yugoslav, American, Maltese and Stateless (that tragic official word) citizens who have poured into this country, assisted or under their own steam, over the last twenty years.

The first thing of which everybody assured me, with conviction, pride, and even complacency, was that I'd see ''some changes in the old place all right''. And they said: ''It's the migrants that've made the difference. We've got a real continental way of life now.'' (Rather in the manner of a Boy Scout earning a merit badge, but certainly a pleasant and praiseworthy modulation of the old screeching note of ''bloody reffos''.)

Well now. At the end of sixteen months I am sitting in a brand new, shoddy, and very expensive apartment built by a Yugoslav landlord with foreign labour. My windows look down, at the one corner, onto an enchanting inlet of Sydney Harbour, and up, at the other, to a hill whose contours remind me of the Mediterranean, except that its curved terraces are planted, not with olive trees, but with red brick bungalows and rotary clothes hoists, all the way up to the high skyline where the home unit blocks are growing taller than the two Norfolk pines and three cabbage palms that have sometimes given me solace.

Change there is, certainly, and certainly a European influence that is obvious in shop signs, in flavoursome scraps of conversation overheard on buses and street corners, in the Polish furnituremaker around the corner, the Dutch framer, the Austrian hairdresser down the street who is a whiz at cutting, and in eating and drinking habits which have improved out of mind. All this adds piquancy to what used to be a fairly dull and conventional dish as a Way of Life.

And there is change too in the look of the city itself. I always thought Sydney beautiful (that is to say the foreshores of the harbour), but now, coming over the bridge from the north side, or across the water by ferry, it looks as romantic in its way as San Gimignano of the Towers. Sometimes I ache with it, and think I would like to live here forever. It is aspiring now, soaring up from the sea, with the intoxicating geometry of angled cranes dizzily high against the hazy Sydney sky (and the climate is awful, incidentally, whatever they say) and the tall skeletons of steel and concrete swarming with ant-sized figures that are marked by the vehement red and yellow dots of safety helmets.

Most of those ant figures will speak English with a foreign accent, and if you came across by taxi it is ten to one your driver spoke with a foreign accent too. If you are coming into town for lunch you will probably be going to a foreign restaurant (small, civilised, and densely patronised at midday by paunchy males in executive-type suits — whatever happened to the lean Australian type? — and groups of ladies in extraordinary hats vying for the attention of the social photographer).

All this is exciting and stimulating, and one has the sense of being in a real city, a big city by world standards, vibrant with the urgencies of busy commercial life, growing at a breathtaking pace. But once the commercial day is over the city empties, and the tide of human activity that has surged and crashed through it in the working hours rushes out at full ebb to the suburbs, where Sydney domestic life is lived — if you call it living.

Returning to our muttons, or the view from my window, I have often thought, with a sort of fascinated horror, of this view multiplied by thousands and minus the harbour inlet, to the south and the west and the north, the red brick and tile going on and on and on and away in a nightmare grid of what must be the most hideous domestic architecture in the world. One feels that the zestful and piquant influences of the Old World have been rejected here, or beaten back, or perhaps have not yet got so far. Excepting for the shopping centres, where the milkbar, the delicatessen, and the greengrocery will almost certainly be run by Greeks or Italians, there is no evidence of a "continental way of life". Sydney suburbia appears to be as stupefyingly dull as it was fifteen years ago, only more prosperous and therefore more smug.

For all that, and for all the terrifying cost of living, which sometimes causes me to break out in a sweat of sheer panic, I think I am glad we came back, and I am only qualifying that statement because I fancy it takes longer than sixteen months for a migrant to adjust — even a home-grown one like me.

It is a queerly tentative place, lacking real definition yet. Perhaps that is what is so exciting about it really. It is a place still becoming, a place where anything might happen, a place — and one feels this with a desperate, wishful eagerness — where one might even be able to *make* things happen if one tries hard enough. Heaven knows there's scope.

It is true that the live theatre is struggling for survival, it is true that the television channels are clogged with the crummiest of the American West, it is true that there is a general political and public apathy toward anything more creative than chasing a quid (dollar now, of course), it is true that young talent is fleeing

Europewards by the boatload and older talent already there is refusing to come home, thank you very much.

Yet there are other boatloads coming in from Europe all the time, bringing all sorts of talents. If they continue to come in at their present rate this country might even have a population of twenty-three or twenty-four millions by the year 2000 (always provided, of course, that we survive that long). Enough population and enough talent to make anything possible, even a cultural revolution, or suburbia blossing into exciting life.

Anyway, as a migrant, I think it is worthwhile sticking around for a bit just to see.

ᖇᖇ *Yasmine Gooneratne* ᖇᖇ

Navaranjini Takes Note of Signs and Visions

I had decided, quite early on, that though I didn't know much about Australia to start with, I was going to learn. Part of the baggage I packed for our visit to Australia, I now realise, was a very strong determination to make a great success of the next five years, for my husband's sake. And so I decided to equip myself early for whatever Australia would put before us.

I began to read, with careful attention, the record my husband's grandfather had left of his travels. A hundred years ago, I thought, this man made the same journey that we are making now. What can I learn from it? What can it teach me?

While Amma took out her own kind of insurance for our safety and welfare, inviting the Brahmin from our family *kovil* to perform the necessary ceremonies for the protection of travellers, I took driving lessons for the first time, and obtained a driving licence. Although I must say, after my first look at the Sydney traffic on the day we arrived, I wondered whether I would ever have the courage to exchange it for an Australian one.

I also learned to swim. Accompanying my husband to Mount Lavinia on Sundays, I had up to that time been usually content to paddle in the waves as they broke in foam a few yards from my beach umbrella, in the shade of which I would then spend the rest of the morning reading a magazine. Observing Barbara and Harry Whytebait and their daughters, however, I soon realised that Australia would require more of me than that.

Evonne and Sibylla Whytebait, who appeared to me to climb out of the High Commission swimming pool only in order to take a short rest before diving in again, represented for me at that time the Australians who would surround us in our new life. It seemed to me that an ability to swim would be as important to us in Australia as an ability to play bridge or tennis had been to my parents in their outstation days: it was, obviously, a social necessity. I decided that wherever we were called on to participate in this all-important rite, be it in river or lake, in a swimming pool or in Sydney Harbour itself, I would not be found wanting. So I took swimming lessons at the Colombo Swimming Club, and despite my terror of the deep end, I had become, by the time we left Colombo, quite a good swimmer.

Though nobody was swimming in it that I could see, the Harbour on the day we arrived in Australia was like a page out of a child's picture-book, bright blue and studded with white sails. Sydney lay shining beneath us, a sunlit version of the cities of spires and towers that the invisible prince flew over by starlight in the fairytale Edward had written into his diary as his last memory of home. It looked as if it had come straight out of a nursery rhyme. Except, I thought suddenly, as our taxi joined the stream of traffic flowing away from Sydney airport, this was no nursery rhyme, and the expressway no fun fair.

People drove so fast! The faces I could see on either side of us were tense and grim. Nobody glanced out of a car window, all communication with the outside world presumably occurring by way of the driving mirror as people rushed onwards intent on getting to some destination from which nothing must divert them, shoulders hunched, eyes focused straight ahead, mouths unsmiling.

It seemed to me that everyone, including our taxi driver who was driving as fast as everybody else, knew exactly where they were going. I felt I would probably not be very good at living, or driving, in Australia.

But though people avoided *looking* at one another, it seemed that some sort of communication was taking place by way of the stickers on the rear windows of the vehicles that, from time to time, drew level with us and passed us on either side. "I'd rather be sailing," said a sticker with a picture of a boat on it. "If you can read this, thank a teacher," said another. "If you toucha my truck," warned a hefty utility piled high with bricks and tiles, "I breaka your face."

I found the stickers amusing, but our taxi driver didn't.

"Racist bastard," he said, of the driver of the utility. He stepped on the accelerator, we drew level with the utility, and passed it. "See that?" our taxi driver said, and spat. "He wasn't even Italiano."

My husband was very interested by this exchange, which yielded, he said, a useful insight into Australian society. He is, of course, very knowledgeable about Sri Lankan society. One look, or a few seconds' listening to a stranger's speech are all that is necessary: he's got the person mentally taped, investigated, classified. It comes of being a linguist, I suppose — he's simply doing his job and doing it well.

"Move up a little closer, honey," said one sticker invitingly; but the next warned, in tiny letters and numerals, "U R 2 close".

I was looking out eagerly on that first day for clues of one kind and another that might help explain Australia to me, and I began to watch for the stickers, which seemed to me to be like the flags run up by ships at sea, being in this case signals of friendship and a shared sense of fun.

Occasionally a traffic light flashed red and brought the charging cars to a temporary stop. At these times I glanced occasionally sideways. The first time I did this, I found myself broadly winked at by the ginger-haired driver of a monster truck. Of course I looked away again hastily, and stared straight ahead through the windscreen. Luckily, my husband, seated in front of me, had been making notes in a memo pad, and had seen neither the truck driver nor his wink.

The next time I looked out of the window at the traffic lights I found myself gazing into a pair of bright blue eyes ringed with what looked very much like my own kohl. The eyes belonging to a young man who appeared to be admiring my earrings, which *are*, as a matter of fact, rather nice: a pair that my mother-in-law had given me as a farewell present. As soon as he caught my eye through the glass, he pointed to the brightly coloured parrots swinging from his own ear lobes, and mouthed something that I couldn't make out. Of course I looked away at once. It was only as we got into gear again that I realised the young man had probably been asking where I bought my jewellery.

Who knows? I've learned since that anything can happen in Australia. In the land of the duck-billed platypus, where reality is stranger than fantasy, why cannot men wear parrots in their ears? But after that, I seldom risked a sideways glance. I didn't want a repetition of the first two experiences; on the other hand I didn't want to meet a stranger's cold, unfriendly eye. But I needn't have bothered about that. People continued to stare ahead. Some drummed with their fingers on the steering wheel, impatient to get on, or maybe they were keeping time with a car radio. A woman reached up, tilted her driving mirror towards her, and checked on her make-up and her hair. A man used the few moments of waiting to glance over papers that lay on the seat beside him.

Then the lights flashed green once more, and everyone shot off again, very much like horses at a starter's signal, ourselves included, for to stop, pause, or even to move slowly amid such frantic intensity would have caused, I thought, someone, maybe many, to die. A massive pile-up, like the disaster on the M1 in Britain that we read of in the papers the day we left Colombo.

Now that could never happen, I reflected, in Colombo. The traffic in that city is crazy, but it isn't death-oriented. There are no multiple traffic lanes, no purposeful movement forward of streams of vehicles. There it is merely swirl, and muddle. People hang out of bus windows and stand on the footboards, nobody takes any notice whatever of zebra crossings, taxis and bicycles describe figures-of-eight in the traffic without bothering to signal, and trapped at the centre of every traffic jam there is usually a policeman whose helpless gestures everyone ignores.

But nobody *dies*. With traffic moving at under five miles an hour, with car horns being used not so much to demand way as to discreetly announce presence, with motorists aware that the motorbicycle moving beside them carries not one man only, but his wife, his child, and very possibly his mother-in-law as well, the accidents that occur are not usually fatal.

I had a sudden mental vision of my husband stepping every day into the terrifying currents of Sydney's traffic — as he would have to do, I realised, if I did not get myself an Australian driving licence as quickly as possible. I felt sick with fear. And then, without warning, the figure of the surfer on the back cover of Amma's magazine came inexplicably into my mind, and with it an image different but not incongruous, because equally powerful and controlled, of Arjuna, the archer of the *Mahabharata*.

I closed my eyes, and the two images merged into one behind my eyelids: surfer turned into warrior, surfboard into chariot, sultanas into Gandiva, the God-given bow. I opened my eyes, and glanced at my husband. He was looking at his watch, apparently calculating the time this first journey was taking us. His right hand was on the seat behind him, a few inches from my knee. Keeping my eyes open, and making a concentrated effort of will, I put my hand on his hand, and deliberately placed the heroic figure my imagination had created between my husband and the oncoming waves of traffic.

Godlike One, Arjuna! I said to myself, as our taxi entered the torrent of cars streaming onto Pyrmont Bridge, You who lived five years in the shining halls of Heaven, learning the use of all the divine weapons! You who are among warriors what the Himalayas are among mountains, what the Ocean is among waters, what the Tiger is among beasts, what the Whale is among the creatures of the deep! May you stand always, his shield and his protector, between my husband and whatever is to come!

I felt better at once. Not only because my husband had responded to the touch of my hand by clasping it affectionately in his own without looking round, but because I knew I had made contact with a supreme source of power. I felt proud that our new experiences, however daunting, had failed to obliterate the famous lines of the *Mahabharata* from my memory.

If anyone can protect my husband in this new and confusing world, I thought, Arjuna can.

If I had told my husband of my vision, he would have been amused, and would almost certainly have reminded me that the picture in the magazine was no shield or amulet, merely the invention of some surfing enthusiast on the Australian Dried Fruit Board. Which, of course, I was perfectly aware of. But that didn't alter the fact that it was an *inspired* invention, productive of hope, and full of divine grace.

I was pleased to find as our journey to the suburbs continued, that the vision did not lose its clarity. Just as the smiling child with her woolly lamb had signified "Australia" for me as a schoolgirl, the heroic image of Arjuna-as-Surfer, rising in power against the waves of a terrifying Unknown, symbolised "Australia" for me on the day we arrived in Sydney, cheering me with its promise of fine weather, cloudless skies and ultimate victory.

So that it came as quite a shock when our taxi swung round a corner, and there on a brick wall I read two words splashed in white paint from a spray can: "ASIANS OUT". Below them was the Smith's Crisps slogan, familiar to me from the year I spent in London with my husband while he was finishing his PhD: "BASH A PAK A DAY".

I wondered whether my husband had seen the slogans too. He

was looking straight ahead, but I knew that he had. I wondered what he was thinking, whether he remembered Charmaine's warnings to me, and the questions Vera had asked him in her letter.

I knew, then, that the welcoming smile on the face of that little girl in the poster at school had been meant for someone else. Whoever it was that she had held her flowers out to so invitingly, it could not have been me.

AWAY

❧

∾ *Kate Jennings* ∾

Aunt Dot's Camel

I arrived in Matane, a town in Quebec, after dark. The motel's decor was the *ne plus ultra* in provincial elegance, orange shag carpet, brown chenille bedspreads, white plastic furniture. The motel restaurant served up food to match the decor, chicken à la king and lemon chiffon pie. The next morning, I stepped out into feeble sunshine and there, beyond a patch of gravel and clumps of grass flattened by a rude wind, unseen in the gloom of the night before, was the St Lawrence River estuary, stretching away without ceremony or shore to the horizon, an infinity of dirty whitecaps and grey water. This, I thought, is a river in hell. I half expected Charon, the ferryman from Hades, to show up and offer to row my soul to the other side. And, as I do when I find myself in a less than alluring place, I blamed my mother.

You'd be right in saying that's taking parental culpability a bit far. It is true, though, that I became a traveller because of my mother. Stifled by domesticity, she encouraged me to a life of independence, education, and travel. She bequeathed me her dreams and her discontent. The times were right, and I set about living those dreams. This has caused all sorts of conflict between us, as it has for many other mothers and daughters. And to complicate matters, her dreams are a bad fit on me. My temperament is not as adventurous as hers. We are partners in a three-legged race, my mother's dreams and I, stumbling out of step and losing our balance more often than not. I want to run the race alone.

My mother yearned to travel. She'd fret and sigh and her eyes would cloud over like Camille on her deathbed, only she didn't have tuberculosis; she had wanderlust. Her life, she believed, would not truly begin until the ocean liner bearing her away from Australia had pulled out from Circular Quay and the last streamer strained and snapped. We always knew she would leave us some day, and so when she finally did, we were not surprised. We only wondered what had taken her so long.

My mother — and I in turn — travelled to broaden horizons but also to escape, be rid of responsibility. As Watanabe Kohan's haiku goes:

> While travelling,
> I am free of care.
> No man knows me,
> No man betrays me there.

She was also, like almost every other woman I know, an incurable romantic. Perhaps in her travels she would meet that ideal companion and have her life transformed by him. It does happen. Take Edwina Prue, a poor girl from a ranch in New Mexico, who was standing on a railway platform in London when a nobleman saw her and fell in love on the spot. He traced her to New Mexico and courted her with orchids, and Edwina Prue became the Baroness d'Erlanger, with homes in London, Paris, and Geneva, and a palace in Tunisia. Unfortunately, you have a better chance of winning the lottery than this sort of thing happening to you. The only romance you are likely to come across on the road is rape or near-rape from some predatory fellow on the lookout for a woman with a suitcase and a head full of moonshine.

Escape and encounters with barons are not the best of motives for travelling, but my mother can be forgiven for wanting to go out and meet life instead of waiting, as women have traditionally done, for something to wash up on her shore. It is significant, however, that women of my mother's generation dreamed more of travelling than they did of having a career. It takes no particular skill to be a traveller. There are no exams to pass. Once launched on your way, the momentum of journey takes over, and no matter how timid you are, there is at least the illusion that you are accomplishing a great deal.

I took my mother's dreams one step further and became a travel writer. When I tell other women what I do for a living, they invariably look wistful and remark on my luck. It is work like any other, I say, but they don't believe me. I explain that most travel writing is advising people on where to go, stay, eat, and shop. In fact, I feel almost apologetic about being a travel writer because members of my profession have a reputation for being outrageous free-loaders. There is a song sung about travel writers, made up by airline stewards I am told, which illustrates this:

> The gratis gang are we
> We only go for free
> If we don't fly first-class
> Then you can kiss our ass
> If you don't comp our room
> There will be no tourist boom.

I do concede that I get to places I wouldn't ordinarily be able to visit. The women I tell all this to think I don't know on which side my bread is buttered. The truth is, while scooting around the world might suit some, I am a terrible traveller, a champion worrywart, a Nervous Nellie of the first order. Will I get to the airport on time? What if the hotel has never heard of me? Have I enough traveller's cheques? And so on. Bob has been heard to wonder out loud how I ever managed to leave Griffith, New South Wales, in the first place. But most of all, I hate to fly. I simply detest it. I wish I could be knocked unconscious and off-loaded at the other end.

Travelling, to my mind, can also be the loneliest of affairs. Philip Levine has written a poem about finding letters and post-cards from a man who had spent a lifetime wandering from place to place:

> . . . each one
> said the same thing; how
> long the nights were, how
> cold it was so far away,
> and how it had to end.

When I travel, I don't stride forth into the world and gorge on experience like a giant feasting on a flock of sheep. Instead I feel quite small and alone, like a child who has run away from home and comes to the conclusion, when the front gate disappears from view, that this might not be such a great idea after all.

Travelling has its lovely moments, of course. In Kyoto, very early one morning, I wandered down an empty street in the direction of the Eikando temple. A shopkeeper in a fresh white apron darted out of his store and deposited a tin filled with sticks and papers in the middle of the road. He lit this impromptu brazier, a signal for monks in wide straw hats and blue robes to materialise. Chanting in counterpoint, they criss-crossed the street as if mapping out their melody. One by one, housewives appeared in doorways. They greeted the monks with deep bows and placed coins in the cloth bags that hung from the monk's necks. A boy in high-top sneakers raced around a corner and screeched to a halt. Little boy and tall monk bowed, their heads knocking together. I fumbled in my pocket for some coins and, with the help of the shopkeeper, also gave alms to the monks. We all beamed and bowed. Bowed and beamed.

While touring Britanny, I stayed in the faded but still gracious Château de Locguénolé near Hennebont. My room had high ceilings, a marquetry floor, low feather bed, a luxurious high-sided tub, and shuttered windows which looked out over a garden of crimson dahlias and purple hydrangeas. The garden sloped down to the moody Blavet River and a *parc* of beech, oak, and blue cedar. Whispers of wind would stir the tree tops and sudden squalls of rain pelt the shiny leaves of camellia bushes and the slate roofs of the chateau's outbuildings, to be replaced by a nuzzling sunshine. *La douce Bretagne*, they call it, and this, I thought, is why I left Australia.

I also shouldn't neglect to mention memorable meals. At Le Moulins du Duc near Hennebont, *langoustine* with a touch of ginger, duckling flavoured with honey and limes, a passionfruit soufflé with an apricot *coulis*. And best of all, as many Belon oysters as I could eat. ("Intimations of the ages of man, some piercing intuition of the sea and all its weeds and breezes shiver you a split second from that little stimulus on your palate," writes Eleanor Clark of the Belon oyster in her rhapsodical *The Oysters of Locmariaquer*, as fine a travel book as you'll ever read.) At the Pousada de Santa Luzia in Elvas, a Portuguese town known for its plums, golden mounds of salted cod fried with eggs, onions, and potatoes — *bacalhau* — which the waiter kept pressing on me by saying, "Another morsel?" and I would give in, blushing at my gluttony.

Lovely moments, and lovely bad moments, as John Julius Norwich called then in *A Taste for Travel*. One night in Kyoto I tried out a chicken-in-the-pot restaurant. The people there spoke even less English than I did Japanese, but with much to-do and cries of "Special, special!" I had mimed being a writer — they installed me in a tatami-mat room. The waitress lit a fire under a cauldron of broth and dropped, piece by piece, into it, a heaping tray of chicken and vegetables. This particular dish is popular with sumo wrestlers, and I believe it. The pot was bottomless. A bowl of chicken, a cup of soup, vegetables, more chicken, rice, until I was awash in the stuff. I wasn't managing my chopsticks well, so the smiling waitress, who sat opposite me and clucked encouragingly whenever I swallowed a mouthful, got up and shuffled out to the kitchen. Gales of laughter greeted her. My ears burned. She returned with a fork. More chicken, vegetables, soup, rice. Enough, I said, as politely as I could, pointing to the appropriate *kanji* in my phrasebook. With a final flourish, a large rice cake went into the pot. The waitress indicated that I should swallow this whole. *Very* bad advice, a Japanese acquaintance said later. The glutinous rice cake stuck fast. My face went red. I gasped for air like a fish stranded on the sand. The waitress was delighted. She clapped and giggled until she hiccuped.

Even if I tell you that for every Château de Locguénolé in a travel writer's life there is a motel with an orange shag rug, for every Belon oyster a plate of indigestible chicken à la king, and for every encounter with Buddhist monks endless hours of listening patiently to tourist industry officials, like the young woman who went on and on about the Bas-Saint-Laurent being the "cruddle" of agriculture, you probably will still think I am being a curmudgeon when I call travel writing "work". And I have to allow that although I hold forth on how everybody should stay home and tend the farm instead of traipsing around the world — I was especially eloquent on this subject after counting eighty-seven tour buses outside Notre Dame Cathedral — I would become as restless as a bear behind bars if I didn't have easy access to travel.

' "Take my camel, dear?' said Aunt Dot, as she climbed down from this animal on her return from High Mass".' The opening sentence of Rose Macaulay's *The Towers of Trebizond* never fails to start me hankering after parts unknown. Like Aunt Dot's niece, I want to climb up on that camel and be off. In moments of enthusiasm I forget the often-depressing reality. The other day I passed an art gallery on Madison Avenue which had a display of 1920s travel posters in the window. "Hotel Quisisana, Teneriffe," said one. "The finest winter climate in the world". I backed up and read the poster again. Teneriffe? I'll just duck home and get my toothbrush . . .

Yesterday, an Australian friend who also inherited her mother's wanderlust dropped by for a cup of tea. Two other Australian women I know, one who has lived in Germany for twelve years and one in Japan for nine years, had written to tell me that they were going home for good, so we fell to discussing the advantages and disadvantages of settling down in Australia. We both felt envious of these women. We miss not having a sense of community, a place where we can stand up and be counted, but we both admitted that it would be difficult to give up the perks of our expatriate lifestyles.

The best trip I ever had, I reminded her, was when I flew the length of the Great Barrier Reef, and on up to Cape York Peninsula courtesy of Air Queensland. For sheer physical beauty, nothing can beat it. The Great Barrier Reef makes the Caribbean look like a used-car lot. At the same time, my strongest memory of that trip was dining in a resort surrounded by casuarinas and laburnum and listening to a group of boozed Australians. The more they drank, the more sullen and nasty the men became and the more shrill and insistent the women. What we should do, they all agreed, with the abos is round them up on an island and never let them off.

My friend had a story to add to this. She had returned the day before from an exhilarating three weeks in Brazil. While staying at a hotel in the city of Salvador, she came across some Australians, "Yobos", as she described them. Their loutish behaviour had got them banned from the Salvador Yacht Club, and they were boasting about it. Ironically these yobos were on their way to Australia for the Bicentennial celebrations. And not surprisingly, they too had definite opinions on what we should do with the Aborigines. In two hundred years, some things haven't changed at all.

"Prawns on the barbie. That just about sums it up," commented another disgruntled friend in a recent phone call from Australia. He lives in the Yarra River Valley, as beautiful a place as you'll find anywhere in the world. "Oh come now," I chided him. "It can't be as bad as all that." Easy for me to say. Where's the camel, Aunt Dot?

～ *Louise Mack* ～

Escape

My dear Family

There is nothing like the first hours at sea to bring out all the latent antagonism of man to man. I have never seen so many plain, homely, uninteresting BODS in my life! What a disillusionment! I thought I would meet all kinds of delightful charming cultivated people on a long sea voyage and we could talk about Shelley and Rossetti and Chopin and Italy and Greece and Paris, or they would talk and I would listen. There would be moonlight thrown in and a great stillness broken only by the murmuring of the waves. But no! They who travel from Australia are the moneymakers, the business people, butchers, bakers and ironmongers, people who don't waste time looking for the unseen but convert the visible into gold or silver as quickly as possible.

However we are going to be sociable. Little men with big heads are already running about on thin legs with pieces of paper asking people to come to meetings and go on committees.

So much for the people. But the journey! The journey! I sit for hours gazing at that great shining stretch all round me. It lies so still, day after day, yet its colour changes — turquoise, sapphire, violet — so deep you feel you could cut with a knife the colour alone. Then on other days all thickness and solidity goes and it lies like a pale blue fragile sky. And the sunsets!

The most beautiful part of it all is that the most beautiful is always to come.

～

What do we do all day?

The first class, which always represents Fashion, gives a ball and doesn't invite the second class. The second class, which invariably represents Intellect, gives a party and hangs up the notice of it in GREEK.

∞

The ship grows suddenly quiet. Her motion is slowed. Many passengers go to look over into the steerage. Many others turn away and bury themselves in books. A few weep.

A door high up in the ship's side is opened. Something wrapped in brown canvas is thrown out. It drops down down into the waves. And we have passed on. Already It is half a mile behind.

For an hour a shadow is cast over the ship . . . then the gloom lifts and life goes on again as usual. It seems a little less important, that is all. The brown bag tossed to the waves gives Death a new simplicity.

∞

Early in the morning I sit up in my berth and look through my porthole and see a foreign sail cut clear against a misty rose and onyx sky; a tall brown curving sail leaning over a low brown dhow and in the dhow a black man. My first glimpse of the East. Yet from the deck Colombo looks like Sydney seen from Fort Denison.

Ashore, the earth underfoot is red. Flame trees rear their great red leafless flowers. Scarlet houses and bazaars all round . . . the greenness of coconut trees, the blue sea and the scent of heavy flowers, the warm electric air. Rickshaws. The Oriental Hotel, The Cinnamon Gardens. Mt Lavinia. The Galle Face . . . Anyone who has been to Colombo will want to forget the temporary insanity of that yellow breeze-blown day, rushing through the scented scarlet city among the palm trees, buying, bargaining, laughing, screaming . . .

At eleven o'clock everyone in a penniless condition gets back to the ship . . . and next morning a ship laden with moonstone brooches, filagree ornaments, ivory elephants, toy rickshaws, half-pounds of Ceylon tea, clean clothes washed in the lake, sunburnt worn-out Australians.

∞

It is in the third week of the journey that the unloveliness of the human races becomes most apparent. The only persons who appear to advantage by this time are the misanthropes who have had nothing to do with anyone. They have been here before. It's

always an old traveller who begins by keeping aloof and ends by
being the only one anyone still wants to know.

Every time the women pass each other they smile. They never
pass without it. Soon it becomes worn to shreds, a mere painful
pressing back of the lips. You learn to dread it as you see it coming towards you.

○∞○

It is only half-past seven but the cabin is worse than an oven.
Every movement is an effort. Our faces, necks, arms, hands,
drip, drip . . . The little brown shutters are over all the portholes
on the sunny side of the saloon. In the yellowy-brown light all the
women look ghastly . . . People say ominously, "Wait till we get
to the Red Sea. *Then* . . ."

We enter the Red Sea. We pass Mocha. Away in the distance
we can see the city at the sea's edge, its palms against the sky. A
thrill goes through this raw Australian breast — Age, age, antiq-
uity, romance. *Coffee!*

○∞○

The Canal holds out its arms to us and we pass through. On, on,
on all day . . . The water before us runs on like a lengthening
green snake. Behind comes the slow procession of stately ships
following us to the Mediterranean with a sort of haughty humility . . . great, silent human-looking creatures, when night
comes shooting silver search-lights over the water and lighting
the ships that move in front of the solemn procession.

○∞○

Naples. *I missed the ship!* A frantic race to catch her at Marseilles,
a strange feverish flight through a new world, infinitely precious
and wonderful. Alone, unprotected, almost no money but I was
glad. In the train I whispered to myself, *"You're in ITALY. You're
going to ROME!"* Morning, before dawn, a green world outside
the window. My heart begins to beat wildly. I had anticipated
brown and grey ruins and ruins and ruins. Here were green
fields and scarlet poppies blazing from fields and roadsides. I
could have been going from Launceston to Hobart. That's the
first great lesson of travelling: the world is just the world. A city
is just a city. The dream place doesn't exist. I didn't expect to
find marble emperors stalking about marble streets but I didn't
expect a railway station and buns and coffee at Rome! *Trains at
Rome!*

. . . Ventimiglia . . . the end of Italy . . . Carried along in a great stream of Italian peasants laden with bags of vegetables and bundles of all kinds. Customs officers . . . midnight . . . a sense of romance and unreality.

Alone among all these Italians. The intoxication of moments like this is what your true traveller must ever seek. Without them one night as well stay at home. But with them the world is a glorious place. And everything I saw, every place I passed called, *"Come back! Come back!"* And I will.

∽

There was never a greater fallacy than the old Bible theory about staying in one's place all one's life. If I had a vote in world affairs I would shift this whole universe about every ten years and in a hundred years what a world there would be. It would be everyone's province and that false prejudice called Patriotism would stand exposed. How we would forage ahead, each nation bursting with the spirit of a new country . . . Exuberance would carry us forward doubly quickly.

∽

May . . . 1901. TILBURY. I had expected an overwhelming throng of ships in a dull yellow fog with a city rising from the very bank in a solid mass. Instead . . . we were the only ship there; no fog but sunshine and pale blue sky. Only a few houses visible and a couple of hotels. And grass and a broken bottle or two and some empty jam-tins. The world's the world all the world over.

A wharf, a dirty wooden wharf with dirty wooden sheds. A common wooden gangway. People walked down and there was England! Green fields, less green than I had imagined, some even a little yellow; then houses, dull, dingy, red, brown but no forest of bricks and mortar. In the train I kept asking "Is this London?" and at last. "*This* isn't London?" "Yes, this is London."

No mighty roar or eternal hum or sickening sea of chimney pots. A big railway station with high overhead a glassed arched roof. Cabs, cabs, cabs . . . driving through a neat clean city with high high houses and flecked trees of the loveliest tenderest green growing in squares with iron railings. Such *intense* surprise to find trees and grass and gay bright leafage in this terrible dreaded city of fogs and everlasting smoke. It gives a feeling of love and reeling happiness.

∽

LATER

Here I am in London!
Is it really I?
Walking down High Holborn
Unconcernedly?
Circumscribing Fleet Street,
Wandering through the Strand,
HERE I AM IN LONDON!
— So I understand.

More later. *With love,*
                    From Lou
                              in
                                  London

❧ *Georgia Savage* ❧

Vietnam

In 1989 and a long way from childhood, I went south to the End of the Earth, the place where river and channel waters meet the Tasman — where hills of mythic blue go gentle into the sea. There I met the Vietnam veteran who'd come home green. I watched him in his pastel windcheater washing dishes like any suburban house-husband, watched him in an oilskin coat digging the potato patch while braced against the wind. I saw his eyes smile with love at the sight of Zoë, his small, bouncing, beautiful wife. But not a word could either of us get from him about his war, about the things that turned him green.

Like the girl, Sam, in Bobbie Ann Mason's *In Country* I felt like getting together a poncho and some rudimentary camping gear and spending the night in a snake-infested swamp in order to find out for myself what the war was like. Knowing that wouldn't work, I went to Vietnam instead.

❧

the French city, 'the Saigon of the piastre' as Lucien Bodard called it, had represented the opium stage of addiction. With the Americans had begun the heroin phase, and what I was seeing now were the first symptoms of withdrawal.

All The Wrong Places, JAMES FENTON

❧

It costs over $2000 Australian to have a fortnight in Vietnam, so one can't stay long. This means the tourist tries to fit in too many experiences and ends up swamped by emotion. For my part, I found this led to fits of laughter when swearwords or tears might have been more suitable.

I was on a tour organised for war veterans from Australia. There were two other takers, a Vet from Brisbane and his wife. We met in the Air France queue at the Bangkok airport and for the three of us it was more or less love at first sight.

Saigon — that's what they call it over there. If you say Ho Chi Minh City, the Vietnamese break up, which isn't saying much because they break up at most things. (Binh, who longed to learn rhyming slang, would give a helpless little scream, grab his slender knees and double up whenever we used it.)

The beauty of Vietnamese women knocks you out. It is an equation of grace and spirit, amber skin and lustrous oriental eye. Seeing it, you begin to believe old fairy stories of women whose looks drove men mad. Nothing had prepared me though for the beauty of certain men. (One should wear chains on the heart in Vietnam.)

At the presidential palace — familiar from television — the top storey was designed for dancing. The floor is parquetry and the walls, screens which open to the seasons. I took off my shoes and humming to myself, did a slow waltz there. Later, looking down into the garden, I saw a man watering a centuries-old tree with a length of hand-held hose. Behind him were the ornamental gates tank no. 843 smashed through and in doing so signalled to us at home that the war was over.

The streets in Saigoon are lined with tamarind trees. Their trunks are whitewashed to waist height to protect the fleet of night-time cyclists riding without lights. Once there was street lighting but much of it is now kaput. The resultant darkness adds charm to the evening and confusion as well. Your cyclo boy, singing a snatch of the *Marseillaise* each time you pass a French building, whizzes you through the traffic with nerve-snapping skill. And the breeze you feel on your face is softer, sweeter than the petrol flavoured variety at home.

People use the footpaths as extensions of the houses which turns them into community verandas. Families — hundreds of them — sit outside in the evening to watch the passing show. "'Allo, 'allo," they called and laughed and waved. We laughed too and could see why the Queen of England enjoys her job. At a softdrink stall I saw a woman with Asian eyes and auburn hair and freckles. She and I stared at each other, *recognised* each other, then I was past.

Next morning at the central market, Chrissie and I turned the tables on a pickpocket by getting behind him to mimic his every move. Finally he turned, shrugged, grinned nervously and hurried away. It was there we saw the woman begging with a drugged baby in her arms. It was wrapped in a khaki shirt and had skin of bluish-white. Only shocked mental arithmetic convinced me it was not the child of an Allied serviceman. The mother cursed us when we averted angry faces and moved on.

At our hotel each room had both an air-conditioner and ceiling fan. The bathtubs were built for two or more and the electric wiring which dodged in and out of the wall was joined with Elastoplast. That wiring caused us to organise a private version of fire drill. But the night I blew the lights in the block with a borrowed infuser, we were too helpless with laughter to knot the sheets, let alone abseil from the fourth floor balcony.

From my window I could look across at what was once the American embassy. It was impossible to see the distinctive double box shape of the roof and not see also a phantom helicopter and phantom crowd of panicked people wanting to board it. On the corner below me the men of the bakery had taken time off from stacking French rolls to squat by the wall for a smoke. In a country where the average wage buys only three days food a month, everyone moonlights. Doctors cook in restaurants, engineers pedal cyclos. Laughing again, Binh told me some Vietnamese parents shock their daughters into good behaviour by threatening to marry them to schoolteachers.

Blackmarket stalls are everywhere. Some have only two packets of cigarettes and a litre bottle of petrol for sale. The better stocked ones indicate that if capitalism was banished on what is spoken of as Liberation Day, it was back in business again at seven the next morning.

ᠵᢆᢣ

Several years ago, after reading Joseph Conrad's Heart of Darkness, *I understood what had happened to the soldiers who had served in Vietnam. We had seen the darkness and corruption and, even though most of us didn't realise it, it had challenged our values in ways we weren't prepared for.*

The Soldiers' Story, TERRY BURSTALL

ᠵᢆᢣ

In Vietnam, the war it seems was just last year. In Vung Tau, it was yesterday. This seaside town, with its famous Back Beach, was once home to squadrons 9 and 35 of the Royal Australian Air Force. It was also a recreation centre for our troops. These days it's full of Russians — tourists come to buy cheap television sets and hairdryers, or technocrats working in the burgeoning oil industry. They are tall, good-looking people, the women dressed, bleached and made up as I remember myself being in the early 1960s. Believing us to be Americans, they'd return a smiled greeting in the hotel lift with a cold nod. At other times we were invisible to them.

At the streetmarket it seemed every stallholder had a sister in Richmond, Melbourne. Because of this or perhaps certain sweet old R. & R. memories, the people they call *Uc dai loi* are extremely popular with them. ('Allo 'allo.) One woman refused to sell me a watch, saying "This number ten watch. You go other place. Buy number one."

At Back Beach — packed with Russians — the skyline was dominated by a bearded and robed figure of marble. It was put there by the Americans to dwarf *Kwan Yin* on a neighbouring hill. They named him St George and said he'd come to slay the dragon. By 1975 the Vietnamese were saying his empty hands showed that he'd sat to play chess with Buddha and through lack of wisdom, lost everything.

∾ *Dora Birtles* ∾

Rescued: and Again Drifting

*In 1932 Dora Birtles joined two other women and two men to sail
in a cutter from Newcastle, NSW to Singapore. The women wrote
newspaper articles on board as a means of financing the journey.
Birtles's later book, from which this extract is taken, frankly
describes the psychological and sexual tensions on board as well as
adventure and mishap.*

Things were getting serious but not so serious, at any moment a blithe wind might come that would carry us to Singapore. Our friend the south-easter. Had we left Macassar a day
or two earlier he might have blown us all the way; but it was no
use thinking of that now. There must be some fairy-tale way of
cajoling him, of coaxing this wind horse to work for us and not
jingle off in a sulk. Take some straw from one of our mattresses
and tie it to the mast? In twenty-four hours two miles to the
north.

The heavy burden of silent collective suggestion made Henery
decide to get out the engine. He and Joan worked on it in the hot
sun, cleaning the plugs. Ruth and I wiped off the vaseline and oil
with which it had been smeared to protect it from rust. Suspicious places in the wiring were bound again with insulating tape.
The two men got it on the out-board bracket and thrust at the
disk to start it. Again and again. It turned but nothing happened.
Again, once more. Give her another try. Another look at the wiring. More turning. Sven thrust. Nothing. Then Henery tried
again and took, as Ruth said he would, the skin off his knuckles.
The engine kicked twice, two small explosions. That was all, two
abortive coughs. The skeleton went back into its cupboard, rat-

tling its parts as it went. It would have been a surprise had they made it go.

In the bright moonlight that night Ruth and I fished, still in twenty fathoms. She caught a fish, a pathetically small fish not six inches long. We talked about fasting. She said we could go for a month on water alone, I did not think a month, not after our prolonged low diet. She said, "People die of fright not starvation," and I did not contradict her but surreptitiously I felt my fattier parts and determined I could fast longer than Ruth. I knew nothing of fasting but I remembered Marco Polo's Tibetan sheep, they lived on their tails in the winter.

I felt pessimistic, relieved that I had made a will, it was a tidy habit, like folding one's pyjamas after sleeping. I wanted to know why Sven was so quietly confident, "In for a deuce of a time but it will be all right," he said. He twisted this way and that, till at last I pinned him down, his mother's prayers would not be wasted, "She prays every night for me." . . . All the mothers praying, "For those in peril on the sea . . ." as good an anchor cable as anything else in mid-ocean.

The next morning's 8 a.m. longitude put us eight miles farther east. East, the eternal drift.

We had no playing cards on board. Ruth amused herself cutting out a pack from stiff paper, substituting bread, cups of tea, butter and chops for the Ace, King, Queen and Jack; and pears, apples, plums and bananas for the four suits. She drew every card, it gave her great pleasure and took two days. When it was finished I played a hand of rummy with her, no one else wanted to or would play. One had to remember that it was the chop of pears one was after or the tea of plums or the butter of bananas, it was unsatisfactory, as a system or a meal. We had only the one game. Our rules were different.

Ten and a half miles farther east. "She has a will of her own," said Sven, and "Sailing under sealed orders", was his joke. He began to tell of ships with hoodoos. The course then was west, or west by south, to bring us into the range of the nearest light. As she would not do it Sven wanted to go north-west by west on a course where we would come to a steamer track, be able to get help and not waste what wind there was fighting the current. This course would take us east and north of the Rhio Archipelago. There was a long argument between the two men, it boiled down to, "You are not being consistent, and Where we made a mistake."

On the other hand, "You have to go as best you can and change your plans according to conditions, you can't do it like a book when you've got no engine. The wind takes you, you have to make what use you can of it." The wind takes you . . . The wind. If only there were wind.

The decision was come to, to try north-west by west for three days and then if it failed to make for some islands, the Tambelans, in the China Sea where steamers sometimes called, and where presumably there was a settlement. We had no sailing directions for them, only the authority of the chart.

The decision had an enlivening effect, Henery and Sven put a light chain on ropes and worked it up and down under the keel to free us from weed and barnacles. We leaned over the gunwale and scraped at the barnacles on the sides as far as we could, hundreds of them tumbled off into deep water like swollen grains of rice. Should a wind come we were ready to move . . ..

Our last tray of kadjong idju had sprouted better than any before. We grew it in darkness on a moistened pad of sacking. It was ready when the tips began to turn green. We had left this trayful till inch-long green leaves had sprouted and white rootlets had pushed up the seeds, smaller than peas and held them two inches above the tray, like the heads of birds, the leaves just opening, the beaks ready to chirp. The brown seed-covers had split and folded back like wings leaving the kadjong chicken-yellow and marked with purple. The trayful of sprouted seeds was a flock of ibis on the point of flying away. To prisoners anywhere growth is a miracle. We ate the kadjong reluctantly and talked of gardens. I wrote a garden poem.

The washing up after breakfast was simple, five plates, a pail of clean salt water and six grains of rice in the bottom of it. "Leave one for Mr. Manners," said grandmother. The last olives were gone. We had saved the stones and crunched them up with our teeth. The candle-grease was done. The ink was almost dried up. It had been watered down till it was so weak it fainted away on the paper. The Child story was at chapter 17. It kept me busy.

Wind. How our ideas of wind had changed. Wind. We would dignify any whispering of air by that name now, our souls were sensitive to wind, after this a breeze would never be altogether commonplace. Wind. What was wind? The theories were all very well where wind was, but where it was not? Here was a circle of sea where winds did not exist. If there was any it went vertical, a balloon could fill with it and go straight up. Winds and currents were inscrutable things, for all Henery's expensively printed four-colour wind charts.

I took pains with the barley for lunch. The last barley and the last kadjong and the last onion, but there was still about three pounds of rice and kerosene for two days. The cheap little cabin light stood disconsolate, it had not been filled for many nights. We had bought it in Macassar, it had a Swiss mountain scene painted on its tin reflector, a chalet, green meadows, snow and red cows. Similar lamps attract the tropical moths in many Malay homes under the coco-nut trees. Snow, green meadows, red cows.

Against the sides of the boat came the slap of water, the exhilaration communicated itself through the boat to us. We were moving. The gradual growing of a whisper of air into something that could be called a breeze. Sven called from the tiller, "It's getting steadier; I think it will last." How eager he sounded. It lasted and something else happened. A steamer. We saw a steamer at about three o'clock the same afternoon.

Henery ran up the signal flags, the ensign inverted and the tiny yellow and blue code flags, "Ship in distress". They fluttered in the wind. Would they be seen? The steamer was going to pass fairly close, they were outwards bound from Singapore. Henery fired six rounds of shot. We were to leeward of them. We dropped the mainsail and raised it again. The steamer changed course, slowed, went astern, it was stopping. Was it stopping? It was stopping! Bless the fraternity of the sea. The second officer on watch had noted the inverted ensign.

When we were close enough the skipper, dark and Dutch, called from the bridge in English, "What you want, boys?" A stentorian call.

"Food. Out of provisions," we replied, our voices thin in the wind.

"Come alongside." He was jovial.

We manoeuvred, they manoeuvred, ropes were flung, fell short, flung again, not made fast quickly; flung, caught and the hawser dragged aboard, twisted round the mast and over the sampson post, once, twice. How she strained. Now we were dancing up and down beside the big cargo boat. Henery scrambled on board.

We were steaming along with them, half speed to them but galloping to us. Waves broke on both sides of our deck, we were almost swamped. The entire crew of the Dutch boat turned out to see us. Women! The "boys" were women. Australians in a little boat and out of provisions. Someone came in a dressing-gown. Another held out a carafe of water, if we were starving we must be dying of thirst as well. The water was so cold beads of moisture formed on the glass even in the hot sun. Cold water. We got it aboard. We had not known there could be anything so cold in the world.

Henery took photographs. News value. Sven got a time check for the chronometer and their position. Malay boys carried tins and sacks down and tossed and slung them aboard. We said goodbye to our deliverers and cast off. The transaction had taken over an hour. Good-bye. We will never forget you — The Rescuer. We sat down to sort out the spoils.

100 Egyptian cigarettes — for the ladies (a gift from the first
    officer, he of the dressing-gown)
cigarette papers
matches
shag tobacco
10 six-lb. tins of beef (Australian beef at that)
20 lbs. of sugar
50 lbs. of flour
100 lbs. of rice
12 or more large tins of sardines in tomato sauce
3 gallons of kerosene
1 lb. of butter resting like a lovely flower on a big block of ice

∾ *Marian Eldridge* ∾

A Sense of Place

(I) *International*

Con walks in the early morning streets of Pretoria and wishes she
had her camera. Now white, now black, the separate groups
throng past. Typists, she guesses. Bankers. Factory workers.
Polisie. Here comes a black girl carrying a bottle of Coke on her
head; slender as the neck of the bottle and as steady glides she.

Con walks in the early morning streets of Pretoria and looks at
people's faces. Curious white men with heavy necks eye her sideways. Black people drop their eyes. A black man accidentally
brushes against her and veers away. "I am so *sorry*, madame!"

Now Con is upset. She can't bear such deference, she wants to
wrench it from him and hurl it back in his teeth.

She hurries back to the hotel. Walter and Paul are already in
the dining room.

It is an international hotel, that is, it is now permitted to take
black guests. Con looks with interest at the two black people who
are seated at a table nearby.

Walter says "If they can afford to stay here they probably
have American accents."

Breakfast at the hotel is delicious — sweet tropical fruits
picked that morning, *matabele* porridge, guava juice. When her
stomach is full Con is no longer so angry.

"What shall we look at today?" she asks over her second cup
of coffee.

(II) Them

Con asks "Do people eat goat around here?"

"No."

"That's interesting. In Nigeria people eat goat's meat."

"Oh! The *blacks* probably eat goat."

(III) Mangoes

People are very hospitable. Con is invited to stay in a country town.

One afternoon after lunch she finds herself sitting by the open sunny window in the van Winkles' living room, explaining herself to the head of the house while in another room his wife packs his overnight case.

"Do speak louder, Con," she calls. "I don't want to miss a thing."

Con in mid-flow about Canberra as compared with Pretoria can't help smiling: back home there isn't one of her friends who would still pack for her man.

"You are going abroad?" she asks suddenly, politely, sensing her host has stopped listening.

She tells herself it's his home, his country, she shouldn't feel niggled if he switches off.

"Oh no," says Piet van Winkle. "I am going to Capetown. Overnight."

"I have no wish to travel outside this country," he adds. "I can see all that I wish to here."

A black maid called Happy appears with coffee on a tray. On her back, in a blanket, sleeps the van Winkles' baby. "She just loves that little kid," Carolyn van Winkle says. Con wonders how many children Happy has had to leave behind in one of the distant Homelands. So, still niggled, as she takes her cup she smiles thanks up at the silent, shut woman, smiles *you can look at me, I understand, I really do*, but the maid's eyes refuse to meet hers.

Drawing herself up straight Con tells herself Before I leave I'll make sure she smiles. And for a moment, until she realises what is happening, what she is doing, she repeats She *will* smile, she *will!*

∽

Out in the street two African women are engaged in loud, cheerful conversation, not in English, not in Afrikaans — Zulu or Sotho perhaps. Piet van Winkle frowns. "You know, that's something I can never get used to. They pass a friend in the street and they continue the conversation for a hundred yards — shouting." He stands up. "I'm afraid it annoys me."

Snap! The window is shut, the venetians closed. Sunshine and voices fade away. He goes out to the kitchen and fetches himself a mango which he eats carefully, slicing it with a knife and paring close to the stone.

He doesn't offer Con a mango.

(IV) Them

At the international airport, two young women suddenly turn to Con, and without any preliminary explanation or identification whip out a sheaf of papers and ask how long she has been staying in South Africa, and why. Surprised, she hedges "Do I have to answer this? Why are you asking all these questions?" "No of course not!" says the first girl, snapping shut her briefcase while the second says sarcastically "Because we just love interrogating people!" And they turn away huffily.

"Relax, girl," Paul says to Con. "They're just a couple of chicks doing a survey for a government tourist agency."

"They could have said so."

"The face of nameless officialdom," Walter pronounces.

"*Them*," says Con, but her comment is drowned by the loudspeaker announcing their flight from Pretoria to Perth.

∽ *Margaret Jones* ∽

Sweet-and-Sour

When I arrived in New York in the summer of 1965, there was a drought, and the whole city was baked dry. It was like living inside a gigantic oven. The city fathers had put up signs saying DON'T FLUSH FOR EVERYTHING, and the button shops had retaliated with SAVE WATER, SHOWER WITH A FRIEND. For the period, this was considered pretty daring.

It was my first time in America, and I had no idea it was possible to be so hot for so long. Unlike Sydney, which has a manic-depressive climate, Manhattan is very consistent. The concrete canyons heat up at the beginning of summer, and stay at the same level, day and night, until the Labor Day holiday signals that autumn is on the way.

"What a brutal climate!" another Australian journalist, also newly arrived, said as we sat sweating over dinner, and the choice of adjective was exact. Because of the drought, there were restrictions on the use of power, and the air conditioning — that indispensable element for surviving the New York summer — only worked part time.

I went to a reception at the Indian consulate, and we might have been in Delhi, waiting for the monsoon to break. Drinking litres of iced mango juice, I acquired a curious sort of high, and became convinced the juice was coming out through my pores in orange sweat.

I needed somewhere to live, and found a summer let, a claus-trophobic apartment on West 46th Street, between Sixth and Seventh. The owners, like all true New Yorkers, or at least those who could afford it, had fled to the beach for the summer. The apartment was a walk-up above a men's wear store, up a dark, narrow staircase, and when I came to know the city better, I thought I was lucky not have been mugged or murdered.

When I ran the carpet sweeper over the floor, it became clogged with coarse yellow hair, and all the time I lived there I had a fantasy of a blonde woman tearing out handfuls of long hair in a frenzy. It was not a comfortable idea, but long after I heard that the couple who owned the apartment had a large dog, very hairy, shacked up there with them.

It was too hot to sleep, and I lay naked night after night on top of the bed, damp with sweat, listening to WINS, a 24-hour station which broadcast nothing but news. It was forced feeding, but I learned a lot about America in those long, sad nights . . .

∽

After I left London I spent some years in Sydney with the anti-Vietnam protest movement threaded through it. On election night, 1972, I was at a performance of *The Merry Widow*, not by choice but to oblige a friend, and it was in one of the dressing rooms afterwards that I heard Labor had been swept into power. We rushed on to a party at the Nimrod, then still in Kings Cross, and there were tears and embraces and celebration drinks until all hours.

It was a fateful victory for me personally. Because of it, less than a year later, I was in Peking, on a two-year assignment as one of the first three Australian correspondents to be accredited to the People's Republic of China.

I had heard some rumours in the office that the *Sydney Morning Herald* was opening a bureau in Peking (I'll continue to call it that; the switchover to Beijing came after my time), but until I was asked if I would go, I had no ambitions in the direction of China. I believed I was thoroughly Europe-oriented and my only acquaintance of Asia was as a tourist.

"Why me?" I asked incredulously. "We think," said the executive who was making the proposition, "that it will do us good to send a woman to China." This was fairly cynical, coming from a paper which had refused to have women on its general staff until the late 60s, and continued the ban on women as sub-editors until much later, but times change, and there is not too much point in reviving old grudges.

After New York and Washington and London, Peking was like another planet, and in those early winter days, with the dust storms marching in from the Gobi Desert and the air snapping and snarling with static electricity, more alien than I could have possibly imagined.

For a while, I felt more nervous in Peking than in mugger-ridden New York, for we were still in the closing years of the Great Proletarian Cultural Revolution, and though there were no signs of the violent turmoil still shaking the country visible in the capital, we were always under threat over what we were writing. Newcomers made the pilgrimage to the house where Anthony Grey, the Reuters' correspondent, was held prisoner for two years as a hostage for Chinese journalists in jail in Hong Kong. The Australian publisher Francis James, an old acquaintance, had only emerged from China a few months before I went in, after three years captivity. "Be careful. I don't want to have to write leaders asking: 'Why don't the Chinese bring Margaret Jones to trial?' " the *Herald* editor said crossly before I left.

On the other hand, there were few worries about physical safety. The only incident I heard of in two years involved the wife of a French diplomat, who was struck a glancing blow over the head by some poor lunatic as she went into a shop. She was not much hurt but the man was executed the next morning, and her husband received a courteous invitation to attend. He declined. Despite all the cloud-cuckoo-land stories you heard about Chinese honesty, there was a certain amount of petty theft, mainly involving money and small antique objects, but things of obvious foreign origin, like cameras and watches, were too risky to touch at that time, and could be left lying about with impunity.

In the 70s the foreign community in China was small and the press corps even smaller, fewer than thirty when I arrived, forty-six two years later, mainly due to an influx of Japanese. There were five women: one a famous British correspondent, a veteran of World War II, assorted Middle East wars and Vietnam; a charming plump Italian; a cool East German who, rather unusually, had brought along her husband; a Cuban who spoke no English and so had a lonely time of it, and me.

The women correspondents were the luckiest on the female side of the foreign community, for at least we had jobs and could keep reasonably busy. Worst off were the diplomatic wives, who had nothing to do, not even housework for there were maids and cooks, and women to look after the children. Most were bored and discontented, and more than one marriage came to grief in that sterile environment.

I found it ironic that I had to come to a communist country to acquire a "staff": a maid, a driver, an interpreter. I could have had a cook if I'd had more space, but the Chinese habit of taking a nap in the middle of the day from half past twelve to two o'clock presented some difficulties. I never got used to tiptoeing round my own apartment for two hours while the interpreter went to bed in the second bedroom, the maid dozed off in the kitchen, and the driver slept soundly in a little room intended for a pantry, but which now held his bed. The sweetest moment of the day was five o'clock, when they all went home, unless I needed the driver to take me to a banquet at the Great Hall of the People in the evening.

Actually, being full of revolutionary zeal when I arrived, I refused to have a maid, thinking it demeaning. I would do my own housework, I said. This idealistic gesture did not last long. Chinese brooms and mops are both home-made — bundles of straw and bundles of rags tied to poles — and they are amazingly heavy and hard to handle. Over everything, for the ten months of the year when it does not rain, lies the diabolical Peking dust, and it was not long before I was applying to the Diplomatic Service Bureau for an "aunty".

My first aunty was youngish, still in her thirties, and I got on with her wonderfully. She was one of the few people willing to try to understand my rough Chinese. ("What language are you speaking?" said my interpreter, who could be very bitchy when she tried.)

But the aunty, like the British, believed if you shout loud enough, foreigners will eventually understand you. And so I did. We were very happy with each other, and we both wept when she was taken away by the Diplomatic Service Bureau, on the grounds that she was too young and active to waste her time working for just one person, and she must go to a family.

My next aunty cast a gloom over the household, as she was a thin, scuttling old lady who claimed to be sixty but looked seventy, and should have been retired. She refused to use any of the labour-saving devices I had so painfully managed to bring in all the way from Hong Kong, and insisted on having a wooden washboard to scrub the teatowels. She spent most of her time in the kitchen drinking hot water and smoking vile-smelling cigarettes, and when I came in she would jump up with such a look of theatrical guilt that in the end I stayed out of the kitchen and did without my morning coffee. Every time I saw her struggling with mops and brooms, I felt guilty myself, especially as I knew that, though the Chinese charged me the going rate for her services, she only got a fraction of the money. It was the same with all the staff.

It was at that time very hard to talk to Chinese because of the rules against fraternising with foreigners. But once, in the company of a good Chinese speaker, I had an enlightening conversation with one of these women who worked as maids. She was astonishingly frank, and said that the influx of foreigners had been the *worst* possible news for many Chinese women. They, once their own children were off their hands, used to find jobs in small neighbourhood factories where the atmosphere was cosy and they had the companionship of other women. Since the foreigners had come, she said, these women had been plucked out of these agreeable jobs, and set to work cleaning foreign houses and looking after foreign children. As there is direction of labour in China, they had no choice in the matter.

Chinese are terrible racists, and find foreigners disgusting anyway, with their body hair and their smell of meat and milk; so the women suffered doubly. (My driver, otherwise a kind and agreeable man even if he did turn out later to be working for the Public Security Bureau, always used to wind the window down hastily when I got into the car. I was tempted to point out that his garlicky smell was just as unattractive as my dairy products one, but didn't in the cause of Australian-Chinese friendship.)

In topography, Peking could hardly have been a greater contrast to the other three cities I lived in over a ten-year period. My winter arrival in this leafless place wreathed in a mixture of dust and smog struck me with a terrible chill. I thought it ugly and physically depressing, and because of this first impression, it was a long time before I came to see its spare, haunting beauty which had not much to do with contemporary buildings, but with the beguilement of the eye by the bleached colours of North China and the way the small *hutung* houses huddle onto the earth.

Unlike Washington, there was a very lively, centralised social life, though rather an incestuous one. As the Chinese themselves were out of bounds, except for official occasions, the foreigners turned inward, and something very nice evolved, which was a return to home entertainment of the Victorian kind.

There was an excellent choir, drawn from all the embassies, which did the rounds for parties, and could be relied on to produce setpiece programmes for foreign festivals like Christmas. Amateur players were recruited for drama and variety turns, and fancy dress evenings on historical themes were regular events. It was amazing what could be run up on home sewing machines, which many diplomats' wives seemed to carry with them, and the theatre shop, where the Chinese sold theatrical costumes to foreigners, proved very useful. The Australian Ambassador once played, very effectively, a NSW colonial governor dressed in the uniform of a Japanese general from the theatre shop, some fake medals, and a plumed hat created from a pith helmet and a feather duster.

It was a great place for losing self-consciousness. For a time, in the evenings, we used to drive out to the Ming Tombs for poetry readings, and lie in the soft grass drinking wine by lantern light, while the readings went round the circle in half a dozen languages. Alas, the Chinese put a stop to these magical evenings by imposing a curfew at the Tombs. It was obligatory for any such gathering of foreigners to be watched over, at a distance, by motor cycle police from the Public Security Bureau, to make sure we were not making contact with Chinese. The police, it seems, had objected to being kept from the' beds by the activities of demented foreigners, so that was the end of the poetry readings.

Of the . . . cities I have written of here, Peking was certainly the one which jolted me most. It gave me the best and worst of times, with periods of intense boredom punctuated by flashes of excitement, with enlightenment matched by equal disillusion, with friendships born out of propinquity but none the less lasting. Its legacy is wonderfully sweet-and-sour.

❧ *Janette Turner Hospital* ❧

Changes and the Things that Don't Change: India 1977 and 1990

The first changes I notice in Trivandrum are the *absences*. I miss the smell of coconut oil, which used to drift like exotic fog, wisping up from every restaurant and kitchen and marketplace. *Breeding heart disease*, the Indian Medical Association warned, and in Kerala, where literacy, public education and health standards are the highest in the country, there has been a sharp change to cooking in safflower and soya, the polyunsaturated oils.

❧

Bureaucracy is something that hasn't changed, except for where it has become more cumbersome than ever. For example, it takes close to an hour to cash a traveller's cheque in the State Bank of India in Trivandrum.

This is how it goes. First I was at the counter for quite some time, as the clerk attends to two other customers. Then I gave him my traveller's cheque and passport. He has to make three entries into a ledger that is surely a parody of ledgers. It is straight out of a Dickens novel, it is the largest ledger I have ever seen. It has a wing span of over three feet. The clerk makes his entries with meticulous penmanship. I think: if he copied out every word of every visa in my passport, and every word on my traveller's cheque, I still don't understand how it could take this long. He stamps all his entries with several rubber stamps. He handles the stamps with a reverence that suggests erotic involvement with the acts of certification. Eventually he gives me a metal token the size of an Australian dollar coin and asks me to sit and wait. I wait. I watch my traveller's cheque and passport being taken by a *peon* to another desk in a warehouse of desks. Again I think of Dickens and *Bleak House*.

As we have often done before, Cliff and I ask ourselves is this passion for the ledger and the rubber stamp something the British bequeathed, those 19th-century Dickensian/Kiplingesque bureaucrats of the Raj? Or is it an expression of the hierarchical and intricate caste system which was already in place, and which the Brits found convenient to use? Or is it both? — a long-lasting marriage of true minds giving birth to a bureaucratic maze with tentacles that Dickens's law clerks might have drooled over.

Meanwhile, back in the second-floor oven of the State Bank of India, Trivandrum Branch, another clerk copies many words into another huge ledger. Another *peon* takes my cheque and passport and growing documentation to another desk, another clerk, another ledger.

Eventually a *peon* emerges from a swing door in the clerk's room. He carries the file of my financial materials across the waiting room, right by my chair, and gives the whole bundle to one of the tellers behind a barred cubicle at the other side of the room. More clerks, rubber stamps and mysterious activities ensue. At last the teller, with a fine show of having no idea of the relationship between the material in his hands and the woman slumped in the waiting room in front of him (it is perhaps not irrelevant to mention here that the mid-winter temperature is 33 degrees celsius, the humidity high and the air pressure equivalent to the wearing of a leaden suit) — the teller calls out the number on my token as though to waiting multitudes, though Cliff and I are the only waitees. By this time I am in a state of mesmeric tranquillity and almost resent the interruption of my reverie. I go to the teller. I hand in my token. The number is checked, my encashment certificate is stamped. I am handed my passport, my rupees, my encashment certificate. I am exhorted to keep the encashment certificate as I will need to show it (for checking and stamping) at the international airport on departure. I wilt at the thought.

∽

The system of trash collection hasn't changed. There isn't one. Not in any city in India. There are two ways of dealing with waste. In the family compound of which our cottage was a part, there was a designated coconut palm: all trash (vegetable, papers, plastics) was dumped at its base. When the pile got too high, too stinking and too raddled with rats, it was burned.

Mostly, however, people simply throw their waste matter into the street. Even in quite wealthy areas, where palatial houses sit well back behind high walls thick with bougainvillea, *peons* dump the household trash over the wall into the street. It lies there and blows about, and gets redistributed by sweeper boys, and eventually, at no discernibly regular intervals, sweeper boys light bonfires along the sides of the streets and burn off the heaps of rubbish.

Traffic hasn't changed. In Bombay there are now traffic lights and lanes painted on the roads. These represent a fantasy of order imposed on chaos. Any taxi driver worth his salt will regard a space on the opposite side of the road as an invitation. In every Indian city we visited, we have regularly, hearts in mouth, been driven at breakneck pace toward oncoming traffic. Somehow, in the last split second, the driver zips back onto his prescribed side of the road.

There is a mad and exhilarating eclecticism to Indian traffic. On one city block in Jabalpur, I tried to make a count: 10 buses; too many taxis to count; too many rickshaws; too many scooters and bicycles; about a dozen cows; hundreds of pedestrians; several ox-carts; half a dozen hand-carts (these are about 12 feet long, pivoted on a central axle and two bicycle wheels, pushed or pulled by a running *peon* and piled high with anything from bricks to bananas); one elephant carrying a load of palm branches in his trunk like celery; one camel. All of this is moving and weaving crazily about in a narrow space without shoulder or sidewalks, crammed between shop-fronts. Everything is moving except the cows, who stand with looks of ineffable peace on their faces while the traffic parts like the Red Sea and sketches polite arabesques around them. At an intersection in the heart of New Delhi, when the lights changed, six cows moved sedately across the road, and the maze of cars adapted instinctively as water flows around floating debris.

ονδ

Our two days in Varanasi (the Hindi name for Benares, which is an Anglicisation), coincided with the Hindu festival of Maghi Purnima, and the sacred city and sacred banks of the Ganges were a magnet for hundreds of thousands of pilgrims. The traffic was even more chaotic than usual. Buzzing down to the Burning Ghat in an auto-rickshaw, I could feel the onset of heart seizure roughly twice per minute as our driver zigzagged between people and cows and buses and cars. (I think there are more cows than vehicles in Varanasi.) Our driver never looked over his shoulder before changing lanes (I use the term ''lanes'' very loosely here). Several times I touched the flank of a passing bus to steady myself as we careened alongside it. I noticed that rickshaw drivers, bus drivers, pedestrians, gave an odd little flick of the wrist at the moment when they moved themselves into the direct path of another lethally moving object. It seemed a ludicrously touching faith in the power of signification. People drive and walk, I thought, as though they have an unlimited supply of reincarnations ahead of them. Or else as though they believe they have an invisible and inviolable forcefield around them.

After surviving for half an hour in this dangerous chaos without so much as seeing an accident, it was clear to me that people *did* have an invisible and inviolable forcefield around them, and that when they gave that odd little flick of the wrist they were simply saying: here it is; here is the boundary of my forcefield.

Thereafter, I used the trick every time I crossed a road or travelled in an auto-rickshaw. I flicked my hand casually. Here is my forcefield, I said. It worked very nicely. I escaped from Varanasi unscathed.

Accidents do happen, however, and rather frequently. But they happen mostly at night, when the chaos is much increased by the terrifying habit of driving without lights, or with only parking lights on, in the mistaken belief that gas is thereby conserved. Accidents also happen between towns and villages on the ''open highway'' (if such a term can be used for the rutted, narrow, potholed roads) since drivers pick up speed when they get the chance, inviting messy impacts with buses and laden oxcarts.

It was clear to me that the forcefield method of death-prevention was intimately tied to the ritual of indicating one's personal boundaries with the flick of the wrist. Since this signal cannot be detected by the dim glow of parking lights at night, it is advisable to stay off the streets after dark.

❧

In Bombay, Delhi, Madras, most major cities, there has been no change in the system of municipal water supply. It is still off for most of the day. You fill all available containers with water during the evening when the water is on. You keep small pitchers beside the tubs of water. You flush the toilet (if you have a western toilet) by emptying several pitchers of water down it. You bathe by tossing pitchers of water over yourself.

When we stay in Bangalore, the water is off for three whole days and nights. There is a wellbore with pump in the grounds of our guest house. We pump ourselves buckets of water and haul them upstairs to flush the toilet. A *peon* brings a bucket of hot water to our room at six in the morning, and we stand in the tiny bathroom (it's five feet square, a bare cement floor with toilet in one corner), lather ourselves, then throw pitchers of water at each other till the bucket is empty.

We begin to have erotic cravings for Canadian bathrooms. We lust after a hot shower.

In Trivandrum, however, we feel rather smug and privileged. Trivandrum is one of the few cities in India with a water purification plant. Also the water goes off only once the whole time we are there. (This is due to the good luck of geographic location at the foot of the Western Ghats. Kerala is green and lush, its rainfall heavy. There are two monsoons a year here, and water shortage is rare.) Our bathroom has a tiled floor, a shower head near the ceiling, a drainhole in the floor. When you shower, the toilet and washbasin get splattered. There is only cold water, but this close to the equator, what else would you want? We have three cold showers a day in a futile attempt to stay cool. Sometimes we get up during the night to have a fourth cold shower in the faint hope that we will fend off heat waves long enough to get to sleep.

∾

The fishing boats at Kovelam have not changed, and this is something I've been waiting 12 years to do again. Just 15 kilometres south of Trivandrum, Kovalam is one of the most beautiful beaches in the world. The fishermen go out in long handmade boats. Four logs lashed together, the boats are buoyant but not watertight: they sit low in the water which rises around the legs and thighs of the passengers, blood warm. I sit in the middle of a long boat, and the fisherman kneels at the rear with his bamboo paddle. We pass through waves like ghosts through walls and head for the open ocean. This is my idea of euphoria.

For an elephant at Kanchipuram, and for the fishing boats at Kovalam, I'd do it all again. For many other euphoric moments too, of course: especially boating down the Ganges; or wandering through the utter serenity of the deer park at Sarnath where the Buddha preached his first sermon; or browsing through the fragrant dusk of Palayam Market. For such moments, I'd fill in every necessary form in triplicate, I'd wait interminably in rooms that feel like Turkish Baths. I'd dose myself daily with Kaopectate. India is exhausting and exasperating but also seductive. Once you've been, you keep going back.

∾ *Stella Bowen* ∾

England Again

*Australian painter Stella Bowen lived in both England and France
with the writer Ford Madox Ford during the 1920s. After their
separation in France, Bowen supported herself and the couple's
daughter Julie by painting portraits from a Paris base. By the
mid-1930s her finances dictated a return to London.*

After the studio was cleared of debt, it took just six months to
convince me that life in Paris was no longer possible. I became convinced for the simplest of reasons; I had no more
money.

In six months I had only two small portrait commissions. I
had the greatest difficulty in finding a tenant, at a much reduced
rent, for the smaller studio, and my chances of returning to
America in the spring became fainter and fainter. Finally the
New York Bank Moratorium put the stopper on all my hopes. I
could not get confirmation of the few commissions that I had
been offered verbally before I sailed home, and the very friends
who had jubilated at my previous success and foretold its repetition, now wrote and said "For goodness' sake don't come over
this year. You will not make even your expenses." So there was
nothing for it but to turn my attention to England, and see if we
should be allowed to creep back there.

This realisation hit me like a sudden blow one lovely afternoon
in early spring as I was standing on the Pont Marie. I was looking
towards the Ile Saint Louis, where I was on my way to see the
paintings Louis Marcoussis had been doing there. He had been
lent an improvised studio by Madame Helena Rubinstein in a
beautiful old house which she was about to pull down. The river

had never looked lovelier nor the house-fronts of the quai de Béthune more warmly golden in the late afternoon sunshine. *"Avez-vous remarqué,"* an old French painter once said to me, *"que la lumière de Londres est rose, mais celle de Paris est dorée?"* I had remarked it, and I was in no mood for London's pink sun, nor for the slack, slow and heavy tempo of London streets and London conversation. London offered no stimulus capable of dissipating your worries, but left you severely alone to build up all sorts of poisonous little phobias and obsessions. Paris on the other hand was an immediate tonic in times of trouble; her hard head and delectable bosom were always at your disposal, for comfort and advice. She could also show you such physical beauty that to leave her seemed impossible. Especially on the island!

That is where the Bradleys lived and where Jenny (now Julie's godmother) had given me the best of my French social education. That is where Julie was at this moment having tea with Madeleine Marcoussis and where, long ago, the *Transatlantic Review* had had its little office. Rich foreigners had bought some of the old houses on the *quai* and filled them with exotic decorations, but these appeared merely as extraneous ornaments on the prow of a tightly-packed ark which, anchored in the Seine, held an insular and even a provincial life peculiarly its own.

When I looked at it from the bridge on that sunny afternoon, it seemed to contain all France for me. In my private imagination, Montmartre usually shared this distinction because it housed the Marcoussis, and in spite of the fact that they were really Polish, to me they represented a considerable slice of French life. Julie and I used to climb what seemed just a busy village street on Sunday mornings to visit them in their tall studio with the great view from the top of the rue Caulaincourt. This studio contained the most charming of treasures — Aubusson tapestries, an ancient spinet, African masks and fetishes, Alice's ivory bracelets laid out in a long row, old faience tiles hung up, and a comic collection of glass bottles — all arranged against the simple domestic background of two hardworking painters. There were also Louis' cubist compositions and Alice Halicka's satirical-romantic decorations, and in particular there was their delightful daughter in person, who was Julie's best friend. Madeleine was as dark as Julie was fair and as quick as Julie was deliberate and they twittered together with a charming mutual devotion. There would be a proper French Sunday lunch with *hors d'oeuvres* and a fine salad and a bottle of red wine and fast and friendly talk, chiefly of painters and painting, and also of such common topics as how to dress and feed one's self without spending money. There was nothing about those Sunday lunches to make one homesick for the roast beef and Yorkshire pudding and the subsequent somnolence of the English Sabbath. On the contrary.

On the day when I saw that we would have to leave Paris, the Marcoussis happened to be all on the Ile Saint Louis, along with those other friends and beauties and joys that I realised I was going to lose. For if Paris offers a good antidote to emotional troubles, she is adamant where money is concerned. She allows no blurred edges or wishful thinking on this stark subject. In London, you can kid yourself that things will come right in the end, that luck is just round the corner and the day of reckoning very far away. Paris permits of no such self-deception.

So I knew that we must go back to where my few pounds were still worth twenty shillings and where there was, perhaps, a market for portraits that no longer existed in Paris for a foreign woman painter.

With difficulty I found a tenant for my studio. He was a rich, neurotic and undisciplined American whose wife had just been trying to commit suicide. I hated leaving them amongst my things, but they paid me three months rent in advance. With deep misgiving I installed Julie — now twelve years old — in a *pension de famille* to finish her school year at the *Ecole Alsacienne*, whilst I went prospecting across the Channel. The day I left, I took her to the Bon Marché to buy some necessary socks and vests and petticoats, and we wandered in a state of utter desolation amid the ugly displays of cheap underwear. That night, I sailed in the third-class women's cabin from Dunkerque to Folkestone. At midnight, listening to the creaking timbers of the vessel, I remembered that it was my fortieth birthday.

∽ *Shirley Hazzard* ∽

Observing the Conventions

Gianni sang. He sang rather well, and quite a lot. When very young he had the idea of becoming a professional singer, but abandoned it because of the battles one had to fight. There were the teachers, the impresarios who did not recognise talent, or were jealous of it; there was the now celebrated cellist who, auditioning together with the youthful Gianni, had talked throughout Gianni's performance.

"*Dunque* — '*Maestro*', I asked him. 'What would you think of someone who talked while you performed?' And, giving me that smile — with his mouthful of white teeth which were not then exclusively false — he said, 'Ah, but you see, when I perform, no one talks'. 'Then,' said I, 'the difference is that *your* audience is composed only of civilised persons'."

Gianni sang as he drove us to Herculaneum in his new car. He could sing arias, and knew Neopolitan songs by the dozens — 'Libero Bovio, Salvatore di Giacomo, those are the names to learn at Naples. Never mind about King Ladislas, or Joachim Murat.' When we approached the royal palace at Portici he slowed down. "Look at this. Who but a Neopolitan would have a country retreat with the road going right through the house? And at the foot of an active volcano." He laughed, and thumped his hand on the wheel, highly satisfied with the folly of the Bourbons.

Gianni was something of a patriot. That is to say that all foreigners, and particularly anglo-saxons, came in for a mauling. "The names these people have," he remarked, although my name was practically the same as his. "Where do they get them from. I had an actress once — I mean, in a film I directed — a skinny-looking thing like you, English, called Sally. Imagine, *salt*. A fine name for a girl.''

I leant forward, my elbows along the back of their seat, my chin bumping on my enlaced knuckles. The nape of Gioconda's neck, rising out of a crimson coat, was whiter than her throat, as if in summer her hair had hung down over it; above this whiteness, twisted glossy ropes of hair were secured by a comb of curved tortoise-shell.

"Your comb. I never saw anything like it.''

Her fingers came up to touch it. "How old is it, do you think? Or an old copy of something old? Here — and here — there must have been stones; diamonds, even, for the rest of the work is so fine. I found it on a barrow in San Biagio — one of those barrows, you must have seen them, where they sell, or try to sell, cracked saucers and broken keyrings, rubbish scavenged from here and there. I took it home and cleaned it. And Gianni liked it.'' Here Gianni gave a possessive, endorsing nod. "I've worn it for years.''

It was a pale, cold day, quiet as a weekday. We were almost alone on the road. At Resina, with the Vesuvius rising over us, we came into a country market where a dozen stunted donkeys, each dragging its own teetering Vesuvius of ill-corded bales, applied their muzzles humidly to the Maserati as it inched among them. Not long afterwards this little town founded on the lava was submerged under the eruption of skyscrapers flung up by a housing project.

At Herculaneum we were the only visitors, wandering unaccompanied through vacant Roman rooms, like guests who have arrived on the wrong day and can take stock of things without having to be polite. Gianni loved my pleasure in the ruins, proud as if the town were his own creation, explaining the arrangement of the houses, the changes of situation caused by volcanic action — "Here was the sea, then, with gardens and cypress alleys leading down to it. All that land down there came much later.'' Every so often he would tell us, "It was a marvellous life,'' as if he himself had been plucked out of it.

"Look at this, for instance.'' Gianni led me away to the foot of one of the corridor-like streets and into an ornate room that had served, possibly, as a private theatre — one end giving a sense of proscenium, decorated with a stone mask set above mosaics of animals and garlands. "What could be more charming.'' He followed me up the room to examine the decorations and, taking me by the shoulders, stood me in the niche intended for some statue. He then kissed me — or attempted to, his mouth roughly glancing over my chin and throat as I spun my head away, dodging his caress like a blow. He dropped his hands from my shoulders but still stood blocking the way, looking at me and smiling, and repeating in a normal voice, "What could be more charming."

I stood in the niche where he had placed me. Even to push him away seemed too much like a response. In an undertone he complained to me, "Why the fuss. I am only, so to speak, observing the conventions."

"Damn you," I said in English, furious that Gioconda's proximity somewhere in this labyrinth obliged me to lower my voice to him like an accomplice. "Damn you and your conventions."

Gianni walked away. Having stepped down through the narrow doorway he turned back, one hand raised and resting on the outer wall, to look at me with the same bright eyes and hard, humorous compression of the lips.

"Just one moment," said Gioconda, out of sight. Gianni stood quite still. In the street beyond there was a tiny sound, and Gioconda appeared beside him winding her camera. "It was so natural," she said. "So like you."

Gioconda later gave me this photograph, along with one or two others she took that day. I have it still, and there is Gianni, smiling ironically out of the picture at something that has momentarily taken his fancy.

I remained some minutes more in that small Roman theatre — that had, I dare say, seen a lot of this kind of thing played out in various costumes.

Gianni made, I thought, a reference to this incident, in the car as we drove on around the gulf of Sorrento — observing to Gioconda that he found me young for my age. "Strange to think," he said, as if I were not present, "that there are only six or seven years between you two. You seem like my contemporary, while she —" tipping his head back in my direction, "might just be leaving school. Or entering it."

Over his shoulder he gave me, too — again as if the matter were crucial and personal to him — accounts of the great eruption, quoting Pliny to us as though to back up his own testimony; citing like fresh evidence the letters of the poet Statius. "You see how it is with us," he said — meaning Italians, or perhaps the human race. "The ships were waiting to take them off. Ash and lava were streaming down on them. But they had dinner, they talked, they went to the baths, they slept. And then it was too late.''

I could see that he thought well of them for this, just as he had commended the impracticality of the Bourbons; and quite expected him to add, as he did, ''There is something to be said, for it, after all.'' And when I, still sulking, made no reply, he most unfairly shrugged at Gioconda as if to give me up as a bad job.

Of that journey, with Vesuvius slowly turning us on its flanks, then releasing us for the long arc of the bay, there remains a childhood sensation of disappointment: my outing had been spoilt, the expedition had shifted character in an unlooked-for way. In memory there is a blur of cold sea and silver fields, and then we are at Sorrento and I am cheerful again, having had my lunch and being excited by the pretty restaurant, the romance of the slopes above and cliffs below, and the great view out to Capri. It is as Gianni has just said, I am as easily diverted as a schoolgirl.

❧ *Nettie Palmer* ❧

Barcelona

May 15th, 1936

How clean everything is here after London! Not merely our
sparsely-furnished cottage itself, which we have taken for a year,
but the air, the fishing-boats drawn up on the sand, the strip of
beach that runs in a long curve to the docks at Barcelona.

Our irregular but continuous row of houses — the Calle
Monsolis — stands against a hill, and the concrete walls of the
courtyards behind the houses are even higher at the back than at
the sides, so as to support the sheer clay cutting over which hang
trees belonging to a wide farm immediately above — a fig over
us, a cherry further along. Just as these houses almost lean back
against the hills and face the sea, so I find myself leaning back
against Spain and looking out on the Mediterranean: I orient
myself, that is, I face the East.

It is good to be in Spain these days. There is a feeling of sap
stirring, of life beginning to bud, and not only because of the
Spring. I feel that the young people who come pouring out to the
beach in their shorts or coloured frocks are heady with the sense
of a new world opening up ahead of them. It is partly a political,
partly a social liberation. They are discovering the pleasures of
"sport", of hiking, of tramping over the hills with picnic-baskets, boys and girls together. A good many of the conventions of
Old Spain must have pressed very heavily on youth. But now —
every Sunday seems to be a fiesta.

Not for everyone. Things are going badly for Roca who keeps
the fonda at the corner, and for his prim, pretty little
"Aragonesca" wife from Saragossa. It is going to be a bad sea-

son, they say, and many of the big houses, like the Torre Monsolis, are closed up; the rich people have gone to France and there will not be the parties of theatre-goers and concert-goers driving out along the beach-road from Barcelona for supper. At least so Roca says dolefully. I feel sorry for him, for he has been very good to us since we came, though we spend very little with him, doing most of our own cooking. He has sunk a lot of money in this fonda of his, making it gay and modern, and he is a wonderful cook. But he takes the bad outlook very lightly; a buoyant, intelligent man, he is more concerned with the general welfare of the country than with his own personal prospects. His wife, though, stands at the door of the empty fonda watching the youthful holiday-makers and their picnic-baskets with narrowed, resentful eyes.

July 4th, 1936

With A. last night to a demonstration in Barcelona on behalf of the young Brazilian officer, Luis Carlos Prestes, who had been imprisoned in Rio de Janeiro for working-class activity. Usually people seem so self-centred here, so remote from the international scene, that I was curious to see how many would participate in this meeting. I was soon enlightened. When we found the Gran Price after going down the narrow Street of the Hospital, a curved slit between high old houses, people were pouring into the building from all sides.

What a gathering! The hall had a wide, circular floor, then three galleries, the widest at the top. Very quickly it was packed. People of all ages and sexes — and, apparently, all classes — though the tone of the meeting was set by the youths and girls in uniforms of shirts and shorts, or shirts and grey trousers, very militant young people of the Popular Front parties.

Señora and Señorita Prestes (mother and sister of the imprisoned man) appeared on the platform and were given the central seats. Everyone rose and cheered them wildly; it seemed that everyone knew the story of this young Brazilian revolutionary. The mother was a dignified woman, dressed in black with sufficient care, sufficiently absorbed and tragic. The daughter, in light-grey with a rose-coloured scarf, was more alert and responsive.

A spirited meeting, with vigorous speeches, mainly in Catalan; but long drawn-out. It had been timed to start at ten; it was ten-thirty before it really started; and when it ended our last tram had gone. That meant a considerable trudge home, but when the outer city had been left behind it was full moonlight and a nightingale was singing gloriously in the tiny wood near our house.

July 19th, 1936

Awoke to the dull sound of firing, but took it to be celebrations connected with the opening of the People's Olympiad at Montjuich Stadium. Not till the milkman came did I notice how still everything was — no trains running, no cars on the road, hardly a soul on the beach. The little milkman's face was very serious: "A military rebellion's broken out in Barcelona." Women and men were gathering in the calle, looking across the bay to the city and listening to the faint rattle of machine-guns. There was uneasiness in their faces, but it was no use asking them what the trouble was; they were emphatic that no one could know anything. Soon cars with determined-looking men in them came tearing out from town; barricades were hastily thrown up along the road and preparations made to blow up the little stone bridge between here and the station.

It was terribly hard to grasp what was happening. Everything echoed with vagueness, nothingness — nada, nada . . . Yet into the bright morning some evil seemed to have suddenly entered, violently shattering the quiet, threatening all the future. The big, empty houses up toward Tiana appeared in league with it, as if they had been waiting all summer for the attack, harbouring conspirators behind their handsome stone walls. I found myself thinking: "This feeling of liberation here was an illusion. The dark forces have struck back; there'll be war all over the world."

But what affected us directly was the thought of A. in Barcelona among the fighting. She had stopped in town to act as interpreter for a huge group of French athletes coming in at midnight, and was to meet us at the station this afternoon. We tried to get in to Barcelona by walking along the railway-line, but were stopped by young men with rifles. All afternoon there were awed groups in the calle, listening to the firing across the water. The loudspeakers on every window still gave no real news, merely buzzing like cicadas: "Tranquilo, Spaniards, tranquilo: we are winning."

After tea this evening we sat on the stone coping near the church, watching the cars being searched for arms as they came in from the Costa Brava, and wondering what was happening across the water. Suddenly the lights came out on Barcelona city (everywhere but on Montjuich Height) and things seemed more hopeful.

∾ *Agnes Hodgson* ∾

Grañen

Agnes Hodgson sailed from Sydney to Barcelona in 1936 to nurse Republican wounded during the Spanish civil war. She was posted to the Aragon front where she served in field hospitals until the end of 1937.

1.12.36   Barcelona

Arrival in Barcelona. First impression at the frontier was of khaki balaclavas and coats. Unshaven men carrying guns and wearing dirty white and black rope-soled sandals. Black of eye, dark skinned and bearded. Everything scrutinised — we realised that we were in a country at war.

11.1.37

Left Barcelona 8.30 a.m. O'Donnell saw us off . . .. The journey was very interesting. The country as far as Tarrasa was covered with young pine woods. The timber was being cut and the soil is red copper coloured. Last season's stubble (corn?) is still standing; vines cut back, thick green crop just shooting; the land looks very dry. There were round haystacks and large white washed stone or stucco houses. The country undulates with a type of fir forest. In valleys there are small vineyards in between olive trees, vegetables in dry river beds and cultivated olive orchards . . ..

We arrived at Grañen all in the dark and asked our way and

were kindly led by a lad to the hospital, slipping in muddy streets by the light of a torch. We were welcomed heartily and shown round the place.

We had a good meal and sparkling wine to celebrate and a ration of chocolate and cigarettes and so to bed pretty tired.

12.1.37 Grañen

Spent the morning being shown about and getting acquainted. Misty morning and cold. It is a large rambling house with a courtyard being filled in with stones. We sleep in a loft with mattresses on the floor. The two male members keep on t'other side partitioned by a Union Jack. The Spanish doctors and *practicantes* (medical students) sleep in another dormitory. There are two theatres and a common anaesthetics room. Two largish rooms adjoining each with two alcoves serve as wards and the alcoves house women patients. Another room upstairs serves VD patients. There is a large dining room and common room adjoining with a ping pong table. The kitchen and bathroom or wash house is more or less underground with three large cellars smelling of wine.

In the afternoon I turned in for night duty. Just my luck — somehow had forgotten such a thing as night duty was possible. Went on duty at nine p.m. An ambulance had arrived in the a.m. bringing several wounded and walking medical cases.

6.2.37

Various cases in the theatre. One lad had been wounded in the abdomen and had shrapnel and three perforations in the small intestine, two in the transverse colon and two in the stomach. A laparotomy was done and the perforations sutured, and four pints of blood were given, and one of saline. Also a bad leg injury admitted with two pieces of shrapnel in one leg. One wound became septic after four days and was opened and drained. Another pneumonia patient admitted but died after four days. The hospital is full to overflowing with influenzas and tonsilitis. We are very busy. The lad with the laparotomy to remove the shrapnel in his abdomen and liver developed bronchial pneumonia. He now has recovered, his sutures have been removed and he evacuated. He was called Pascual. Several hands and thumb wounds, mostly accidents, admitted last night, some suspected of being self-inflicted. A bullet wound through the eye arrived and was cleaned up and sutured. Very busy on the ward but managed to get out for one or two walks.

20.2.37

Tonight our lights have failed, and my pen likewise, but I'll carry on, and by candlelight. Tonight I was over at a house across the street where most of us go for coffee — the doctors took their gramophone and played it. Some of the records are of flamenco songs. It's not quite gypsy and it is very similar to what we heard in the summer of 1932 in many ways. I hope some day to be able to do it. Some of the men here sing flamenco duets quite well. They sing with their heads together looking very solemn and a little as though it is hurting them; and we all shout *'olé'* when they have managed to be particularly flutey. Our chief doctor is quite good, and very naive and sweet, giggling a little with mixed pleasure and irony when he has finished.

Last night when we were at the *Comité de Investigación* my dentist friend arrived for the evening. He went on leave to Barcelona and was then sent to Barbastro; he hopes to be coming back to Grañen in a few days. I shall be very sorry if he stays at Barbastro because I regard him as my particular crony and I was learning Spanish much more quickly with his assistance. He is engaged to an American and wants to learn English. We had a cheerful gathering in our kitchen afterwards opening the package his grandmother sent him (he doesn't look as though he should have a grandmother) of dried fish, and very high sausage, squashed butter, chocolate, oranges, and Barcelona nuts. Then we danced to the new records he had brought up. Just as we were going to bed the dentist's chauffeur came down to the kitchen livid with fury, he had put his leg through his bedroom floor and the ceiling of the common room. We had to take off his puttee and inspect his knee, no damage done, and then we all trooped up laughing, I'm afraid, to see the damage done to the floor. People are always going through floors here.

21.2.37

Chas Hunt returned from Barcelona with stores for the hospital and the medical ones go to Poleñino. He tells me that my trunk is missing, and that Lowson is still in Barcelona. She has an X-ray plant from Australia and is waiting for a transformer and asked whether we would like it here. I spoke to Aguilo and of course he was delighted as it saves them buying one. He requested that the machine be held in Barcelona until our hospital is moved to Polenino. I received no letters and am feeling a bit mouldy.

I copied a leaflet dropped by fascists over the nearby republican line, saying that they (the fascists) had captured Malaga with guns, cannons, machine guns, warships, etc., and that the men who had deceived the poor people had fled, robbing the banks and leaving the poor fools who believed in them to follow. The leaflet asked how long people will believe in the Red Deception and urged people to open their eyes and read the papers that we (the fascists) send you and from them see the truth of the catastrophe. Profit by these moments, it said, to present yourselves in our lines abandoning those who command you if they won't come too, and so obtain the clemency in which all penitents who presented themselves can believe. [*sic*] Printed in Saragossa.

A quiet day otherwise, sitting in the sun.

❦ *Blanche d'Alpuget* ❦

Chaos and Confusion

When Judith arrived in Kuala Lumpur her luggage did not. Or perhaps it did and was mislaid somewhere in the terminal building. The Malay girl from Qantas was winning in her smiles, but uncertain.

"You are the unlucky one tonight," she said as Judith stood by the baggage roundel. When she climbed on to the machinery and peered down the chute she could see a group of Malay boys lying at the bottom, playing cards. They smiled and waved at her.

"They are on go-slow," the Qantas girl explained. "The government is threatening to put the ringleaders in gaol."

A northern Indian Malaysian, a passenger from another flight who had already questioned Judith closely with that extraordinary presumption which was as much a part of Asian good manners as was the soothing lie, said, "Go-slows! Now we are developing the diseases of Western affluence," and he went on loudly to attack the Qantas policy of cheap fares to Europe, which did not extend to ASEAN member states. He had discovered Judith was a journalist half an hour earlier and now lectured her on her responsibility for arguing the ASEAN case in the Australian news media. He ended quietly, pleasantly, by offering a lift in his Mercedes.

When he moved off an Australian businessman pressed his card on her and invited her to dinner at his hotel for the following night. "You need friends in a place like this," he said and patted her shoulder. She heard him calling the Malay girl "Little Blossom" and she and the girl later exchanged looks of shared resentment.

"The company must give you seventy-five dollars a day if your luggage is lost," the girl murmured to Judith when, after an hour and a half, it became clear that the suitcase with her typewriter, her background notes, her very *raison d'être* had vanished. Judith walked out of the terminal to find a taxi thinking, It looks different but underneath it's the same bloody chaos and confusion.

There was a system for hiring taxis from the airport now. One paid the fare to town in advance at a kiosk and handed the receipt slip to the cab driver. By midnight only a few old black-and-yellow Peugeot taxis were waiting outside. Judith approached the car at the top of the rank. A Chinese, whose body was shaped like a squashed loaf of bread, levered himself from the front seat and stood looking at Judith with his square head lowered, as if preparing to charge at her.

"Hotel Malaya, please," she said and handed him the receipt slip. The driver took it. Judith got into the cab. The driver got into the cab. Nothing more happened.

"Hotel Malaya," Judith said.

The man nodded and sat there.

"I want to go to the Hotel Malaya," Judith said.

"We wait," the driver said.

"No. You give me back my receipt," Judith said.

The driver shook his head. "We wait."

Groups of people were getting into other taxis and driving off. Judith opened the door; the driver turned around.

"You get out? You no get out!" he shouted. "I sick man. I very sick. I work."

She managed to snatch the receipt from him and scrambled from the back seat. The driver ran after her down the roadway, towards the one remaining taxi.

"I take four persons only! I need money. I very sick," he yelled.

The driver of the other cab looked at her and made the honking sound which puzzled Malaysian Chinese make.

"Please take me to the Hotel Malaya," Judith said, thrusting the receipt at him.

The driver shook his head. "You, him," he said, pointing to his huge colleague.

The first man had caught up with Judith. "OK, OK, OK, OK," he panted. They returned to his taxi and set off at irate speed.

There was nothing to see except an occasional ghostly row of rubber trees. The old plantation stretched for kilometres, then there was complete blackness again, and after a while a luminous glow, then factories with the names of British companies on them. Independence or not, the colonial master held still, as Judith knew, the lion's share of the economy. She glared at Crosse and Blackwell in neon lights. Houses and a hotel — the Sahid — appeared. The driver swerved into its drive and stopped.

"This is not the Malaya," Judith said.

The driver opened the door. "You get out. You get other taxi."

They had a scene about the receipt slip but Judith, through the sheer energy of desperation that is the traveller's aid, won. Somebody who was asleep on the front steps of the Sahid, when tempted with a *ringgit* note to do so, got up and whistled her another cab. Half an hour later she arrived, shaken, in the centre of Kuala Lumpur at the Hotel Malaya. The left-hand back door of the second taxi had, on a curve, flung open and Judith had saved herself from falling out on to the roadway by clinging to the seat. The driver, a Malay haji, had chuckled, addressed Allah, and reached back with one arm to slam it shut again. Judith was too flooded with adrenalin after that to pay attention to the streets they were passing. The stupid, unfocused feeling that compounds from physical and nervous exhaustion and which reduces concentration to small nips at the environment had overtaken her. She noticed the red-and-gold *Kong Hee Fat Choy* signs plastered in the foyer, the plastic New Year peach and mandarin trees, and a sign by the lifts saying "Special Raw Fish Dinner", but not much else.

There was no room booked at the Hotel Malaya for Wilkes or Wilkinson or Wills. The desk staff seemed thrilled about her lost luggage. "Qantas. Lot of trouble, la!" they said, grinning.

A young Malay escorted Judith to her room and he stood grinning at her when he had — more for his own amusement than for her education, she thought — operated all the electrical gadgets there. She was too stupefied to understand his instructions about the airconditioner.

"You travel alone? You stay alone?" he asked.

Judith nodded.

"You like a drink?" He was a very pretty boy and his expectations of success were evident.

"No. I just want to go to sleep."

He looked from her empty hands to the bed and grinned some more. Half an hour later when Judith was just dozing off he knocked on the door. "I bring you nice drink. Still early, la. You have nice drink," he called.

Judith tiptoed to the door and put the safety chain in place. She could hear him muttering nastily outside and was shivering with nerves when she got back into bed, naked. She was unable to go to sleep for another hour and in that time her brain jitterbugged with ideas so dejected and bitter that at one stage she began sniffling in misery. She thought, When women everywhere were downtrodden at least they were in the main treated gently, like pets, because they were so vulnerable. Now we have claimed equality but we've not won respect, merely hostility. She recalled suddenly what it was that she had disliked about the Singaporeans. They had been no more brusque than Australian airport staff; they had, however, not been submissive. One expected Asian flunkeys to be submissive, like women. I'm a class traitor, she thought, and, I should have been more supportive of Minou to those drunken bums in Singapore.

She awoke with a jolt from the sound of something being slid beneath the bedroom door. The room was in darkness. She lay still, waiting for the next noise, taut with the sense of vulnerability that nakedness causes.

Nothing happened.

After a few minutes her fright abated. She switched on the bedroom lamp and saw that a newspaper, printed in Chinese characters, had ben pushed into the room. It must be morning. A photograph of Deng Xiaoping shaking his fist accompanied the lead story. Judith found her watch on the bedside table. It was six o'clock local time, which meant she had had about three hours sleep after being awake for almost twenty-four. She felt ratty, as if her brains had been fried, and when she recalled the events of the previous evening she snivelled with rage.

∾ *Mabel Edmund* ∾

The Only Black Woman at Ealing Station

In the middle of 1982 I accepted an invitation from the International Biographical Centre in Cambridge, England, to attend an Arts and Communication Congress at Queens College, Cambridge. I had to pay my own way and all expenses while over there. I shall never regret having made that decision to go, because I met some wonderful people there. Some lasting friendships were formed at the college and in London where I stayed a while with friends of my Canberra friend, Professor Audrey Donnithorne. I also spent some time in Dorset and Oxford. The congress is a great opportunity for delegates from around the world to meet and get to know each other better through the art of communication. Each year it is held in a different country. The time that I spent at Cambridge was very valuable to me. I learnt so much in the discussion groups and plenary sessions that were held every day.

Every night we were taken by bus to enjoy a cultural night out. One night, after attending a recital, we went on to an English manor for dinner. It was unusual eating roast beef and baked potatoes, then plum pudding and custard at two o'clock in the morning! We didn't get back to our rooms until three in the morning. I had seventy-two steps to climb up to my bedroom. Most of the delegates were in a large modern building, some of us were billeted in an early century building, a lovely old place with very old antique furniture. I think it had three storeys, with six sets of twelve steps with landings in between. That is why I remember the seventy-two steps that I had to climb two or three times each day. They were so old and worn that they were the color of driftwood. I became good friends with a lady from Benin in Africa, a tutor in a large maternity hospital, and a gentleman from the Philippines who was head of a college. The three of us spent a lot of time together, and shared our experiences.

There were over three hundred delegates from forty different nations and they all had letters after their names or titles. I checked the list of names and I think I was the only one there without a degree. On the last night a large banquet was held, and in his speech the director general said that for the first time the congress had the honour of having a descendant of the original Australians attend, and he invited me to stand and everyone acknowledged my presence. You don't have to have degrees to be important, you just need to be yourself! People accept you.

Catching a bus from Cambridge to London, I asked the driver if he went near the station. He said yes, but I meant the railway station, and he meant the bus station. I was left about a mile from the railway station. I picked up my heavy suitcase and started walking the longest and most humiliating mile I have ever walked. About ever six steps I would have to stop for a rest, my arms felt like they had been pulled out of their sockets. I had to get to Ealing to phone Mike and Kay, the people I would be staying with.

Halfway there, I sat on the suitcase and burst into tears. I didn't have a clue where I was, I couldn't see a railway station in sight. Then a young West Indian girl came along and stopped and she told me where to go. She said if she were going the same way as me, she would have carried my suitcase. I asked a cab driver if he could take me there and he said the station was just around the corner and he did not want to lose his place at the front of the taxi rank. I battled on and made it to the underground platform, bought my ticket to Ealing and waited for the train to come flying along out of the darkness. A young girl helped me throw my suitcase in when the doors flew open and dragged me in with her. I tell you, you have to be fast, the doors just open and shut again so quickly then the train is gone again. When we arrived at Ealing, I grabbed my suitcase and went to throw it out on to the platform and I lost my balance and fell out of the train and rolled over the suitcase on to the platform. As I picked myself up, a lady asked if I was hurt and I told her, no, just my dignity, that's all. By now I was thoroughly fed up with the suitcase, but I dragged it up the stairs to ground level and rang the number by Canberra friend had given me. Mike answered and said he would be straight down to pick me up, but what colour dress was I wearing, so he could recognise me?

I started crying and I told him I did not know what colour my dress was, but "I am the only black woman waiting at Ealing station!"

We had a great week together, every day I caught a train and went out to explore London. I watched the changing of the guards at Buckingham Palace and all that. The only problem I had while there was that my bed had satin sheets on it and nearly every night I fell out of bed! Another surprise was the thousands and thousands of West Indian people living there, all spoke with "plums" in their mouths. They held jobs in high positions and no matter where you went there were West Indians working there. This was very different from Australia, where only the selected few Blacks got good jobs and only then because their relatives ran the committees.

I went from London to Dorset with Mike and Kay to attend a Catholic People's week. Families get together and hold discussion groups, to enlighten themselves and try to bring about better understanding and raise the standards of the church. One subject that was interesting was women priests in the Catholic Church. I guess while this present Pope is in office that will never be so. While in Dorset I became friends with a lady from Chile who was living in Oxford. She had been held a political prisoner over in her country and she had escaped with her young daughter and got safely to Oxford where she was living. She walked with a bad limp from the torture and punishment she had received while she was a captive in her country. Night after night she was still having nightmares and would be dreaming she was being tortured. She sobbed when she saw the tiny room over the stables that she was to sleep in while we were there, it reminded her of the small room that she had been locked up in over in Chile. I wrote to her for a while after I returned home, but I have lost contact with her now. She was a woman with great courage.

∞ *Vasso Kalamaras* ∞

Translated by David Hutchison and Vasso Kalamaras

The Anchorage Was Not Blue

It was chilly; it was autumn, you see. The waves were rising and our plucky boat seemed like a phantom. *Boo-oo, boo-oo . . . boo-oo-oo-oo* it whistled. Then silence again. I was hearing the rending of the waters. The wind shrieked, chilling our skins.

It must have been past midnight, but we could not stay asleep. We had become ghosts, awaiting a sign.

The children were afraid to sleep on their own in the cabin. They could not bear the waiting. They stretched out in a big arm-chair, with myself in the middle, my lap their pillow. I held their little heads for some time as they slept deeply. Their father covered them with raincoats.

No one wished to talk. Mr Manolis, the cook, came in suddenly and gave us the news, "Hey you! Come! We are entering our own waters. The Greek sea!"

We looked at each other as if frozen. Most of us cast our eyes down fearfully, from shyness or weakness. I did not move. That was not for me. My skin prickled, and my eyes stared expressionlessly at the big dark window of the saloon.

Everyone had got to their feet, going up to the poop-deck to catch a glimpse, from afar, of the black shadow of a little island, in the night. To send the first kisses . . . the thought . . . what?

I stayed alone in the big armchair with my two children in my arms.

The enormous saloon was filled with light. It was night outside, night; the first night after suffering ten whole years of homesickness. I had become such a small, lost and unimportant creature.

You would have thought that tears had petrified, compressed by a sudden, immeasurable pain. I believed so. I could not shed even a single tear. The endless waiting in the depths had opened a bottomless cave . . . where everything perched noiselessly. They were lost! Feelings, emotions, thoughts, expectations.

I looked at my children, bent to kiss them, looked at them again, kissed them, caressed their little heads warmly; kissed them again and afterwards rose to look about a little — as much as I could with my two children in my arms. But it did not satisfy me. It did not satisfy me to look at her, to look at her . . . so dark, as profoundly sweet as the breath of my children. Mr Manolis had called her the Greek Sea!

In the morning everyone was up and about. Preparations, commotion, a beating heart.

We had become intoxicated, because our giddiness left little margin for mundane matters and our needs.

Nellie had become very beautiful. My husband was glowing, an endless smile of happiness playing about his lips. And the children were celebrating the event like old Greeks!

They argued with their father that he should put on a smarter tie, and they drew lots for the three best.

I was not feeling well; a slight shivering. It must have been from weakness. Our Australia had worn us out with work, I'm not joking . . . so much for ten years, day and night, night and day. Work had not stopped even on festivals or Sundays. It was the body's first relief. It was reacting!

But I also had a strong obstinacy, and I did not want to faint in front of the others. I held myself upright by force, holding my body straight, talking and joking.

At that time passionate Lefteris seemed to have forgotten his love pains. His eyes were taking in Peiraias Harbour. Dusk greeted us: grey, without rain. We asked would it rain? It did us a favour. It was moved; it heard the song of our souls and revelled with metallic noises. My ears buzzed. They were dancing all around: the gunwales, decks, funnel, aerials. I would not see such a celebration again.

It was not possible to escape the eyes of the cook. He noticed me with surprise, and called to the others good-humouredly, pointing to me, "See the metamorphosis!" How could I forgive him? I was embarrassed.

"What are you saying mate?" I said something like that to him, stupidly angry with myself. I had forgotten how to converse.

"What do you expect? Haven't we come from the wild bush of Australia?" Leon was teasing.

But it was Peiraias.

There, rising up before us, its hills, and the stairways climbing up to its houses, its churches, its streets.

We, our yearning, the warmth of our first kiss — all belonged to it. We scattered them open-handedly at this unbelievable meeting. We did not believe . . .

Perhaps those scalding inward gulps were to blame, our eyes suppressing the tightly-shut springs of tears. Besides, there were strangers! The tears turned about, taking the back way; tumbling inwards directly to the heart.

Leon took me by the hand.

"What is holding you back? Come to the railing. The boat has stopped and the gangway has come in."

I was laughing but I wanted to cry. I was afraid. With much courage I looked down. Some people were waving handkerchiefs and, there among them, I made out — as if in a dream — my granny, my brother, my aunt, my own people.

My God! How did we bear it?

✎ *joanne burns* ✎

out of order

i suppose you wonder why i write to you. who always laughed at
the anachronism of letter writing in the electronic age. but the
telephone has its inadequacies. i speak into an ear so far away. to
a voice at the other end. such illusion of being in the same room.
there is no time to refine, to define my words. monosyllabic
blurts. verbal indiscretions. syntactical, lexical imperfections
embarrass me. the immediacy of your breathing. the tone of your
responses. are you watching the tv news. reading the paper,
stroking your lover's brow as you reply. i feel vulnerable. blushing. this invisibility. and the problem of cost. the webs, the quick-
sands of goodbye, farewell. keep in touch.

✎

a huge avocado tree hangs over the fading terra cotta tiled walls
of one of C's last surviving mansions. it is at present laden with
large fruit. yet no one ever sees an avocado hit the street. none of
the genteel poor who dwell in this locality ever manages to obtain
one. the rich inhabitants must cultivate this tree to drop its produce after dark. or perhaps the twenty four hour security guards
do an excellent job protecting their employer's property.
    watching the occupants arrive and depart these last few days i
have considered the special relationship the rich have with silence. how quietly their limousines slide into the driveway, how
silently the vast metal gates rise and fall. i consider the word
''necropolis''.

✎

adjacent to my latest lodgings is a small park like the one we used
to sunbake in way back. i sometimes go there if i remember. but

honestly i still prefer to embellish nature with my own impressions. as i've told you many times a park is more real to me, more beautiful, if you like romantic, when i lie down and imagine it.

i am renting just one small room, warm, comfortable, light. a kind of nursery, i like to think. i eat out or get take away. i have no time, no inclination for the preparation of food. i have no time to waste. this afternoon on my way back from my daily walk through the streets of this city, i was drawn to the park by the dazzling display of the elements, the sun radiant across the harbour in the foreground. as long as you stay back from the harbour walls you can avoid looking at all the rubbish lolling at the edge like mutant seaweed, floating trashgardens. i read in a local paper that some people were recently caught trying to roll a woman's dead body wrapped in the city flag over the side of the harbour wall in the full light of day. they do some strange things here. the newspapers seem to present them as forms of entertainment. they use coloured headlines. i suppose people here need to be distracted from reports of the city's disastrous economy. do you know that kung flu slippers and rubber thongs are six to ten times the price they are in Y.

∽

although the bus broke down three times on the steep mountain slope, a tyre went flat, and the driver had to attach a torch to the front of the bus for the last half hour of the journey after the light failed, we finally arrived. this is a town i have always dreamed of visiting. as i stepped down from the bus i knew it wasn't the first time i had arrived in this place. i picked up my bags and strode into the darkness, avoiding, rejecting the porters' intense demands to take my bags to the hotel of their choice. i walked for at least a mile till i came to my destination. i slept that night under silk sheets, dreaming i was sharing a joke with the seven armed god who danced on the table in the hotel foyer downstairs. the next day i took morning tea alone in a large chintz drawing room, underneath the mounted heads of tigers as if it was the most natural thing in the world to do. in the guide book i was reading it said that when people in the region die a sheet of fine gold leaf is placed over their mouths.

i have come to this town for its reputation. this place of prophecy where the wind slides up and down the steep mountain sides rubbing the tongues of ancient ravines. sitting in the terrace bar overlooking such a view i overheard two women say they came

here every year for the honey. it promotes longevity of the com-
plexion.

ᏬᎾ

i write to you from the heat. from a hotel balcony looking out at
palm trees and a swimming pool. a postcard morning. i am
watching a group of travellers, grown men, running round the
pool, squirting each other with cans of what looks like shaving
cream. they disturb a flock of coloured parrots with their shouts
and screams. i can almost hear the sound of flesh slapping flesh as
they wrestle to grab the cans from each other. their girlfriends
come out and join in. when the cream runs out they all jump in
the pool and leave remains of cream floating on the blue surface
when their breakfast is served in the pavilion by the side of the
pool. the hotel staff stand round smiling but from this distance it
is hard for me to get an accurate interpretation of their smiles.

these travellers like to be well cared for on their visits. they insist on having beer from their home region even if it is twice the
cost. they bring tapes of their own music for their evenings in the
bar. i have listened to them talking to each other. using terms like
dickhead, bastard, cunt. as if they couldn't decide whether they
were enemies or friends. the use of these terms appears to have
little to do with libido.

the locals are now used to these types of travellers who visit
their region so frequently. they pay well for all services, spending
their money as if they were playing a game of monopoly.

ᏬᎾ

i have noticed in a number of places how people, even children,
walk around the streets clutching portable telephones to their
chests like lifebuoys. not many seem to be actually engaged in
conversations but those i have observed either tend to hunch
their mouths into the device in conspiratorial postures, or yell
into the mouthpiece like pseudo autocrats. i think the correct
word for these phones is cellular, which is most appropriate for
these virtual prisoners of communication. i love the way language defines a situation almost inadvertently.

ᏬᎾ

while still on the subject of phones i have been amused by a novelty phone advertised in one of the endless brochures that fall out
of newspapers here in F: the shoe phone, a phone set into a genuine shoe. a black lace up. private eye style the description reads.
to entertain your friends, to have fun with. strange concepts. i

would have thought that the odours one associates with shoes would have been quite a deterrent to any sort of pleasure.

∾

i have visited N's department stores. the amount of space devoted to specific categories of merchandise can be a surprise. what impressed me, if that is the accurate verb, was the considerable area of the ground floor devoted to photo frames, picture frames. from the purely functional basic, to the highly formal, ornate, decorative. so many sizes, shapes. edged in plastics, metals, fabrics. so many frames with no faces in them. a ghostly expectancy.

in the evenings i have taken to walking around the streets of the suburbs of N. it is reasonably safe here. everyone seems to leave their curtains open. you can see clearly into their living rooms. at the rows of photos of family, friends, selves. on cabinets, shelves, tables. lined up like ancestor shrines i have seen in other regions. however most of these photos look new. they are of contemporaries. the living. some sitting right there in the same room as their photos. my binoculars tell me this. it has occurred to me that people must be living with deep and powerful fears. of loss of memory, of mortality. psychic loneliness. i wonder if they are irritated by the amount of dusting required.

∾

today while i was waiting for a bus i watched a group of young men playing some sort of game on a small patch of grass. i think it must have been their lunch break from the building construction site nearby. wherever you go in this city you see such groups intensely engaged in kicking, throwing, clutching, grabbing balls of various shapes and sizes. serious in their ferocity, they flex and move like parodies of sculptures from ancient gymnasia. what caught my attention this time was the object of their competitive desires: a large glass bottle. they leapt out thrusting for it, as if the future of each individual's life depended on touching it and holding it to his heart. the concept of the bottle's breakability, its potential as an instrument of damage seemed irrelevant. these physical pastimes appear to almost be compulsory. perhaps in this region there is the belief that to sit and merely talk or quietly gaze at the space ahead might produce a stain of imperfection, of emasculation, something approximating terror. i'd like to ask your opinion but i know you would never reply.

∾

don't be surprised that these letters i send to you are undated. it is part of a deliberate strategy. i write letters to you frequently, but i send them randomly, out of order. i send you a letter about L during my visit to Z, you read about Z from a letter posted in J. i avoid your expectations of my reactions to M in an envelope postmarked M. instead you hear about T. i may not yet have visited T. but it is not untruthful to say one sometimes knows more about the essence of a place prior to one's actual visit.

this method of communication gives me a certain robust sensation. i have never enjoyed the concept of unity, order. straight correspondence. this way i can be in at least two places at once. as i move round it has a cumulative effect. in A i am also in D; in F, W; in C, S. and so on. i start to comprehend omnipresence. no wonder humans invented gods so long ago.

∽ *Marion Halligan* ∽

Hard Sausage

I am a person, she said to herself, when she woke up early in the
morning as was her habit these days. I am a person. I do not
need to be half of a couple to exist. She hoped that by saying it to
herself often enough she would come to think it as well as believe
it.

It was important to behave normally, to behave as always.
They — she — had always gone to the market on Sundays since
they'd lived in St Germain-en-Laye, and that was what she
would do. She didn't feel like eating at all, but must still go on
shopping, and there was no more reason than ever for having
dealing with industrial food. She would be, or pretend to be, a
good little housewife and get to the market early; that would be a
change from staying long, luxuriously, loving (but what had it
meant?) in bed and suddenly jumping up and rushing off before
everything was sold and the market people were shutting down.

Mornings in bed. That was a taboo thought. Her mind was
not to go there. She walked up the steep hill, anxious to tire herself, aiming for a state of perfect exhaustion by the end of each
day. She walked up the hill, a dull walk past shuttered houses and
in the dreadful ceaseless roar of cars speeding up the cobble-
stoned road. They'd usually taken the car . . .

It was funny how easy the plural pronoun came. It is I, she
said, not we. The mind was full of pitfalls, traps, treacherous as
a Rotorua, blasted valley. There were paths, ashy grey and
trodden, but not always clearly discerned; a stumble, a slip, an
uncareful moment, and the slowly boiling mud would have you,
would swallow you up, or a steaming geyser would open under
you. Hot and bitter and corroding and destructive was that land-

scape of the mind, and worse than the real one only in that the evil boiling mud of thought didn't kill; you could struggle out, maimed certainly, but fit to fall in another day. She needed to put a lot of energy into following the blighted but fairly safe paths. Into trying to avoid hatred and anger and the evil demeaning desire for revenge that were the result of his going. Sometimes she wondered if she resented more his having opened her life to these ugly passions than his actual abandonment.

She left the noisy road for streets where there were some quite beautiful buildings, classical and large, soothing in their solid calm. She walked down the main street of the town, the rue du Pain, Bread Street; it pleased her that the main street of this wealthy and extravagantly-shopped town should have such a simple necessary name. Past the rich tidal stench of the fishmonger to the market place in front of the post-office.

She paused to look at the basketman's stall, which sold every possible object made of cane. But she didn't need another basket. A tall Arab tried to sell her a bedcover exactly like her grandmother's, in white thick honeycomb cotton; he dogged her path for a while, refusing to believe her refusal. She passed by displays of *charcuterie* which seemed a bit rich to her, she wanted only simple plain things. But made an intellectual decision to buy some Roquefort. The first cheese stall had some, but it wasn't their — her — favourite kind; she went on until she found a really blue and creamy one. There were some Provencal tomatoes, round and soft, and a mound of red and yellow nectarines as gaudy as a church treasure. Fruit slid down easily these days, and there was a certain sensuous pleasure in eating such beauty.

She looked at the meat: not attractive at all. She didn't feel like it, she didn't need to have it. After eleven years of cooking for a husband she had only herself to please. Almost a good thought for a change, a tinge of green in the blasted valley. No fish either, that was a bore to cook too. Carelessly she wondered: what would he and she — the new *they* — be having for lunch today? And back she was in the boiling bitter mud again.

When she crawled out of that, grubby and trembling, she was standing near a trestle table of products of the Auvergne: sausages, pâtés and hams. A tall man like a peasant in a black widebrimmed hat was shouting his wares at the same time as serving a small queue of customers.

"The taste of the soil," he cried. "The genuine fruits of the earth."

He kept up a sort of double patter, crying his products at the top of his voice at the same time as he coaxed loudly but intimately his line of customers.

"Excellent, excellent, *ma cousine*,"he said to an old lady. "Excellent choice there, superb piece of ham."

She looked drily up and down the line of customers and said, "Is that so, *mon cousin*, is that so," and laughed away at her riposte.

"*Saucisson sec*!" cried the man, "*saucisson sec*. Cured in the mountains of the Auvergne. All the flavour of the countryside."

The old woman — not at all a St Germain type but it is never possible to generalise in France — went away with her package and the queue moved up. She seemed to be in it, and considered what to buy. A little pâté, after all, however rich, some of that creamy one with the mushrooms on top, it was always good.

"Here," said the peasant, playing up his ethnic role (he is probably no more a peasant than I am, she thought), chopping off slices of sausage between thumb and forefinger, "try that. Tell me if you've tasted anything better", passing out chunks to his audience.

So when it came to her turn she thought a morsel of pâté — "like that?" said the peasant, poising his knife. "No," she said, "less." "Here?" "No, less . . . Yes, that's exactly right" — and a piece of sausage, "like that", holding her fingers several inches apart. He chopped it off and wrapped it up and took her money and was already serving the next customer.

"A *saucisson sec*," said the young woman, stout and knowledgeable. "Good and hard," she said.

"There you are, *ma cousine*," cried the peasant, picking up a sausage and banging it down on the table with all his might. "How's that! Nice and hard." He smiled. "Nice and hard. Just how you like your husband, *ma cousine*."

The young woman glanced rather consciously at the man beside her, and bought the sausage. Some of the customers grinned lewdly, others looked blank. "Products of the soil," cried the salesman. "All the flavour of the countryside. Come, come."

Her basket was still not very full, but she had bought enough at the market. There was a man selling books, including one of Auvergnat romanesque churches that took her eye for a moment, but she did not want to acquire so solid an object as a book. And all the amazing array of kitchen things; who needed them any more? So she wandered off to the bakery, and bought half a baguette, which she certainly wouldn't eat, but would add to the statistics — at least one out of every three baguettes bought in Paris is thrown away, she'd read in *Le Monde* the other day — and then on to the Nicolas Shop. No point any longer in looking at rare interesting or expensive wines; she bought two litres of good honest red, a *vin du pays de l'Aude*: more taste of the soil, this time the south.

She walked home, down the hill, and the cars still roared past. She unlocked the gate and locked it after her and went down the stairs to the pretty comfortable convenient flat with its garden safely shut away from the roaring traffic, small cossetted flat that she had loved. Poured herself a glass of wine and drank half quickly in little sips, she liked drinking wine. Its warm red flavour spread through her. Like oil soothing her troubled insides. She took a thin thin wicked sharp knife and sliced the sausage, sliced the hard sausage into rings, and picking one up bit with sharp teeth into its spicy flesh.

❧ *Betty Roland* ❧

Smuggling

[London, 1934]

"We want you to take something back with you to Moscow," Harry said. "We think you look sufficiently respectable to avoid the attention of Hitler's Brownshirts."

It was said with a smile but the words contained a barb. I did look "respectable" in my smartly tailored suit, expensive shoes and hat, and consequently I felt they despised me. Nevertheless, they were quite prepared to make use of me and gave me yet another of those large sealed envelopes and a sizeable parcel of books. I was to take these through Germany and deliver them to somebody in Moscow. Bourgeois or not, that called for a considerable amount of nerve, but I was determined to do it and perhaps win their respect.

I laid my plans carefully, concealing the envelope in a large cabin trunk which I proposed to have sealed at Liverpool Street Station. This would enable it to pass through all the borders without being opened and it would thus escape the attentions of unfriendly customs officers. Once it reached the Russian border all danger would be past.

The delay in getting a visa had seriously disrupted my timetable and it was the day before Good Friday when I finally got away. Aware that I must be at the station a full fifteen minutes before the boat-train left in order to get the seals put on the trunk, I hired a taxi and set out, imagining I had allowed myself a good margin of time — but I had failed to take account of the Easter traffic jam. Liverpool Street Station is a long way from Bayswater, and in a growing state of panic I watched the hands of my watch creep past the hour and I was still no further than Trafalgar Square! I shall never forget that agonising journey. We crept along the Strand a few feet at a time, and by the time we had passed Australia House I had abandoned all hope of getting the trunk sealed, and had begun to wonder if I would even be in time to catch the train. Finally, the nightmare drive was over and we were at the station with briefly five minutes to spare. Thrusting some money into the taxi driver's hand, I managed to grab a passing porter, gasp out my predicament and race behind him down the platform, almost falling into the train with all my belongings, including the incriminating trunk, hurled in after me just as it moved off.

It took me some minutes to regain my breath and steady my shaking knees but I finally managed to do so and groped my way along the rocking corridor in search of the compartment where I had reserved a seat, the parcel of books in my hand, leaving the trunk to take care of itself. A sense of fatalism settled over me. There was no way of disposing of that trunk. It could be searched at every border; all I could do was hope that my luck would hold.

I had no hesitation about travelling first class. If I had to be a bourgeois, I was going to act like one, so I enjoyed my dinner on the train, the cabin on the boat to the Hook of Holland, and a corner seat through Rotterdam to Berlin. The trunk was now in the luggage van. Carefully placing the parcel of books on the floor I draped a rug around my knees, hoping that it would not be noticed when the checkpoints came. Apart from the trunk, I had one suitcase, which was on the rack above my head.

There were five other passengers in the same compartment — well-dressed, untroubled, taking not the slightest notice of the woman seated in the corner next to the corridor. Why should they? There was nothing to distinguish her. She just sat quietly staring out the window, and if she was a little pale she seemed otherwise quite normal. We approached the German border; the train slowed down and drew to a halt at a deserted platform. Then came the sound of voices, loud authoritative voices. "Passports, please!" The wheels began to turn, the train rolled on again. There was a rustle and a slight air of apprehension as the sound of military boots and peremptory demands came steadily closer, then a young man, brisk, alert, wearing a green uniform and a revolver at his hip, stood in the door of the compartment.

The moment had arrived. I sat quietly in my place hoping that my heartbeats were not as audible to others as they were to me, and that my hand would be steady when I presented my passport. I was the last to do so. The pages were flipped over and stopped at the hammer and sickle stamped so prominently on the latest visa.

"What is your destination, madam?"

"Moscow."

The effect was instantaneous. Five startled faces turned in my direction and all conversation ceased.

"What luggage have you?" I pointed to the case above my head. "Anything else?"

"Yes. I have a trunk in the luggage van."

"I would like to see it.

I now felt partly paralysed and my mouth and throat were dry. Slowly getting to my feet, I dropped the rug from my knees so that it concealed the parcel of books. Then, like one walking in a dream, I moved into the corridor and waited for the next development. Meanwhile, the young man in the jackboots and green uniform was examining passports in another compartment.

I hoped I showed no sign of the panic that I felt. Thoughts went racing through my mind. The contents of the envelope might be innocuous, but that seemed unlikely, and there were the books that I had managed to conceal. They alone were enough to cause me trouble. At the very least, I would be taken off the train for further questioning. I would probably be searched for hidden messages. There would be nobody to help me. Neither the British nor the Australian consul would be inclined to intervene on behalf of a woman who had so blatantly attempted to smuggle revolutionary material through Hitler's Germany. I was beginning to feel sick.

Finally, the last passport was inspected and I was beckoned along the corridor. The train rocked and swayed, which disguised the fact that my knees were trembling so much that I could scarcely walk. We passed through several carriages and finally reached the luggage van. The young man asked me to identify my trunk, which I did, then I handed him the keys. The first wave of panic had passed and I felt detached. What would happen next was beyond my control. The only thing I could do was to keep my head and remain calm.

He found nothing in the top layer of the clothes, then moved the tray and began to rummage through the remainder, looking rather surprised when he discovered the new overcoat and shoes I had brought for Guido.

"They are for my husband," I said briefly. He seemed satisfied and continued with his work. I had concealed the envelope in the sleeve of the coat. Now it comes, I told myself, too engrossed to notice that the train was slowing down.

It stopped with a clash of buffers and hiss of brakes and I saw that we were standing at a station. Scarcely crediting my eyes, I watched the officer replace the tray, close the lid and put a chalk mark on the end of the trunk. Then, with a murmured goodbye, he opened the door of the van and was gone. I had been saved by the simple circumstance that the customs officers boarded the train as it crossed the German border, carried out their routine inspection and got off again half an hour later at a temporary halting place. It was as simple as that, and had I not been semi-paralysed with fear and delayed so long in leaving my seat, I might have been dragged off with them. As it was, my luck had held and we were now roaring on our way towards Berlin. Returning to my seat, I saw that one of my fellow passengers, no doubt with the kindest of intentions, had picked the rug up off the floor and placed it on the seat, exposing the parcel of books to all observers!

There was a two-hour wait before I made my next connection to the Soviet border, but Berlin was no longer an enchanted city to me so I spent the time sitting on the platform with the rug around my knees, using the parcel of books as a footstool. Every passing man in uniform made my heart miss a beat, but no-one took the slightest notice of the solitary woman waiting for a train. I looked far too respectable to be carrying revolutionary literature. Harry Pollitt had been right.

I had a good night's sleep, broken only when we crossed the border into Poland — no passport difficulties there, only a polite apology for having been disturbed. Breakfast in the restaurant car and, finally, Negoralia where a red flag with the hammer and the sickle fluttered in the wind and told me I was safe.

I had barely stepped onto the platform when a man in the familiar uniform of the OGPU appeared beside me.

"You have something you have brought from London?" he enquired. This took me by surprise, as I had not expected such efficiency. The parcel of books was in my hand.

"Is it this?" I asked of him. He shook his head.

"No. Something else, I think."

We went to the customs shed, where I unlocked the trunk and

handed him the envelope. He glanced at it, nodded his head, then thanked me and went away.

There was one final incident. Aware that I would now be travelling to Moscow on a Soviet train and that meals were not to be relied upon, I took a cake of chocolate from the trunk and slipped it into the pocket of my coat. Walking back along the platform, I heard footsteps running after me. It was my friend from the OGPU to whom I had given the envelope.

"Would you show me what you have in your pocket?" He was no longer as friendly as he had been. With my brightest and most obliging smile I produced the cake of chocolate.

"Your pardon, comrade. It was my mistake," said an embarrassed young man.

A few more hours, then Moscow, Guido waiting on the station and myself triumphant. Member of the despised petty bourgeoisie though I might be, no party member could have carried out the mission more successfully. I felt that I had won my spurs and was entitled to respect.

❦ *Jessica Anderson* ❦

Reckless, Cynical and Frivolous

When I went to book my passage I discovered that some-body *could* stop me. Colin. We were not yet divorced, and my "husband" must give signed permission for me to go. He gave it, of course. What better evidence of desertion than a wife who went tripping, traipsing, gallivanting overseas?

While Ida was making my travelling clothes I went north to see my mother and Grace. It was an uncomfortable visit. Some families have an almost uncanny power of forcing an alienated member to behave according to its opinion of him or her, and as soon as I divined, in their reserved greetings, their questions, and their set reproachful mouths, the discussions they had had about me, I began to act in a manner to confirm them in their opinion. In Ida's rooms I could bow my head and tell my woes, but at my mother's table all I could do was to sit upright and make smart cracks about marriage and divorce. She and Grace would have been ready to console me for being broken and rejected, but could not forgive me for my apparent gaiety, for wearing the first trousers they had even seen "in the street," or for painting my toenails pink. Reckless. Cynical. Frivolous. Those were the words they used about me. And rebuttal seemed so hopeless, and the thicket of misunderstanding between us so old and dense and dusty, that it was less exhausting simply to be as reckless, cynical, and frivolous as they said I was . . ..

Having gone to so much trouble to deceive them about my feelings, I should not have been made so bitter by my success. On the long train journey back to Sydney, torpid and exhausted, I kept hearing those three words — reckless, cynical, frivolous. Reckless I was, and cynical and frivolous I sometimes felt, but even at the very top of that bent, even as I was walking up the gangplank of the ship, with a tiny hat clamped to one side of my silly head, I was weighted by a sub-stratum of sadness. I knew that like fruit affected by hard drought, I was likely to be rotten before ripe. Sometimes I believed it was already too late, but at others I was seized by a desperate optimism that expressed itself in spates of chatter and laughter and hectic activity.

Ida Mayo and the watercolourist came to the ship, and Colin sent a bunch of roses with a card on which he had written *"No hard feelings."* "They're like bloody pink cabbages," I said, and threw them overboard. Ida and the watercolourist looked shocked.

⌘

Those roses, as I see them now, rocking on the thick green water of the dockside, do pose a question. Although I still believe that Colin sent them to demonstrate his nobility to Pearl, and although at the time I could feel, almost as if I were there, the exudation of his self-satisfaction as he wrote "no hard feelings", other reasons do occur. I consider regret, even shock at the realisation of how we had wasted each other. And because I can still ask the question, I must ask another. Have I given an accurate account of Colin Porteous, or have I merely provided another substitute? At number six our speculation on the roses always ended in laughter.

"Well, it was certainly very *cryptic* of Colin."

Perhaps the real man has been so overscored by laughter that he will never be retrieved. As a rule, when we can't find even one good quality in a person, we are prejudiced, and by that rule I must admit my prejudice. Pearl may have been able to mine seams in him disregarded by me, or may have been practical enough to disregard the ones I mined. She certainly would have a better chance of happiness with him than I had. According to Una Porteous, she had money of her own. And she was pretty, too, in her outsize way — not fat, but with a large frontal area and a strikingly large face. Liza had a dinner service, with outsize plates, that she used to call her Pearl china. "Now at last Col will be able to have children," said Una Porteous. But I am fairly certain he didn't, because, when I left the ship at Southampton, I was pregnant.

He was a middle-aged, squat-bodied American, of considerable honesty and charm. He began by making me laugh, and laughter weakened me easily to love. Hilda, out of her varied experience, used to say that of all aphrodisiacs, laughter is the one most unjustly ignored, and I, out of my limited experience, my very limited experience, used always to agree.

He was an engineer who had been engaged in bridge building in Australia, and awaiting him in England were his wife and two eldest children. With five children already, he was delighted by my barrenness. I didn't have a cabin to myself, and he did, so it was in his cabin that we made love. But it was usually on deck that we talked, walking slowly in our engrossment, and sometimes, in disagreement or perplexity, drifting of one accord to the ship's rail to rest on our folded forearms and resume our detailed, halting exploration of one another. Neither of us had ever known anyone resembling the other, and this exploration so thoroughly engrossed us that when we sat in one of the great public rooms of the ship, it occasionally happened that we realised only by the silence spreading around us that we had forgotten to go down to lunch. By this time I had read a great deal about love affairs, but again my knowledge had been theoretical, and it came as a surprise to me that the reality far surpassed the theory.

"None of those books ever said," I told him, 'that it was such a marvellous way of getting to know people."

He looked at me sideways. "Think of the people you will get to know, now that you are free."

"Oh, I shall."

He grimaced slightly, but said, "Yes, you will."

In those days the voyage lasted for six weeks. One day in the Mediterranean he remarked that if he had been free he would have liked to marry me. It is an easy thing for a man to say in such circumstances, but because he was not a man who said easy things, but rather who scrupulously avoided them, I believed him, and in retrospect, I still do. All the same, I would have been afraid to marry him. I felt it was precisely the absence of a future together that enabled us to love without cruel possessiveness. The voyage was peaceful, with calm seas and skies, and as day succeeded day, and I continued to keep this friend and lover by my side, and to wake up each morning to the instant realisation of his presence in the ship, I grew incredulous of so much luck and happiness, and would not have dared to risk it by extending it further. The definite break on arrival — goodbye and no addresses — was at my insistence, and the argument it caused confirmed me in it.

"You see?" I said. "Now we are almost quarrelling. The only way to keep these things intact is to give them up."

"You are either a mad pessimist," he said, "or a mad perfectionist. I don't know which."

"I am neither. I am a preservationist."

He threw back his head and laughed and laughed. I grew angry and walked away. He caught up with me and walked at my side.

"But what you are preserving?"

"This."

"But if you have your way it will be over. You will be preserving nothing."

When I continued to insist, and he to oppose me, we had a real quarrel, followed by a reconciliation during which I wept, and he agreed at last to my terms of goodbye and no addresses.

His wife came down to Southampton to meet him. He had not expected her, and his disconcertion on seeing her on the wharf below, his quick glance from her to me, made me say, "You see, *this* is what it would be like." They were the last words I ever said to him. I moved away and stood at another part of the rail.

I saw them later as we passed through the customs. I passed them without turning my head, but I heard her pleasant southern voice, and his reply, and saw out of the tail of my eye that he had also resisted turning to look at me. Against all logic, I suddenly felt discarded. It was a bleak moment, but my cowardly spirit was consoled by not having put him to any sort of test. And I was consoled as well by gratitude for what he had taught me. I believed that our candour and loving freedom had shown me a happy sexual pattern by which I could live. At last, I thought, I knew how freedom could be reconciled with appeasement.

Six weeks later, certain of pregnancy, I remembered Daff and the abortion car. "As easy as puff," I remembered her saying. "The police are fixed. All you need is about fifty pounds and the doctor's address."

∿ *Nancy Keesing* ∿

Once I Rode an Elephant

I was four years old and it happened like this: we had been living in Auckland for a year, where my architect father had become my fisherman father. I too had become a skilful hauler of garfish — called "piper" in New Zealand — from the harbour to the jetty of Cheltenham Beach. My record catch was seven in one morning.

Dad was not visibly ill and I have no idea why he took this long holiday in the city of his birth. And now we were aboard SS *Wanganui* sailing back home to Sydney.

Also on board was Wirths Circus returning to Australia from its annual tour of New Zealand. In the dining saloon my parents shared a table with the tall man and the dwarf who were great friends and excellent company, they reported. Children ate at an earlier sitting so we did not meet the fabulous pair directly, though we saw them from a distance promenading the deck reserved for grownups, and very incongruous they were, for the tall man was strikingly thin and the dwarf a roly-poly.

The circus animals travelled in holds below deck. The decking above the elephants' quarters had several largeish holes cut in it for, I suppose, light and air but also for the delight of children who, carrying apples and bits of bread, were taken to feed the jumbos. Through each hole elephant trunks, three or four I think, sprouted like strange prehistoric growths. Each tough, leathery, sinuous sprout ended in a gaping aperture, pink and red and runny with mucous — and into this mysterious mouth, that according to my father was not a mouth, but a sort of nose, we thrust our offerings. Holding food the trunks withdrew briefly, to where? To what? I'd never seen and could scarcely imagine, Elephant.

How fortunate the elder daughter of table companions of the tall man and the dwarf. One morning I was escorted (by father? by whom?) to the elephants' hold where monstrous shapes loomed in brown glooms and pachyderm legs rose like vast but flabby tree trunks, supporting flanks like the shapes of old coats that slowly move in a cupboard when an opened door admits a draught. High above me their ear-flaps, and their great docile heads from which trunks uprose to the pinholes of light far away, down which peered the eyes of ordinary children holding bread and apples in ordinary sunlight.

And one trunk snaked down. "Hold your apple out. See, she's putting her trunk down to your hand. Now place the apple in her trunk and see how she gets it to her mouth." Her mouth was a smiling cavern, her yellow, sawn-off tusks . . . There is a smell, warm and foetid rather than rank, and of bodies rather than manure. The hold becomes more visible as eyes adjust to its darkness. It is very clean. The elephant keeper and the trainer, with scraping brooms and buckets of water and mops, swab living leather and moist flooring.

The trainer, a saturnine man, calls something to the hugest elephant and oh! horror! her trunk is around my waist. I had never then seen a snake but atavistically I sensed, and invented, boa constrictor. I was too shocked to make a sound. I was twisted away from the floor sideways; nearly upside down. I was near the roof. I was on her back and somehow — ladder/ rungs in the wall? — the keeper had perched on her rough, rock rump and held me securely. I rode the elephant.

The face of a child I knew in another life appeared close by through one of the holes in the deck. I returned its stare seriously. This was no moment for poking grimaces. For I am supreme. I am the lord, I am the lord, I am the lord of everything.

The trainer utters another call. His hands guide me back to the trunk. Head upright I am enclosed; lowered; reduced . . .

Against injustice, failure, sheer laziness. For ever after, for evermore, I say to myself: "*Once* I rode an elephant. *When* I rode *the* elephant . . ."

❧ *Drusilla Modjeska* ❧

To Crete

In the autumn of 1961, Madeleine took Poppy to Crete. Cecily went too. Cecily lived with her children at the end of a lane on the other side of the main road from the village. Her husband was usually abroad. She was a family friend, not yet a rival. She was going to France and said she'd take Poppy with her. Poppy had come back from Pilsdon for the school holidays and she was still *weepy*, Richard said, *and not herself.* Another break was suggested from a routine that was both familiar and not; so Richard wrote to Madeleine, and Madeleine said Crete. She had never approved of Poppy's romance with France. She wrote to her about de Gaulle and Algeria. That is France, she wrote, describing for Poppy the internment camps of North Africa which had been reported in the French press while Poppy was in hospital, and the young Arabs she'd seen loaded into police vans in Paris. That is France, she wrote, but for Poppy Paris remained the city of Victor Hugo and Colette. Of Crete she had no opinion. She went where she was taken.

Poppy, Cecily and Madeleine arrived in Heraklion by boat on a clear morning at the end of September 1961, just before Algeria's independence. When they had left Piraeus and Poppy could no longer see the coast of the Peloponnese, she stood at the stern where sea birds flew above the foam. It was the first time she'd seen the sky meet the horizon in a clean curve. Like a new moon, she wrote. It was also the first time she'd left England since she'd visited France with China.

The three women took rooms in a small hotel above a covered market. Poppy lay on her bed listening to sounds from the street below, as strange to her as the bright slats of light in the room, and while Cecily look at the shops, Madeleine read her an account of Sir Arthur Evans' excavations at Knossos; but Poppy's attention was on a small, almost transparent lizard that was basking on the edge of a slat in the shutters that accounted for the strange arrangement of light and shade. All she remembered from Madeleine's reading was that Sir Arthur Evans was looking for an early Greek script, and found the ancient palace by chance. Looking for the origins of a culture we recognise as a foundation of our own, he stumbled on evidence of an earlier lost world.

"Read me that bit again," Poppy said to Madeleine, and she did. When Poppy turned back to the light, the lizard had gone.

∾

Before Poppy died she told each of us there were two things she wanted us to be sure to do with the money she left. The first was to buy a washing machine; the second was to visit Crete. May already had a washing machine, and now Phoebe and I do too. Poppy was right; apart from the work it saves, there is the satisfaction of order that hanging out a load of washing can bring to domestic life. As to Crete, only May hasn't been. With young children she hasn't had the chance. But Phoebe has, and so have I.

The April after Poppy died, Thomas and I took a cheap flight from London to Heraklion. As a consequence our first sight of the island was of mountains and a small perfunctory airport, not the Venetian fortifications and long harbour wall that Poppy saw from her boat. But we had dinner that night on the terrace of a café overlooking the harbour, already seduced by the grace and hue of Crete.

Like every other tourist, we collected our guides to the remains of Minoan culture and went to the Archaeological Museum. Unlike Poppy I had already read about Minoa, not only because of her, but because it has become part of the iconography of contemporary feminism. I was already interested in the riddle of a culture that is hidden under the acknowledged history of our own, almost as long before Christ as we are after, a culture about which we know little, but in which women were priests and acrobats and, it would seem, where there were no defences or equipment for war. But I was not one of those who claim Minoa as a matriarchy, suspicious of a tendency to validate the present struggles of women by an appeal to past rule. In this frame of mind, and having taken measured preparations, I was not expecting the shock that made me sob out loud when I stood in front of the figurines that Poppy had described so well: the agile, the squat, the working women of Minoa: mothers, priests, animal handlers, acrobats, preparers of food. *Where do such women come from*, Poppy had written. Where indeed? Their images are quite unlike any we are used to from Hellenic Greece, the idealised classical feminine. I sobbed, as Poppy did, out of shock, and also recognition, as if in those figurines and frescoes, still singing with life three or four thousand years later, there was something I already knew; and that something ran counter to everything I'd learned.

In his work on the puzzles of female sexuality, Freud writes that the early pre-Oedipal attachment to the mother by the daughter, which lasts much longer in girls than it does in boys (the model for his *normal* Oedipus complex), *comes to us as a surprise, like the discovery, in another field, of the Minoan-Mycenean civilisation behind the civilisation of Greece.* This first attachment to the mother in girls, which Freud admits to finding hard to grasp, *so grey with age and shadowy and almost impossible to revivify*, would seem to be the foundation of a femininity which is subsequently overlaid by another order, as Minoa was by Greece. These are thoughts I've had since. At the time I simply stood and looked, reminded perhaps, as Poppy must have been, though neither of us knew it, of something every daughter once knew, a dim region, an ancient possibility that has long been surpassed, and yet lives on, shadowy and grey with age, and yearning to be revivified.

The next day Thomas and I took the bus to Knossos, the palace excavated by Sir Arthur Evans and said to be the site of the labyrinth where Greek legend placed the Minotaur that Ariadne and her thread gave Theseus the power to destroy. Why was this Hellenic myth of an insatiable monster built on the traces of a culture, apparently peaceable, which the Greeks defeated or at least superseded, possibly as early as 1300 BC? Did terrible things happen there? There is some evidence of ritual sacrifice. Surely the Greeks wouldn't have been squeamish about that? What was so powerful about Knossos, about Minoa, about the feminine, that a monster had to live in a maze at its heart, appeased only by the sacrifice of Athenian youth, seven boys and seven girls fed to him every ninth year? Was the monster already there? Is there something monstrous at the heart of femininity? Or did Hellenic legend put it there for us?

With no answers to these questions, Thomas and I hired a car and drove across the island to Phaestos, the southern palace of ancient Minoa, where Poppy had gone with Madeleine when Cecily had returned to the mainland, bound by some other itinerary. Like Poppy, I sat at the top of that wonderful citadel, looking out across the plain to mountains that still had snow on their peaks. But unlike the parched grass and bare rocks Poppy had described in her diary, I saw a hillside covered in flowers; and on the altars of shrines and tiny churches along the road there were bunches of small red poppies.

∽

It was on Crete that Madeleine told Poppy the full story of Ariadne. She knew that Theseus, the son of the Athenian King Aegeus, was among the shipment of youths who'd arrived on Crete for sacrifice to the minotaur. She knew that Ariadne fell in love with him and gave him the ball of thread that would guide him to the monster and bring him back from the labyrinth to her. Theseus killed the monster, and claimed Ariadne as he promised, escaping with her from Crete and her cruel father, King Minos. But Poppy hadn't realised the significance of Ariadne being Cretan, coming from the same island as the minotaur, and she didn't know that Ariadne never reached Athens. On their triumphal way home, the Athenians put in at Naxos where Ariadne fell asleep on the beach. When she woke Theseus had sailed without her. Some accounts said he loved another, others that Dionysius ordered him to abandon her so he could marry her himself. Whatever the reason, Ariadne was left behind and Theseus, distraught with loss, or shame perhaps, forgot to raise the white sails to signal his success to the waiting Athenians. His father, King Aegeus, saw the black sails, presumed the worst and threw himself off the rocks, giving his name to the sea that Poppy had cross by ferry, watching its colour reflected in the sky.

"When Madeleine told me that story," Poppy said, "I cried at the distance between those sturdy Minoan figures which I understand without knowing how, and Ariadne holding the thread for a man who abandoned her. Madeleine said the myth of Ariadne came later. We don't know what her own myths were, on her songs, or her prayers. No one knows her story."

∽

Something moved in Poppy on Crete; and something moved in me. I don't know how else to put it. As if for a glance, or a moment, future and past lost their separation. Poppy took the story of Ariadne as emblematic of her own, a gesture I first understood simply as a tart comment on her life as mother and wife, and I'm sure that's part of what she meant. But on Crete I could see there was more to it than that, for underneath the Ariadne of Hellenic legend lay the girl who was heir to a silent and mysterious world.

Poppy went back to England and a situation which required her continued attentions as mother and wife. One could say it is unreasonable to expect that a brief visit to a Greek island as one of thousands who pour there every year searching for renewal could change anything, and I don't suppose it did. The daily round exacts its toll, and there were six more years before the rift that had opened between her and Richard was acknowledged in separation. But that visit gave Poppy a way of imagining herself. Or maybe it's only me who is given that, for my task is to find pattern and shape in her life, hers was to live each day.

∽ *Mary Gaunt* ∽

By Pack-Mule and Litter

*Mary Gaunt travelled north from Peking to the hunting palace of
the Manchus in 1913. She had planned a further journey along the
Russian caravan route but was foiled by brigands. Instead she set
off for Vladivostock and across Siberia to Norway and Sweden,
hearing en route about the outbreak of World War I.*

I was to ride a pack-mule. Now riding a pack-mule at any time
is an unpleasant way of getting along the road. I know no
more uncomfortable method. It is not quite as comfortable as sitting upon a table with one's legs dangling, for the table is still, the
mule is moving, and one's legs dangle on either side of his neck.
There are neither reins nor stirrups, and the mule goes at his own
sweet will, and in a very short time your back begins to ache,
after a few hours that aching is intolerable. To get over this difficulty the missionary had cut the legs off a chair and suggested
that, mounted on the pack, I might sit in it comfortably. I don't
know whether I could, for the mule objected.

It was a sunny morning with a bright blue sky above, and all
seemed auspicious except my mule, who expressed in no measured language his dislike to that chair. Tsai Chih Fu had no
sooner hoisted me into it than up he went on his hind legs and,
using them as a pivot, stood on end pawing the air. Everybody in
the inn-yard shrieked and yelled except, I hope, myself, and then
Tsai Chih Fu, how I know not, rescued me from my unpleasant
position, and thankfully I found myself upon the firm ground
again. He was a true Chinese mule and objected to all innova-
tions. He stood meekly enough once the chair was removed.

I wanted to cross Asia and here I was faced with disaster at the very outset! Finally I was put upon the pack minus the chair, Buchanan was handed up to me and nestled down beside me, and the procession started. My heart sank. I don't mind acknowledging it now. I had at least a thousand miles to go, and within half-an-hour of the start I had thoroughly grasped the fact that of all modes of progression a pack-mule is the most abominable. There are no words at my command to express its discomforts.

Very little did I see of the landscape of Shansi that day. I was engaged in hanging on to my pack and wondering how I could stick it out. We passed along the usual hopeless cart-track of China. I had eschewed Peking carts as being the very acme of misery, but I was beginning to reflect that anyhow a cart was comparatively passive misery while the back of a pack-mule was decidedly active. Buchanan was a good little dog, but he mentioned several times in the course of that day that he was uncomfortable and he thought I was doing a fool thing. I was much of his opinion.

The day was never ending. All across a plain we went, with rough fields just showing green on either hand, through walled villages, through little towns, and I cared for nothing, I was too intent on holding on, on wishing the day would end, and at last, as the dusk was falling, the muleteer pointed out, clear-cut against the evening sky, the long walls of a large town — Taiku. At last! At last!

I was to stay the night at a large mission school kept by a Mr and Mrs Wolf, and I only longed for the comfort of a bed, any sort of a bed so long as it was flat and warm and kept still. We went on and on, we got into the suburbs of the town, and we appeared to go round and round, through an unending length of dark, narrow streets, full of ruts and holes, with the dim loom of houses on either side, and an occasional gleam of light from a dingy kerosene lamp or Chinese paper lantern showing through the paper windows. Again and again we stopped and spoke to men who were merely muffled shapeless figures in the darkness, and again we went on. I think now that in all probability neither Tsai Chih Fu nor Mr Wang understood enough of the dialect to make the muleteers or the people of whom we inquired understand where we wanted to go, but at last, more probably by good luck than good management, somebody, seeing I was a foreigner, sent us to the foreigners they knew, those who kept a school for a hundred and twenty-five boys in the lovely Flower Garden. It certainly was lovely, an old-world Chinese house, with little courtyards and ponds and terraces and flowers and trees — and that comfortable bed I had been desiring so long. As we entered the courtyard in the darkness and Tsai Chih Fu lifted me down, the bed was the only thing I could think of.

And yet next day I started again — I wonder now I dared — and we skirted the walls of Taiku. We had gone round two sides and then, as I always do when I am dead-tired, I had a bad attack of breathlessness. Stay on that pack I knew I could not, so I made my master of transport lift me down, and I sat on a bank for the edification of all the small boys in the district who, even if they had known how ill I felt, probably would not have cared, and I decided there and then that pack-mule riding was simply impossible and something would have to be done. Therefore, with great difficulty, I made my way back to the mission school and asked Mr Wolf what he would recommend.

Again were missionaries kindness itself to me. They sympathised with my trouble, they took me in and made me their guest, refusing to take any money for it, though they added to their kindness by allowing me to pay for the keep of my servants, and they strongly recommended that I should have a litter. A litter then I decided I would have. It is, I should think, the very earliest form of human conveyance. It consists of two long poles laid about as far apart as the shafts of an ordinary cart, in the middle is hung a coarse-meshed rope net, and over that a tilt of matting — the sort of stuff we see tea-chests covered with in this country. Into the net is tumbled all one's small impedimenta — clothes-bags, kettles, anything that will not conveniently go on mule-back; the bedding is put on top, rugs and cushions arranged to the future inmate's satisfaction, then you get inside and the available people about are commandeered to hoist the concern on the backs of the couple of mules, who object very strongly. The head of the one behind is in the shafts, and the ends rest in his pack-saddle, and the hind quarters of the one in front are in the shaft, just as in an ordinary buggy. Of course there are no reins, and at first I felt very much at the mercy of the mules, though I am bound to say the big white mule who conducted my affairs seemed to thoroughly understand his business. Still it is uncomfortable, to say the least of it, to find yourself going, apparently quite unattended, down steep and rocky paths, or right into a rushing river. But on the whole a litter is a very comfortable way of travelling; after a pack-mule it was simply heaven, and I had no doubts whatever that I could comfortably do the thousand miles, lessened now, I think, by about thirty, that lay before me. If I reached Lan Chou Fu there would be time enough to think how I would go on farther. And here my muleteers had me. When I arranged for a litter, I paid them, of course, extra, and I said another mule was to be got to carry some of the loads. They accepted the money and agreed. But I may say that that other mule never materialised. I accepted the excuse when we left Taiku that there was no other mule to be hired, and by the time that excuse had worn thin I had so much else to think about that I bore up, though not even a donkey was added to our equipment.

Money I took with me in lumps of silver, sycee — shoes, they called them — and a very unsatisfactory way it is of carrying cash. It is very heavy and there is no hiding the fact that you have got it. We changed little bits for our daily needs as we went along, just as little as we could, because the change in cash was an intolerable burden. On one occasion in Fen Chou Fu I gave Tsai Chih Fu a very small piece of silver to change and intimated that I would like to see the result. That piece of silver I reckon was worth about five shillings, but presently my master of transport and one of the muleteers came staggering in and laid before me rows and rows of cash strung on strings! I never felt so wealthy in my life. After that I never asked for my change. I was content to keep a sort of general eye on the expenditure, and I expect the only leakage was the accepted percentage which every servant levies on his master. When they might easily have cheated me, I found my servants showed always a most praiseworthy desire for my welfare. And yet Mr Wang did surprise me occasionally. While I was in Pao Ting Fu I had found it useful to learn to count in Chinese, so that roughly I knew what people at the foodstalls were charging me. On one occasion I saw some little cakes powdered with sesame seed that I thought I should like and I instructed Mr Wang to buy me one. I heard him ask the price and the man say three cash, and my interpreter turned to me and said that it was four! I was so surprised I said nothing. It may have been the regulation percentage, and twenty-five per cent is good anywhere, but at the moment it seemed to me extraordinary that a man who considered himself as belonging to the upper classes should find it worth his while to do me out of one cash, which was worth — no, I give it up. I don't know what it was worth. 10.53 dollars went to the pound when I was in Shansi and about thirteen hundred cash to the dollar, so I leave it to some better mathematician than I am to say what I was done out of on that occasion.

There was another person who was very pleased with the litter and that was James Buchanan. Poor little man, just before we left the Flower Garden he was badly bitten by a dog, so badly he could no longer walk, and I had to carry him on a cushion alongside me in the litter. I never knew before how dearly one could love a dog, for I was terrified lest he should die and I should be alone in the world. He lay still and refused to eat, and every movement seemed to pain him, and whenever I struck a missionary — they were the only people, of course, with whom I could converse — they always suggested his back was broken.

I remember at Ki Hsien, where I was entertained most hospitably, and where the missionary's wife was most sympathetic, he was so ill that I sat up all night with him and thought he would surely die. And yet in the morning he was still alive. He moaned when we lifted him into the litter and whined painfully when I got out, as I had to several times to take photographs.

"Don't leave me, don't leave me to the mercy of the Chinese," he said, and greeted me with howls of joy when I returned. It was a great day for both of us when he got a little better and could put his pretty little black and white head round the tilt and keep his eye upon me while I worked. But really he was an ideal patient, such a good, patient little dog, so grateful for any attention that was paid him, and from that time he began to mend and by the time I reached Fen Chou Fu was almost his old gay happy little self again.

∽ *Lolo Houbein* ∽

Pacific Sidetracks

Eventually I went on a trip up the rivers on a double canoe with one of the crocodile hunters, whom I had earlier considered as just about the ideal living partner, considering my inclinations for tropical adventures. I tried to revive this old interest, but it was of little use, although we were friends of course. He had his children and his eighteen-year-old nephew up for a holiday. With three of the Papua New Guinean boys, who worked off and on for The Lodge, and Joe, his Sepik cook, we steamed down the Aramia into the Bamu and up the Gwari River, which came tumbling from the Southern Highlands. This is the heart of the country. Rainforest stands like a green tapestry screen on both sides. Birds of a beauty unsurpassed fly through the tree tops. Cries of wildlife unseen cut through the stillness. Crocodiles splash in the water. There are leeches at every landing place and mosquitoes everywhere. You accept that you will be bitten and stung and sucked to a pulp for the privilege of just being there.

Dusk was the hour of the flying foxes; they wheeled low over the water in a dance of dalliance until it was time to hang upside down from the branches of trees, the likes of which did not exist anywhere in the world. I drank it in. The beauty, the strength, the vigour and energy of that world.

Each village housed a different tribe, each with its own language. Papua New Guinea has over seven hundred languages and the cultures they represent differ widely. One language on the Gwari sounded superficially like Swedish and I would have investigated but for falling ill with malaria. It was a beauty of a bout. I ran a fever which sent me into delirium. At the same time a cut on my right hand festered into a tropical sore and my right arm, which had its lymph glands interfered with during a cancer operation in 1974, swelled up to twice its normal size. When I was lucid, I crawled from my bed to the edge of the deck to dip a towel in the river. Wound around my throbbing arm, it would dry to a tinder within an hour. I was horribly, horribly sick and the skipper later told me he feared I would "kick the bucket". Having a sick woman on board tarnished his idea of a trip up the river and our friendship cooled off rapidly. Joe the cook cast me a glance of pity now and then and this was the only compassion I was aware of.

The double canoe was lumbering on its way back to the Bamu, loaded with empty oil drums, when I recovered from the fevers. I wanted to wash the sweat off my body but privacy was hard to find, so I settled for a good hairwash. I was sitting in the sun on deck for the first time, feeble, but still alive, my arm a monstrous purple-blue-yellow-green, drying my hair, when the skipper yelled. "Women and children on the aft deck! The bore is coming!"

I had heard plenty of stories about bores and placed them in the same category as fishing stories. I looked ahead, and what I saw coming rolling towards us over the wide, wide waters stopped my breath! The bore was a rolling wall of water, a metre and a half high, advancing at the speed of a running casowary. This was the tide from the sea forcing its way up the rivers. We had just entered the head of the Bamu, where it is at its narrowest, but still easily five hundred metres across. The bore, squeezed by the banks, roared towards the landspit where the Bamu divides into the Gwari and the Wawoi and we were floating mid-river in between, with the jetty of Emeti just coming into sight on the righthand bank.

It took less time than it takes to tell this, before the bore hit us with the force of a tornado. Nephew Peter was eating a bowl of cornflakes in the galley when the roof fell in. The right-hand dugout canoe split fully down its length, before most of the deck splintered off the left-hand dugout. Eight people were hanging on to the wreckage and sinking, while I was being swung in the air by a deck pole. I tried to grab the little boy's hand, as he was nearest, but his leg was caught. His father freed him and both children clambered up. Soon we were all in the left-hand dugout, shaken, but uninjured. Drums and wreckage floated over the width of the river, which was again as calm as on a lovely summer's day.

We floated back up the Gwari with the tide for four hours, before we could turn and float back to the Bamu. All the men had performed heroic deeds to rescue belongings from the wreckage and, because I always packed my things in plastic bags, most of mine were retrieved. The skipper's moneybox was delivered back to him a year later, completely intact, by local villagers.

Arrival at Emeti, six hours after our ordeal, was heaven on a mudflat. Squeezing the soft, brown, waterlogged earth between my naked toes, I knew I was an earth person, a landlubber, a true Capricorn.

❧ *Dulcie Deamer* ❧

India's Alleyways

Now, I'm not going to drag anyone who, so far, hasn't skipped the Prologue, through a step-by-step description of the Far East in 1908-1909. Nothing is worse than that antedated "family album" stuff.

But there are a certain number of high-lights that I don't want to skip. They contributed to the knocking-into-shape of the person (me) who, so very much later, was supposed by some to have been "born at King's Cross", and to have acquired my whole experience of life in that square mile.

My first sight of the Indian East at Colombo was an irrational homecoming. I belonged — not to New Zealand, but to this. And I was to tolerate the fermenting ripeness of India's alleyways as if I'd been reared there.

Frank Fox had suggested that I might send woman-interest articles from the East. Albert enthusiastically agreed. So much so that he whisked me in a hired gharry, on our first evening in Colombo, to a top-bracket house of illfame, so that I could meet the little Cingalese girls and write-up the experience.

We got in all right, and the girls scarcely more than children, were sweet, and called me "darling". But as clients, sahibs in rickshaws, began to arrive, the saturnine Tamil proprietor blocked our exit, demanding ransom-money if we wanted inconspicuously to get out. We literally fought our way through a side door. I was enjoying myself — it was so new and exciting — but my partner panicked properly. I must not — oh, heavens — be seen.

Thanks to the side door I wasn't.

If he'd had a pennyworth of horse-sense he wouldn't have

taken me within a mile of the place at night. And a "house of illfame" article for a reputable Australian magazine in 1908 was unthinkable.

It's really wonderful that we usually survived undamaged, in view of the crass errors of judgment to which he was enthusiastically prone. And it was a long while before I, green as grass, knew enough to attempt to deflate him.

In Bombay, in the company of a couple of journalists — Albert being on duty at the theatre — I had another night-time experience, as raw and real as the Colombo one was just plain silly.

We visited a burning ghat. The dead woman, twelve years old, and married, lay on crackling faggots, between perforated iron screens that controlled the draught. The smell was if a joint had caught in the oven. In the heat large bones cracked like pistol shots. A foot had been consumed to a mere lump, and was turning slowly round on the ankle bone.

I said within myself, "If it drops off I might scream." But we left before it did.

I'm pretty certain I wouldn't have screamed. I'm not the type that does, except at a fun-party. Basically I've always been the avid observer, soaking up new experiences.

That's why I wasn't shocked when the same journalists, knowing I was looking for possible copy, took me in a gharry, at a walking pace, along Grant Road. (Kipling mentions that long-time notorious street in one of his poems).

Each lighted doorway exposed a tiny room with a double bed. Seated on a chair in each doorway, her feet not touching the ground, was a little dark-skinned girl.

"They're finished by the time they're fourteen," I was informed. "Only fit to be thrown on the rubbish heap."

No, I wasn't exactly shocked. Mother, a generation ahead of her time, had told me all the facts of life, including prostitution, before I was in my 'teens. I was startled and indignant. But there was nothing I could do regarding this time-honoured massacre. A green seventeen, who hadn't yet cut her journalistic teeth, and the magazines heedfully obeying Mrs Grundy, I couldn't even write about it.

When, also in Bombay, a bomb was thrown into our gharry as we drove slowly through the native quarter to view the three-storey tenements and the temple fronts all blazing with lamps to celebrate a religious festival, everything happened too quickly for me to be more than excitedly surprised.

Our driver slewed round, threw the bomb out of the gharry, and a Sikh policeman leaped forward and stamped out the lighted fuse. Then the horse was whipped up, and we broke out of the seething street at a gallop.

There was nothing dull about my honeymoon.

India, in 1908, was riddled with explosive nationalism. Riots flared, rioters' corpses filling bullock carts; secret bomb factories were raided by the police. The Press didn't write up these things, but of course all the journalists knew. And, being pally with them, we acquired a lot of undercover information.

While the London Comedy Company was showing in Calcutta (where, incidentally, I *did* have a small part in one play) the Viceroy's daughter was married, and we saw the royalty-style wedding procession; not dreaming that the bride was weeping in nervous terror behind her veil, and that the watching crowds were heavily infiltrated by security agents in all manner of disguises to forestall an "incident".

Having become friendly with Inspector Frizzoni, a power in the police force, we were confidentially enlightened after the event. And when, deep in a Hindu quarter, we visited Surendra Nath Bannerji, a benevolent looking, grey-bearded little Bengalee, smiling behind his spectacles, who edited a violently anti-British newspaper, and was suspected as an active bomb-plotter, the Inspector told us later that some of his men had shadowed us protectively.

Albert thought he might get some copy out of the visit. I'll hand it to my husband — he took risks with the unconcern of a small boy who doesn't recognise them.

But he really shouldn't have taken me to Kali's famous temple at Kalighat on the outskirts of Calcutta when rioting was breaking out in the vicinity.

Right in front of Kali's image, Kali, the Black Goddess, whose necklace is of human heads, we were caught in a jam of worshippers who became suddenly anti-British. The din of the temple gongs was overscored by cries of hate, and arms reached towards me. A young Brahmin priest, by some quick-witted miracle of authority, got me out. I don't know how Albert got himself out, but he did.

I wasn't scared. Whenever violence has exploded in my vicinity my reaction has always been exhilaration, combined with an instinctive certainly that nothing will happen to *me*.

Outside, in the temple courtyard, came another spurt of

trouble. An educated young Bengalee shouted "What are these English people doing here? — Give us our national liberty!"

My husband kept his nerve (which, as I knew by this time, couldn't always be depended upon), and shouted back that we were not English — we were Australians — we were *sympathisers* with his rightful aspirations.

It worked. The young Bengalee jumped on the step of our waiting gharry as it started to move, calling down blessings on our heads.

To revert to quieter matters, I wrote another Stone Age story while in Calcutta, being still too possessed by that climate, in spite of India, to tackle anything else.

Cremation, bombs, vice — but also an alabaster idol with an enormous diamond in its forehead, a Rajah's palace with caged birds-of-paradise flanking the doorway, a lovely girl (a high-class courtesan) with a thin gold nose-ring set with pearls banging low to frame her lips. But over all the *feeling* of India — like the thin, sweet piping of a flute behind a wall: heard once by me, and never since forgotten.

Kate Grenville

The Space Between

The banana-shaped tourists lie in chairs by the swimming pool and stocky Tamil waiters on bare feet bring them drinks. The daring ones have ice. The manager himself has assured us that yes, the water for the ice is boiled. Boiled and then frozen. Oh yes yes. Boiled, of course boiled.

For myself I avoid the ice. It's not exactly that I don't believe him. But I prefer to smile and shake my head. No ice, thank you.

Outside the cool marble corridors of this palace-turned-hotel, beyond the graceful arches framing the sky, the streets of Madras are hot. Out there the sun is a solid weight on the top of the head, a heavy hand across the back of the neck, but beside the blue water of the swimming pool the sun has been domesticated by umbrellas and palm-leaf screens. Where the guests sit turning brown or scarlet, Madras is as far away as a travel book.

Here by the pool, under a blue umbrella, Mr and Mrs Partridge involve me in kindly conversation.

— Travelling alone are you? You don't find it a bit . . .?

Mrs Partridge's crepey old face puckers as if encountering a bad smell.

— A bit, you know, unpleasant?

Mr Partridge tries to clarify his wife's query. He rubs a hand over his bald head, red from the sun, and says:

— You don't find that these chaps. Ah. They don't let their own women out on their own. Of course.

They're kindly folk who do their best to conjure up the girl in white frills who must be underneath my baggy shirts. They even have a go at a little matchmaking. Mrs Partridge leans in and murmurs while Mr Partridge stares off across the pool.

— Sandra dear, we were talking last night to the young man who's here with the tour. A very nice type of young man.

Her husband brings his stare back from the middle distance and speaks energetically.

— Nice group of people here. The McFarlands. The Burnetts. The Pruitt chap. Good company helps, doesn't it? In this heat?

Mrs Partridge nods and shows me the pink plastic of her gums.

— That's him. Ted Pruitt.

I've seen Ted here by the pool carefully browning himself like a chop on both sides. I've seen the way the water pools around his body on the cement and the way the hairs on his legs stay flattened to the skin even after they've dried. I've enjoyed watching the hairs on his legs, and the shell-pink soles of his feet, that the sun makes translucent. In the small of his back is a dark mole, pleasingly symmetrical, the kind that can turn into a cancer. I have avoided looking at his face, filled with too many teeth, too much flesh, eyes of too knowing a blue.

On cue, Ted appears at the edge of the pool. His muscular arms glint with ginger hairs as he hauls himself out. The water streams down his head and makes it as flat as a dog's. He flicks his head sideways and glittering drops land on the concrete. As I watch they evaporate into the dense sunshine.

— Ted, we were just talking about you, says Mrs Partridge. Come and meet Sandra.

He stands over me, blocking out the sun. I squint up at him, at his face invisible against the glaring sky.

— Hi. What was it again, Sandra?

— Sandy, actually.

He stands above me, legs apart, water running down his body and spreading in pools around his feet.

— Sandy? Used to know a bloke once called Sandy.

He runs a hand over his shoulders, where skeins of muscle lie side by side under the skin.

— I mean, no offence of course.

He gestures and grins and watches me under cover of rubbing his head with his towel. I see him looking at my baggy pants and shirt, and my face half-hidden under the hat. When he stands up to dry himself, the muscles of his chest flex as he rubs his back, and twinkling water is caught in the hairs of his curved thighs.

He bulges heavily, thickly, unabashed, into the taut weight of stretched red nylon between his legs.

Mrs Partridge looks away as he rubs the water off his legs. Mr Partridge breaks the silence.

— I was just saying to Sandra . . . Sandy?

— Sandy.

— Ah. Just saying what a good bunch of people we've got here. Lucky, really.

Ted shakes water out of his ear.

— Too right.

He sits down, leaning back on his hands. I see his chest gleam in the sun but have to look away from the red bulge offered towards me.

— You been going around on your own all this time?

— Yes. It's been a lot of fun.

My voice sounds prissy in my own ears.

— Yeah?

He doesn't quite close his mouth after the word, so I can see blood-pink inner lip.

— Why'd a good-looking chick like you want to get around on your own?

He stares at me, waiting for an answer, but although I wet my lips with my tongue, I can't find one.

— You must have a bit of, you know, from the fellas.

He glances again at the shapeless pants and I wonder if he's thinking, on the other hand maybe she doesn't.

— Anyhow, any time you want to come around with us, just say the word. We'll look after you. No worries.

He smiles. It's the wide blank smile of a man who's looking down his own strong legs, safe in muscles and red nylon.

When the waiter comes over to pick up our glasses, I recognise him by the moustache, such a thin line on his upper lip that it might have been drawn with a ballpoint. Each morning this waiter brings my breakfast, knocking inaudibly before coming in immediately with his tray of pawpaw and the dazzling smile that makes his moustache go crooked. I put a hand over my half-finished drink and he bows. He wonders too, when he sees me each morning lying in splendour in the canopied bed, why I'm alone. His black eyes dart from Ted to me and he bows again before padding off. He shouts in Tamil across the pool to another waiter and their laughter echoes between the arches.

The Partridges excuse themselves. They walk off arm-in-arm,

slowly, like an advertisement for retirement. Ted and I sit in silence, and watch the waiter remove a toothpick from behind his ear and clean his fingernails with it. When he has finished, Ted sighs and says:

— Well, where you going next?

His voice seems very loud.

— I thought I might go to Bombay.

— Yeah? Look, we're all going there too, for the silver. Why don't you come with us? No good being on your own. For a girl especially.

He's watching me and I'm conscious of the size of his very white front teeth. His hair is starting to dry, fluffing out around his temples like down. I squint into the glare of light off the pool and picture myself diving in, trying to drown. Ted would rescue me, using the approved hair, chin or clothing carry to pull me to the side of the pool before administering artificial respiration. It would take determination to drown beside Ted.

— Well, thanks. But I don't think so.

Ted has not heard properly, shaking a last drop of water from his ear.

— Eh? That's settled then? We'll have a ball.

I have to raise my voice to say again:

— No. No, I don't think so. No.

Ted is in the middle of winking at me, thinking of the ball we'll have, when he understands that I have refused. The wink goes wrong and all the features of his face fight each other for a second. When they have resolved themselves into a coherent expression, it is one of suspicion and dislike.

— Okay. Suit yourself.

He gets up, flings his towel over the chair with a flourish, and dives in. He is a powerful swimmer, reaching the end of the pool in a few strokes and showing those pink soles in a flurry of water as he turns. He would hardly be able to imagine drowning.

— You've lost your young man!

Mr Partridge beams down at me. He and his wife are no longer arm-in-arm, but Mrs Partridge tweaks a thread off her husband's shoulder as he speaks. Behind the kindly uncle, winking at me from under white eyebrows, a sharp voice can almost be heard. Some people just don't want to be helped.

— We were counting on you to look after him!

Mrs Partridge's eyes disappear into a web of kindly wrinkles as she smiles teasingly. Behind the smile, embedded in the lines that pucker her mouth, is doubt. They both watch me, but I have nothing to tell them, and my smile is exhausting me.

~

Not far from the hotel, there is a cluster of shacks that squat in the dust, lining a path of beaten earth. Hens scatter under my feet and skeletal dogs run along nosing the ground. Pieces of cardboard cover the walls of the huts. DETER UPER WASH. They *are* the walls, I see when I look more closely. Women sit in the shade, picking over vegetables, while beside them their other sari hangs drying in the sun — tattered, dust-coloured with age, but washed. Is there another one in the dark interior of the hut? Is there, somewhere, the wedding sari, best quality cotton or maybe even silk, with the lucky elephant-border or the brocade border that reads GOOD LUCK GOOD LUCK GOOD LUCK all the way around the hem? As I pass, the women look up and stare, their lips drawn back to reveal stained teeth. They are not smiling, but only staring, and they look away when I smile.

Out of the doorways a few small children appear, staring shyly, their huge dark eyes full of astonishment as they look at me. They curl one foot behind the other in embarrassment when I look at them and twist their bodies away as if fleeing, but their eyes never leave my face.

As I pass the huts the children drift out after me and at each hut more emerge. I can hear their feet padding in the dust behind me. When I turn around to smile they all stop in mid-stride. They all stare, motionless except for a hand somewhere scratching a melon-belly, a foot rubbing the back of a leg, a finger busy up a nostril.

On the fringes of the silent group the girls stand, curious but listless, holding babies on their hips. They stare blankly, shifting the baby from one hip to the other, automatically brushing away a fly.

At last one of the boys lets out a nervous giggle and the tension breaks. Suddenly they're all shrieking, dancing around me, bravely reaching out to dab my arm and springing back, squealing and giggling.

They seem to know a bit of English. They yell:
— Good morning! Good afternoon! Good night!
When I speak to them they explode and cover their mouths with their hands to keep so much laughing hidden. They don't point, but they nudge each other and gesture around themselves,

miming my clothes. One boy, bigger than the rest, wearing only a tattered pair of shorts that hangs precariously under his round belly, sweeps his hands around and stands before us in baggy trousers and big shirt. He stares up at me and says:

— You boy or girl?

His voice does not prejudice the question one way or the other.

— Girl. I'm a girl.

He stares, not believing. After a moment he grins enormously and laughs in a theatrical way to show how well he understands the joke. Then doubt clouds his face. He ducks his head as if overwhelmed by his question, but pulls at my sleeve:

— You boy or girl?

He stares up at me waiting for the answer. His round head, under its short fur of hair, seems too large for his frail neck. He cranes up at me for the answer.

— Boy. I'm a boy. Like you.

He considers that, but after a moment of looking at the front of my shirt he bends over with laughter again. Now he's embarrassed and won't look at me. He says something to the other kids and they all stare at me. They're waiting for a proper answer. It's very quiet in this back lane. The horns of the taxis on the main road seem puny and very far away. It seems the kids could wait forever for an answer.

I start to walk back to the main road, but the kids follow, straggling after me along with the dogs and a hen or two. When I walk faster, some break into a run to keep up, even the girls, with the babies on their hips bouncing and crying. One by one they dart around in front of me and run backwards for a few yards to watch my face as they try again.

— You boy or girl? Boy or girl?

They're all doing it together so that the words have become a chant. Bah yo gel bah yo gel bah yo gel.

At the edge of the shack village they stop as if on a line drawn on the road. I walk on until finally I can wave goodbye before turning a corner that takes me out of sight. But they are still calling out even after I've disappeared. Bahyogel bahyogel. Their voices carry a long way down the quiet street.

∾ *Barbara Hanrahan* ∾

Some Girls

To be popular on the ship you had to be willing to iron, and men came along to the ironing room looking helpless, and some girls were good ironers because they had brothers to iron for at home. I'd never ironed a man's shirt. I hadn't even ironed my own clothes. My grandmother and Reece had always washed and ironed everything for me, but on the ship I was even washing my own pants and hanging them on the nylon traveller's line in the cabin to dry.

The sort of men some girls went after were the insolent blond ones who wore checked viyella shirts and ties with shields or old-school stripes. They were cocksure little boys, but they were men, with jumpers that rode up over their stick-out bums; and they had hard sunburnt faces with sunny sunshine smiles when they wanted something like a shirt to be ironed, but other times they didn't see you; and their ears stuck out on either side of their private school haircuts, at each port they wired home for more cash. Though one of the checked viyella men was a bachelor farmer (some said a pastoralist, a grazier): big and ugly, blistery-faced, with a sandpapery voice. Flap-winged galahs, white stones that dried-up rivers didn't run on, the Halloween-mask faces of steers and mama-bleating lambs waiting to be butchered were in his voice. He was big and clumsy and boring, but he was rich and umarried. The blond men's arrogant old-school voices turned smoothly conspiratorial when they chatted up the flash girls who sat at the captain's table. But the farmer's voice didn't need to pretend. He stood there in his baggy sportscoat and the trend-setting girls from Toorak and Double Bay in their classy strapless playsuits with built-in bras hung on to his every word.

A shirt to iron was a badge that meant you had a man, and you sprinkled on water drops and rolled the bundle up tight, then ironed with your elbow sticking out. Dot gave me an ironing lesson — you did the little bits, collars and cuffs, first; then went on to the open stretches of sleeves, front, back. But I was a failure on that ship: I didn't get a shirt. Alfred, the Austrian boy, giggling and gossiping in his short shorts, might have been my girlfriend. After I drank whisky for the first time at Julie's twenty-first birthday party, I slid down the wall and fell on the floor and kissed the vegetarian intellectual we called the Professor — but next day he didn't seem to remember. I invited the English boy into the cabin to see my drawings; he only sat on Gwenyth's bunk beside me; we had to sit with our heads bent so they wouldn't bump against my bunk overhead. When Gwenyth came in, he jumped up and went away. She nearly died. She said never to bring a stranger to the cabin again, he might steal something.

I hadn't known Gwenyth before I got on the ship. She was an older woman from Adelaide who knew the name of every London bridge and was a friend of my Aunty Margaret's. She thought it odd Aunty Margaret hadn't told her she had a niece going to England on the same ship as she was (Aunty Margaret didn't know — she wasn't speaking to us because my mother had forgotten to send a card for my cousin Averil's birthday). Gwenyth hadn't wanted us to sit together at meals — we had to share a cabin, but she wanted us to go separate ways outside so we'd meet different people; but we'd been placed at the same table, so she had to put up with me, and Gwenyth took a quarter of a teaspoon of Father Pierre's Monastery Herbs with all her meals for the pain in her lumber regions. She was always going on about her black-bristled prophylactic clothes-brush, but I could never understand what she meant. She had a complete wardrobe of miracle wash-'n'-wear clothes. She'd brought *The Diamond as Big as the Ritz* with her to read, but didn't think much of it, so gave it to me. She wouldn't have the fish baskets I bought in Aden in the cabin. When she was sitting on the top deck in her deck-chair a man came up and asked was she a virgin.

And some girls needed a man to buy them a drink — it was another thing you did on a ship. You sat in the lounge at one of the little round tables, and you could drink cappuccino and eat continental cake, but the best thing was to have a man buy you gin and tonic or scotch on the rocks. Scotch was the right drink, and I winced at the taste but drank it down: I drank it because it meant I was the same as Dot and Julie, though I had never seen girls drink as much as they did.

Alfred couldn't afford to buy them drinks, so they didn't talk to him for very long. Alfred was going back to Austria to see what it was like. He didn't stop smiling his big white smile and he collected girls and was always kissing them on the neck, on the cheeks, by the mouth — but only in a friendly silly way, never seriously. "Us girls," he said — and "Us girls" included Alfred. He spent a lot of time sitting and talking to me and he took me to the dances on the ship and warned me about the way I looked at men (he reckoned I gave them the come-hither look, though I didn't mean to); and everyone thought I was his girlfriend, but I wasn't. Alfred would have looked perfect in leather shorts with embroidered braces and a feather in his hat, and when I asked why he didn't kiss me in any sort of way he said he just couldn't, and it was as if Alfred had a secret and wanted me to guess it. And a boy called Bill would often come and sit and talk with us and his girlfriend, Wilma, ironed his shirts. Wilma was nut-brown-maid innocent with freckles and a pretty Dutch smile, a girl nice and good enough for Bill, and they walked round holding hands. Wilma's mother was frizzy-haired, sly-eyed, she spoke with a foreign accent and she had diamonds all over her fingers because her husband, Wilma's father, was a jeweller. Wilma and Bill went to the ship church service on Sunday, and Wilma didn't know her mother was always sleeping in the daytime with one or other of the two German boys who shared Alfred's cabin.

And girls were on the ship to cut boys' hair; to lie round the pool in their bikinis with the oh-so-smart Paris look so the strolling officers should see them; to dance cheek-to-cheek or jive in the glass-walled bar on the top deck (if you were outside, looking in, it was like madness: the ship sailing on a wide black sea and inside the glass cage the silhouette figures flung apart, come together to the beat of soundless music). And girls were learning to do the Twist — you were supposed to wriggle round as though you were wiping your back with a bath towel. And there was a sad-faced orchestra that played "Santa Lucia" at afternoon-tea time; and Miss Schneider, the Adelaide migrant artist, walked about with her sketch-book, long-nosed and aristocratically foreign. She had her photo on the Women's Page of the *Advertiser*, the Governor opened her exhibitions that featured society-girl debutantes and vases of snowball hydrangeas. Miss Schneider gave private lessons and was a Fellow of the Royal South Australian Society of Arts, and Gwenyth went up to meet her, excited — Miss Schneider was a real artist, and Gwenyth even introduced me. I told the blond boy in a viyella shirt who kept wiring home most often for money that I was an artist, too; he looked at me and laughed: "Bull artist, you mean."

In Auckland I wore my dark glasses going down the gangplank, and felt flattered when I got stopped by an immigration officer at the bottom who wanted to look in the cardboard box I carried — I supposed he thought he might find drugs, but it only held the letters and card to post to my mother and my grandmother and Reece. They played "The Maori Farewell" when the ship left and then we went back to Brisbane, and that leavetaking some girls were getting drunk and standing on the top deck crying because they were really leaving the last lights of Australia behind.

JOURNEYS WITHIN

∾

∽ *Olga Masters* ∽

The Getting Away

The getting away was terrible.

Kathleen was very white and Patricia buried herself in the corner of the couch and cried quietly like a grown-up. Lebby had a fever and May had put her into the double bed under the speckled eiderdown. It was ironic that May should spare Lebby from witnessing the departure, since she was the one least troubled by it.

When Amy came into the kitchen with her luggage, Patricia made for the corner of the couch and Kathleen ran to Gus and clung to his leg. He lifted her up, with a brief look of hate towards Amy, across Kathleen's tangled head for it was quite early in the morning, and May had not found time so far to comb Kathleen's and Patricia's hair and wipe their faces with a damp cloth. Kathleen thought how strange it was to see Amy dressed up with a hat on at that hour and a thick coating of lipstick. Beside her the kitchen seemed in even worse confusion. The teacups from the first pot, made when the boys and Gus had got up for the milking, waited beside the stack of porridge plates and rounds of bread, ready for what the farming community called second breakfast, taken in more leisurely fashion when the chores were done.

Amy took a piece of bread and ate it dry, pushing it through her red lips, eyes very round.

"If Fred is finished I'll get him to carry my port down," Amy said, laying the bread on the tablecloth.

"Come on," Gus said to Kathleen and hitched her higher, to carry her nearly at a run towards the dairy.

May scooped Patricia up and ran after them. "We'll see the poddies fed!" she cried.

Amy set off for the gate, bent sideways with the weight of her case. Fred saw, and ran to catch her up and take it, while she ran ahead to stop the car, wobbling down the rough track on her high heels. The car made a great deal of dust stopping suddenly. Climbing in, Amy got a showering on her navy skirt. Since she had not said any formal goodbyes to the others, she was too embarrassed to say goodbye to Fred and fussed with her handbag, looking inside it and snapping it shut and slapping at some imaginary dust on it. Only once did she lift her head to see Fred's round hungry face under his round felt hat, and beyond him Patricia running screaming towards the road (she couldn't hear the screaming but she saw it) — and Kathleen standing stiff like a small stone statue, and May with her fist raised shaking it in the air.

Some of the passengers in the centre of the rear seat, with others obscuring their view, thought the driver was receiving a reprimand. The driver, who had known May from childhood, thought so too. He lifted his hands from the wheel and raised them palms upwards and swung around to look for an explanation from Amy. But Amy had shrunk in her shame and misery between a small boy bearing signs of car sickness and a man bearing signs of a traveller in tea, for his attache case was across his knee and he was utilising travelling time by going through papers.

In spite of herself Amy was impressed by an illustrated spill of tea from one corner of a sheet of paper, the leaves growing fainter as they crossed the page. She wondered if she might get to know the man, perhaps he would find her a job at the place where he worked. There would be jobs for a lot of people surely, because of all the tea sold. She had a swift vision of the big brown enamel teapot in May's kitchen, nearly always full and hot, and felt her chest and throat begin to tighten. She decided to imagine a handsome tin of tea which she would send home as a gift. She saw Kathleen and Patricia bent over it, only their backs showing. Lebby was in May's arms looking down on it too, her eyelids lowered.

Amy and the man exchanged one glance. His eyes were cold and a pale grey with very pale lashes and sandy brows that grew in a little tuft near the bridge of his nose, and didn't bother going further. Amy looked again to make sure she wasn't mistaken.

She thought there must be hairs above his eyes, too faint to see clearly. But there were none, only skin shining and faintly blue, stretched tight on the bone without flesh to nurture growth.

Amy looked away from the glare of his unfriendly eyes. Oh my goodness, she thought, up till now I've only seen one kind of eyebrows. There must be a lot of things I haven't seen. An excitement crept in faint shivers from her thighs upwards to pump her heart harder. I'll see things, I'll do things! Keep your old job in your tea factory! The farm houses flew past, the cows leaving bails in bored little knots, the dead timbers of great trees white against the green of grass-covered hills. Goodbye to all that! Amy ran her hand down her side raising a buttock, tucking her skirt under it, no longer touching the tea man.

"Pardon *me*," she said, and the small boy in spite of advancing further into his state of squeamishness raised respectful eyes to her face.

～

Nearing Sydney, Amy had begun to worry, aware that she must leave the train at Central Station and find her way to Annandale. She left her case in a locker at the station (wishing she did not have to spend money this way) and took only her handbag and a bag crocheted from string, a method taught her by a hotel guest, and inside this wrapped in brown paper a nightdress, toothbrush and hand towel. Her aunt would surely allow her to stay overnight and a few subsequent nights until she found work and a room or board somewhere cheap. Sydney was cheap, she knew that, and there was proof of it visible from the train she was riding in — a great sign on the side of a building that said three course meals for sixpence. One of those meals a day would be all she would need, with a cup of tea and a slice of bread and butter for breakfast and a twopenny pie at midday. That would mean eating for ten shillings a week, and if she got a room for ten shillings there would be money over from her wage (she hoped for thirty shillings) to buy some clothes. She had to jerk her thoughts away from clothes, remembering a pleading promise to send things home for the little girls when May shouted to her about their thin jumpers and the absence of warm singlets for the winter.

She had asked the tram guard to tell her when Wattle Street came up. Intrigued by her big blue eyes, he hovered near her and put on an air of authority, giving tickets and change with a flourish and saying "Fares, *plis*," even when he was aware there were no new travellers on board. All of it was put on to impress Amy, a girl from the country as she had told him, who might be seen on the tram again and would be good for a squeeze of the hand when they exchanged money, nothing more, him a married man with four children and a good Catholic. He snapped his bag open and shut for nothing, then when the tram started up after a stop, he held up two fingers and she didn't know what he meant and looked frightened, which gave him cause to bend over and say he meant there were two more stops before she got out.

A nice man, Amy thought, gripping her bags tightly in case she left them behind. People were helpful in the city, they minded their own business too, as she had been told by travellers through Moruya. Amy looked for verification around the tram but saw only solemn and frowning faces, many of them pinched looking, wedged between shabby hats and coat collars. They are hungry for their tea, Amy thought generously, wondering what hers would be. She stood now, for the guard had given her another signal. I know he's sorry to see me go, she thought, feeling loved and wanted and happy so far with Sydney.

But number seventeen did not look welcoming, not being favoured with a street light close by and looking resentful of this, crouching dimly with only a faint light showing behind the glass top of the front door like an orange in a fog.

More light came from a May bush near the front gate, scattering petals on the path as the wind rushed about it, reminding Amy of the shower of confetti two giggling young cousins threw on her and Ted when they walked out of All Souls. She shook the memory off as the May shook off the surplus blooms, finding a bell to press and hearing slippered feet growing more distinct as she waited.

"Aunty Daph!" Amy said, squashing her crochet bag in both hands.

"My goodness me!" cried the woman, who looked a lot like May. She peered around Amy, looking for Amy's children, and appeared to Amy greatly relieved when there were none emerging from the gloom.

❧ *Rachel Henning* ❧

The Ascent of the Blue Mountains

Rachel Henning's letters from Australia, most of them to her sister Etta in England, are packed with descriptions of journeys, beginning with the voyage out. Once in Australia, Rachel continued to travel a great deal. This letter from New South Wales is to her sister Annie in Queensland.

BATHURST,
APRIL 17TH 1856

My Dearest Annie,

I have been longing to write to you, because from the last glimpse I had of your dear face at the railway station, I am so afraid you vexed yourself thinking I hated the journey so. It was not particularly pleasant, certainly, but like everything, far worse in anticipation than reality.

I got on famously and had nothing disagreeable anywhere. The ride to Penrith that night was rather pleasant, as it was very fine and there were only two people besides myself in the coach, an old farmer and a young digger. The latter went all the way, and was very civil to me in helping me and my goods in and out of the coach.

He was not quite a gentleman, nor yet a common man. The roads were in a most awful state. The driver from Penrith to Hartley said he had never seen them so bad. The ascent of the Blue Mountains on the Penrith side was almost impassable. We went along for four or five miles with the axle-tree buried in mud. I cannot think how ever the horses did it at all.

We passed a carriage stuck in the mud, which two horses had

not been able to pull out, so they had been taken out and were standing by the side of the road, while a gentleman, up to his knees in mud, and a stupid Irishman were trying to fasten four bullocks to the carriage. Our coachman got down and helped them, remarking that very likely we should want to be dragged out soon. However, we managed to get along, and only came to grief once. We went through the bush to avoid the sea of mud in the main road, and one of the leaders got frightened and turned off among the trees, dragging the coach against some saplings and nearly upsetting it. The restive horse was taken out of the harness, and the passengers got out while the coach was backed out of the scrape.

The road was better when we got to the top of the mountains, though bad enough everywhere. It was a cloudy day and yet there was no rain, or none to speak of, and as we did get along I preferred the mud to the dust.

There were only three passengers besides me: the young man going to the diggings, and two women. One seemed like a shop-keeper and the other was, I think, a girl going to service. Both were going beyond Bathurst.

The view down Mount Victoria was very fine, certainly, but not equal to Snowdon by any means.

It has rocks and woods and is more extensive perhaps, but it wants water. I should have enjoyed it more, also, though I am no great coward, if we had not been going at a hard trot down that steep hill with an unguarded precipice on the left down which a coach was upset some time ago, and eleven passengers either killed or maimed.

I was fortunate in getting a comfortable room to myself at Hartley, while the other two "ladies" had to sleep together, and as it was clean, I had a good night's rest. Supper I had none, as there was nothing eatable — raw beef and bad pork, but the bis-cuits and wine were a resource. The last day's journey was the most tiresome, as the sun came out very hot and gave me a head-ache, and in the afternoon there was a heavy thunderstorm. It did not last long, but it come down a pelt while it did. I was not very wet, however, owing to the shawls and umbrella, but you may fancy I got in a great state of mud.

How curious those Bathurst plains are, when you first see them, so many miles without a single tree. Although there had been so much rain elsewhere, the road was quite dusty within fif-teen miles of Bathurst. Mr Sloman did not drive to meet me, as he could not leave the office, but he met me at the coach office and walked home with me. Amy was looking very well and very glad to see me, and I was rejoiced to be there and have some tea and go to bed early, which I did. I was not so very tired, however. I can bear shaking about better than most people, all my bones are set so loosely!

Bathurst is an ugly place enough. All brick and dust. Amy's house is not beautiful, but it is comfortable inside, and I think I shall like being here for a time very much.

The piano is a capital one. I had no idea it was so good. Amy has a very bad servant who does not know anything, and has just made an open tart without putting any fat in the paste. Of course it has dried up to a cinder.

Ever, my dearest Annie, your affectionate sister,

RACHEL HENNING

✒ *Leanne Hollingsworth* ✒

Reflections on a Black Childhood

We lived at Twenty-nine Mile Crossing, a couple of miles out from Walloon, which is outside of Ipswich. I was living with my "real" family at the time. Our house was the only one around for a couple of miles. We lived in a very old, two-storey house near a railway line, surrounded by bush and a river.

It was here, at the age of five, that I experienced embarrassment and humility but learned pride.

Being always the last one in the family to make a move, I remember lying drowsily on my mum's bed, one eye open, watching everyone else scurrying around, getting ready to catch the train to Brisbane for a day of shopping. I remember Mum repeatedly telling me to get a move-on if I wanted to go. It was really no big deal to stay home on our own; each of us had at one time or another. Besides, we had the television to keep us company! But as I lay there, my decision whether to go or not moved more positively towards the excitement of the big city, lunch in a cafe, lollies, and persuading Mum to buy this or that.

Busily chewing the decision over, I didn't notice everyone leave the house, yelling half-hearted farewells in their hurry for the train! Its whistle blew loud and clear as it rounded the bend! Man, did I move!!! I rushed around at blind speed trying to find suitable clothes. Of course, the inevitable occurred — I couldn't find any! So I grabbed Mum's old house dress from the end of the bed, slipped it on (inside out) and raced out in time to see Mum talking to the conductor, obviously asking him to hold on a second. How she knew I was coming, I'll never know. Maybe it's that thing that all mothers are supposed to have — intuition?

I raced dow   the front steps and took a short cut through the barbed wire fence, snake style, on my belly; but I didn't flatten my bum on the way through. Hmmm! you guessed it! I ripped Mum's dress, my panties and scratched "it"! Ouch! But I was in too much of a hurry to notice pain! I reached the train with great relief.

I climbed the stairs, facing the knowing smile of my mother. I remember the quiet humoured whispers of the other passengers as they noticed my bared piece of anatomy; and do you think I was going to show them how utterly embarrassed I felt? No way baby!!

I turned to them and smiled my best toothless smile with an air of poise as if I was wearing my best blue dress with the oversized bow at the back!

∾ *Jean Devanny* ∾

Inland

At the request of Jack Henry I went inland after the strike, despite the approach of hot weather, as far as 600 miles north west. Here, the towns and settlements were based on sheep and cattle stations, farming, mining and kangaroo hunting. Mostly, I talked about the international situation, linking it up with the Soviet Union and Peace issues. Occasionally I stayed long enough in a place to establish a Peace committee.

Financially as well as politically, the tour was very successful. At the end of it, I was able to provide myself with a badly-needed new typewriter.

My success was due to the fact that I had left nothing to chance. To the Party contacts in each place, many of them non-communist, I forwarded advance publicity, with detailed and explicit instructions on how to go about exploiting my visit to the utmost. Those days, the idea was widely prevalent that communists were down-at-heel types, different to the norm and, to combat this, I stipulated for the provision of good platforms and that only persons of unimpeachable repute in the localities should be permitted to associate with me. In lack of a good home offering hospitality, I would stay at a leading hotel.

Thus instructed and directed, the comrades without fail did an excellent job. In some places the Methodist parson took my chair and assisted me in other ways. Elsewhere the Mayor officiated. Also to my advantage was that the general secretary of the Australian Railways Union, Jack Chapple, had preceded me in some areas, and left instructions with the branches of his union to render me every assistance possible. The officials of these branches organised some of my meetings. Travelling by slow goods train from place to place, the conductor would lock me into a carriage or compartment by myself, thus enabling me to study or rest. On long stretches the wives of railwaymen, notified by telephone of my arrival, would turn up at isolated sidings with a tray of refreshments for me.

The meetings themselves in the inland did not tire me much; the thin winey air was like a tonic to my lungs and vocal cords. It seemed to double the power of my naturally strong voice. Not until near the end, did I uncork the bottle of cod liver oil I carried.

Some experiences of that tour for one reason or another were memorable. My first meeting at Charters Towers, for instance, eighty miles inland. Here, I was wakened to the need for a sliding scale of tactics, as it were, in breaking new ground. The hall was packed. Some in my audience had come along, doubtless, to hear a novelist, writer of books they had read per medium of the local library — and the opening remarks of my chairman shocked and repelled them. Letting his enthusiasm run away with him, he alluded to my terms in jail! Consternation among the crowd was evident. A jailbird; one could imagine them thinking. What sort of writer was this? One woman went out. It took me quite a time to break down the mistrust that, all unwittingly, had been aroused.

Cloncurry, 500 miles west, was noteworthy for quite other reasons. My meeting here was organised by the officials of the Australian Railways Union — with misgivings, for they had set out two forms in a street as meet to accommodate the audience. "You don't expect much of a crowd," I remarked to my chairman, when early on we went along together. "Well, no," he replied, "the left is not popular out here." We would not, he thought, bother to take up a collection. He and his mates would pay all expenses, and make a contribution to my further tour as well.

But a good half of the population, about 800, turned up, and gave me an attentive hearing. Still my chairman was diffident about a collection — "we didn't want to knock them back" — but I insisted. And several pounds were contributed, in addition to which a pile of Soviet and Peace literature was sold. This, I jumped down from the truck and took round myself.

At Mt Isa, silver-lead mining town 600 miles west, I was met at the station by the Mayor and a group representing the various trade unions. I was escorted by the lot to the leading hotel. Here,

I was astonished to learn that I was expected to sleep, not in the room to which I was conducted, but on the balcony to which it led. I glanced out through the french windows. A long row of stretcher beds stood out there. "Do all the women boarders sleep out there?" I asked. "We haven't any women boarders. But those things don't count out here. You couldn't sleep in your room." "Indeed I shall, thank you." The maid laughed.

The next morning I confessed myself defeated. The heat within doors overnight was overpowering. I got no sleep. Thereafter, I slept on the balcony, in company with twenty-seven men. Even here, the conditions were hard to take. Not the heat, but the fumes from the mines bothered me — sulphur fumes. I lay in bed and admired the beauty, in the midst of the ugliest and most sordid town in Australia, of the mighty mine works. Sprawled along the side of a central hill, all lit up and sprayed at intervals by the brilliant colourful flare of the blast furnaces, they took the form of a colossal battleship en fête.

The hotel was good, the ice plentiful, but the daytime heat prostrated me. The Reverend Hobbin, of the Methodist Bush Brotherhood, took me in his car to visit the dam twelve miles out and when, on returning to my hotel, I rose from my seat I left a pool of sweat behind me. I went under the shower in my clothes.

My largest meeting here, the happiest of my tour and the most lucrative financially, was held in a disused stadium, the Reverend Hobbin in the chair. Question and discussion time made me realise the amazingly cosmopolitan nature of Mt Isa's population; men taking part announced themselves as having come from different areas of South America, the Middle East, the Far East, even from the land of the midnight sun!

The Party branch in Mt Isa was strong, numerically, and in influence. The weekly roneoed sheet, the *Plug*, was accepted as the town's newspaper. And no wonder, I reflected, on scanning some of the items featured. Mingled with articles dealing with industrial matters were comments on the local scandals, in semi-ribald fashion.

In most areas inland, cow's milk was unprocurable: the people relied on goats and the tinned product. At Winton, a small town on the far-west plains, the goat population seemed to exceed the human. Vari-coloured, the flocks made a fine sight when streaming in at evening across the plain and along the streets, to pack themselves into the back yards. I stayed here in a private home. When she wanted milk, the housewife went to the back door, jug in hand, and up to her would rush the goats, competing for the privilege of first milking.

The white cockatoos made a great spectacle in Winton. All water here was artesian and, morning and evening, myriads of the great birds would come in to drink at the bore drains. Instead of flying straight in, they would hedge-hop, as it were, from field to field.

For drinking, I found the bore water distasteful. It came out of the tap smelling musty, and piping hot, and had to be left to cool. A midnight swim in the dam, after a meeting, exhausted me: the water was almost unbearably hot and *heavy*.

My contacts in Winton put themselves out to entertain me. I went dancing, with ringers and other station workers. A Sunday picnic was arranged. Away out over the plain we bowled in trucks, to spend the day beside a creek-bed dotted with slimey pools and edged sparsely with drab gums.

Yet the Wintonites loved their funny little town. Not for anything would they leave it. A young school-teacher told me that once he had gone to Brisbane for a three-week holiday: after two days, he was driven by homesickness to board the train again for home.

⤫ *Thea Astley* ⤫

Why I Wrote a Short Story Called 'Diesel Epiphany'

Thea Astley read this at Writers Week in Adelaide, before reading her short story 'Diesel Epiphany'.

I should explain, I suppose, that I'm not a very accomplished traveller. Some people are expert at it, but things, awful things, seem to happen whenever I board a plane train bus. Actually, I don't do too much plane boarding because I can never afford to travel more than cattle class. This is the sort of thing that happens when I leave the safe perimeters of my patch: once when I was staying in the Marlborough Sounds and had gone driving with friends in the afternoon, I came back to my motel room at four o'clock and the Ambassador for Lebanon was asleep in my bed. Now I didn't think for a minute that he was one of those courtesy presents they sometimes give you in hotels like the shower cap and the two pieces of fruit and the mending kit. It wasn't a hotel like that. So I went down to the office and I said there's a very large dark man — and I'm almost sure he's foreign — asleep in my bed and they said oh that is the Ambassador for Lebanon. We have changed your room. And then they moved me to a kind of spare room they used for the gardener. And the year before that there was the moose. Somewhere between Calgary and Regina our Greyhound bus hit a moose. There we were at two in the morning shuddering in the autumn cold of the prairie caught up for an hour while the driver inspected damge to his headlights and waited for the west coast bus to come through. Anyway, after this hour of half-doze the lights suddenly snapped

on and the driver went right down the bus handing out question-
naires for us to fill in: nature of accident; estimated speed of bus;
estimated speed of moose; nationality (of moose?), sex, purpose
of travel, visit. Signature. Can moose write? There was one of
those hissed domestics going on in the seat in front of us. The
husband kept saying, Will you forget the goddam moose. The
moose is just fine. Why don't you worry about the goddam bus,
for Chrissake. You're riding the bus, aren't you? You're not
riding the goddam moose. The seat in front of us was full of sniv-
els and as if this wasn't enough we're an hour late into Regina
and four passengers crawl in from the bus shelter and there are
only three seats and the driver says, Will that woman who got on
with her husband mind getting off and the woman who was big
and black says, I aint got no husban. Ah'd like a husban. And
this snaps the bus wide awake and a voice cries from down the
aisle, You get her a husban. And there's a general cackle and
then the whole bus starts calling, Don't you get off till he finds
you a husban and I hear the woman in front of me say, She can
have mine and then this couple sulk all the way to Chicago. I
mean you can FEEL their sulks.

I think buses are worse in Australia. Or maybe it's the drivers.
There are those bus captains who seem to be training to be sit
down comics. They have a mike and a PR system and it's like the
breakfast show all night or they play country and western and
metal rock or conduct community singing. They crack funnies.
There was one driver on the southern run who used to say at
comfort stations, Now don't forget the number of the bus. Write
it on the back of the person in front and don't let them out of your
sight. I remember a party of lady bowlers who sang hearty songs
with risque choruses non-stop from Gladstone to Brisbane. And
another time on the Gold Coast run a young man behind (what
was it Bob Ellis said about the beauty of the monologue?) told his
life story loudly to an uninterested grunting passenger. By Surf-
ers he'd covered his life to eighteen, his father's life to fifty, his
first six jobs, his father's one job. By Grafton he'd gone thoroughly into four girlfriends and was metaphorically examining
the failure of relationship with his fifth when this gentle little man
across the aisle from me swung round and snarled, Forget her,
son and let me forget her too. I can't stand it, he said. I can't
stand it another minute. I'll kill him. I'll kill the driver. I'm sev-
enty-one and I don't have to stand it. The last time I went to the
Centre I told the driver either you lower that music or you put me

off and I'll walk. Right here in the middle of nowhere. And I started to tug at the door and I said, You ought to be ashamed. When the newspapers get hold of this it won't look too good, an old bloke of seventy put out to walk from Oodnadatta. So then he lowered the godawful music. And then the old man gave up trying to sleep and he told me he had this fantasy about buses that did the Wagner run and the Brahms run or *something*, and he liked to think of all the passengers getting excited when the driver said, Now folks, we can have a bit of hush? I'm putting on the Elgar second and all the Norms and Berts get all worked up and say, Shut up, love, it's the Elgar second. Hey, Ron, did you hear? They're gunna play the Elgar second. Then he stopped talking suddenly and began to wrestle with his ear plugs. I'd like to think he got his dream but maybe he had to ask to be put off. I'll never know, because we got off at Macksville at four in the morning and then the horror began from a different angle. We'll leave the key to your room on the table near the office, the hotel had assured us by phone. There was no key. Maybe they've left it in the door, I suggested. Country pubs do that. So we went upstairs and Jack went down one corridor while I went down another and I found a door with a key in it and I opened the door and felt for the light switch in one efficient movement and the naked bulb blazed down and there was this terrible moaning from the bed and I said oh God I'm so sorry and shut the door smartly and then I realised I'd left the light on so I un-locked the door again and the man in the bed let out a sharp cry that cut right through my apologies so I took my humiliation away to the smoking room and lay on the floor with my head on my overnight bag and after a while, a long while, Jack came back and he said, Hey there *was* one door with a key in it. I guess you heard him shouting.

I really don't want to think about buses. Trains have the personality, the tension, the romance of all travel — of waiting-rooms and tea-rooms and the music of the rackety lurch. And with luck you can sleep on trains. And here's another one. First class this time somewhere between Augsburg and Nuremburg and Germany is in darkness though there are lights across the swept fields and the pruned hedgerows. I have the compartment to myself, my bag's on the rack, my shoes off, and I'm hoping for sleep all the way to Hamburg. But just then one of the attendants comes in to check my ticket and he's an elderly frayed man and despite the pressed affirmations of his uniform he looks tired as if perhaps he has done this run too long. He has little English and I have no German except Lieder titles, but in a major effort to communicate, as we pass through Nuremberg without stopping, I point out at a fierce blaze of townlight and neon. *Die Meistersinger*, I say. His whole body seems to awake as if a finger has prodded nerve spots of his nostalgia.

Opera, he asks. You like?

I shake my head and say Lieder. Lieder. I like Lieder. Dietrich Fischer Dieskau, I say hopefully. And then to my surprise he smiles fully, widely and leans forward.

Gerhard Husch, he says. Ah.

Elisabeth Schwarzkopf, I offer. It's like a competition.

Hans Hotter, he says.

Irmgaard Seefried, I say.

Anneliese Rothenberger, he says. And I laugh.

In Australia, I manage with difficulty, train conductors don't Anneliese Rothenberger.

Ah, he says. They know the Beatles?

We are filled with mutual delight.

On and on the train goes. On and on go we, offering singers' names to each other like small bouquets of respect.

Wilhelm Strienz.

Lotte Lehmann.

Christa Ludwig.

Gottlob Frick.

I remember the old man on the bus. Ah, I think in my turn. Ah.

❦ *Joan Colebrook* ❦

A World of Water

As soon as the railway was built and linked up to our own area, we could get to the coast by making the slow daylong journey to the small but growing port of Cairns, which had once been only a row of tents and wooden huts on a sandy ridge, surrounded by mangroves and almost completely flooded at high tide. But before we could set out, there was the ever-present farm and milk work, the supervision of the dairies and the crops, and the keeping up with orders for the mill — to which the huge logs drawn from the scrubs were pulled, slowly, slowly, on the bullock wagons, and then cut up into timber to be shipped down to the coast. To watch the infinitely dilatory progress of these wagons, to catch on the air the long-drawn echo of the bullocky's litany, and the crack of his greenhide whip, was to be forcibly reminded always of the tedious pioneer lifestyle.

In our time Cairns had a "real" hotel, which was known as Hides. Its wooden passages were a little uneven, its verandas sloped slightly toward the street. In the dining room the tables were spread with damask cloths, and starched serviettes sprouted like flowers from the glasses. On the walls were photographs of the premiers of Queensland and local celebrities with beards and watchchains draping their shirtfronts. Outside the hotel the streets were sandy and white in the glaring tropical sun, which hurt our eyes after the soft light of the tablelands; this sharp sun contrasted with the gloomy darkness of the huge fig trees under which women, walking slowly in the heat, encountered each other, unfurling their umbrellas for a moment to exchange the latest news. These streets were lined with primitive but spacious wooden buildings — their iron roofs glittering, their long stairways plunging down from latticework verandas to the ground. In the main street a draper's shop predominated, with old-fashioned merchandise in its windows. A machinery shop carried cane knives, and guns and farm implements, cream separators and small water pumps. There was also a teashop, with "Caf?" written in gold script across the windows, where dust gathered on tired-looking chocolate boxes.

We loved to visit the tiny shrine of the newsagent, which had blocks of pink and white coconut ice for sale, and sticks of licorice in glass jars, as well as out-of-date weeklies from further south — that is, from Townsville or Bowen or Mackay. Here we would occasionally buy a bag of cherries — a romantic fruit, because cherries were grown only in the cooler uplands of New South Wales and Victoria. The cherries would have been kept on a piece of ice wrapped in sacking, to prevent them from deteriorating during the long trip to the tropical north. When we bought them we would stroll along the streets together popping chilly cherries into our mouths, while my father scanned the weeklies as we walked, making comments about how empty they were of real news, and about how badly propaganda for the north was handled ("Go North, Young Man" and "Be a Man and Have a Go at the North").

Toward the end of town the buildings grew smaller; their roofs were slanted and made of rusty iron. Some of them were owned by Italians and others by Chinese. The Chinese shops had a certain mystery about them — they were dark and smelled of overripe bananas, and sold tea and scarlet-papered boxes of crackers, and lichee nuts, and, perhaps, opium.

In Cairns, when we didn't stay at the hotel, we sometimes spent a night or two at a certain rambling wooden boardinghouse on the Esplanade, where many beds were placed on the verandas and festooned with snowy-white mosquito nets. We would get up at six in the morning, and if the tide was high, we would join the early risers in the public baths, where we splashed and dived in the warm salty water, were pushed by wavelets against the rough pilings and wire netting, got sand and seaweed in our hair, and finally walked back along the edge of the inlet, past gardens filled with brilliant flowers and speckled crotons, with cascara and jacaranda trees showering petals onto the lawns. After that came the hearty boardinghouse breakfast — porridge and eggs, bacon and sausage, hot strong tea in coarse china cups. My father would deplore the thin powdered milk they served (milk from the tablelands would not keep during the long hot journey to the coast) and he would enlarge upon one of his future projects, which was to institute a freezing plant so that milk could be chilled and sent all the way down to Townsville, where, during those years, the big white P&O liners were beginning to carry travelers around the world.

On those days in Cairns our father would also expatiate about the "Great White Way" — a dream road he hoped to see descending the gorge of the Barron, winding from the tablelands to the future "city" of Cairns, and so not only carrying down the produce of the pioneer farmers to market but also bringing up ignorant southerners to show them the beauties of the inland north. Enamored of ancient history as he was, I think that he imagined the "Great White Way" as the Appian Way — the highway from Rome to Brindisi, the oldest and most famous of Roman roads, built there centuries before the birth of Christ. He continually boosted the idea of such a road, stretching majestically from our own humble muddy red tracks on the tableland to the soon-to-be-enlarged wharves of Cairns, and perhaps far down the eastern coast. He spoke with wonder and awe of what the Romans had done. How could we in the North do less! It was clear that such a road would simplify our lives, although it seemed, at the time, an impossible dream. (The cost of the railway had been bad enough. "A million and a quarter," our father said. "But that was nothing compared to the patient toil, and the great avalanches of earth sliding down during the wet season, and the lives of men lost on those perpendicular cliffs, and the attempt to put up the strong but frail-seeming bridges over the abyss of the Barron!")

⁓

Road or no road, the railway provided tablelanders with a very epic descent. The long journey would land us, just at twilight, at a little station called Redlynch, where a buckboard with horses would be waiting to carry us to Trinity Beach, the site of a small-ish wooden cottage on top of a cliff, looking over the sea. At this point of the coast, a channel of perhaps ten miles separated us from the Great Barrier Reef, and against the horizon rose the curious shape of what we called Double Island — looking like two hills joined together, or like the two humps on the back of a camel. This island, which had originally formed part of the mainland, owed some of its beauty and its character to that fact — to the long-ago geological uplift and subsidence, some of the land sinking and some uprising, so that the large islands of the immediate coast were simply pieces of the old continent sticking up above the water. Beyond them, in a complex rhythmic pattern, spread the reef proper, two hundred or more cays and atolls formed by coral and detritus anchored by vegetation, and enclosing in smooth crystal-clear lagoons thousands of forms of reef life — anemones, starfish, and tiny darting coral fish of brilliant colors — as a garden might hold flowers. On the seaward side, the delicate many-colored life ceased abruptly; the resistant coral wall sloped quickly to great depths, and was met by the whole force of the ocean, so that it was loud with the roar of leaping surf.

The buckboard, on its way to Double Island, moved slowly along the sandy road, which was white under the moon and bordered on either side by pale, mysterious paperbarks. The horses splashed through little creeks, and we smelled the rank smell of mangroves. At last, we reached the cottage outlined against the sky, where a man holding a lantern waited on the veranda. To visualise those holidays was to obliterate what was more mundane, and to remember only the brilliant shining path of the moon burning its way across the Coral Sea, past the humped shape of Double Island, and straight onto our veranda.

"What are you staring at?" one of my sisters would ask.

"I can't help staring."

"It's only the *moon*."

"I know it's only the moon. But look how bright it is! It's like magic . . ."

"It reflects the light of the sea," suggested Hazel sensibly.

"Besides," our brother Tracey added, "the moon is full tonight." He sat sprawled on the veranda ledge, his legs stretched out in front of him. He had been given the little outside room to sleep in — the room with no proper ceiling, just bare rafters beneath the iron roof. But he didn't complain, only shrugged his shoulders and smiled his kind smile. Something told me that I didn't really know him; in my childish way I thought of him with pain and guilt.

By the time we were all falling asleep, subdued after the long day in the train, the jolting journey in the buckboard, we were already feeling that sensual battering which holidays meant to us then — a rhythm of wild running and leaping and climbing, up and down the rocky face stretching up from the sea to the cottage on its summit; a cycle of sleeping and swimming and eating embellished only by the ritualistic burning of our skins. Soon the

coarse wool bathing suits would be perenially damp, would hang
— smelling of salt, in scorching sun and pelting downpours — on
the little line near the woodpile where Tracey chopped the box
trees to turn in the iron stove. Under the smoky walls of the
kitchen, her face reflecting the heat, my mother cooked the fresh
fish we ate each morning and most nights.

Behind the house there was a path which led to the bay. It was
actually called Chinaman's Bay, but I never saw a Chinaman
there, only an occasional fisherman who rowed out to the traps,
or into reef waters to catch the coral cod, bright red, with markings of electric blue, or the king snapper, with its bands of scarlet
upon pinkish silver scales. The fishermen brought their catch up
to us early in the morning in a wet salty bag. Sometimes they
brought blue crabs — as large as dinner plates, with enormous
heavy claws — and these my mother (shutting her eyes in pain)
dropped one by one into a kerosene tin of boiling water. I would
hear them give one long last sigh as they died, and a string of sil-
very bubbles would rise to the top of the scalding water. Because
it seemed odd to observe my gentle mother taking part in this
cruel operation, I held my breath as she did it, trying to pretend
that it had not happened. Afterward all dark thoughts were forgotten, for the coral cod had a rich white flesh that tasted wonderful in golden batter, and the crabs were eaten with a thick lemony
sauce or failing that, served cold with vinegar and parsley.

As we walked down to the bay we smelled the rank rotting
smell of the inlet and felt under our feet the white sand of the
track, over which hung huge tamarind trees, heavy with furred
brown pods that could be boiled or crushed to make a pleasant
acid drink. Long before the British reached the northern shores,
these trees had been planted, probably by the Macassarmen,
who arrived every year with the trade winds, looking for dugong
or trepang (sea cucumbers, as they were called), swept along in
their raftlike boats, mounted with one small cabin in which men,
women, children, and perhaps dogs all huddled together. These
early traders made their seasonal camps on Australian shores.
They built fires to dry their trepang, mingled and traded with the
Aborigines, and along with their Eastern features, they left tiny
tamarind trees to mark their passage. We didn't care much about
the tamarind but thought, instead, of the big old crocodile who
lived in the mangroves, where a tiny salt stream trickled out into
bay waters. It was a huge estuarine crocodile, like those we had
seen and heard on the Daintree River, and I hated it when my

older and bolder sisters beat with a stick on one of the paperbark trees, and called out loudly, "Come out . . . Come out there . . . Let's have a *look* at you!"

Even the placid shut-in bay had its dangers. One day when our grandmother was at Double Island with us, she sat beside a gum tree, and I remember the white splash of her button-up blouse under the speckled shade, and a long hatpin with a shiny bead at the end, which held the hat she wore perched over her forehead. Suddenly she said that she would give a prize of five shillings to whoever floated on their back for the longest time. We at once took up the challenge, and I was determined to win. I remember that I almost fell into a dream of floating in the warm still water, until I was lonely enough to open my eyes, and saw my grandmother on the shore, waving her hat wildly in the air. Everyone else was out of the water, so I ran out too, and asked, "Granny, did I win the five shillings?" They looked at me with a kind of horror.

"You won all right!" Hazel said. "There was a shark circling round and round you."

"I *saw* its fin going *round* and *round*," one of the twins added solemnly.

"We *did* shout, darling," our grandmother said in a faint voice.

"I would have gone in," Hazel said, smiling with relief, "but it wasn't *necessary*."

❧ *Marnie Kennedy* ❧

Hit the Road

S am and I saved enough to buy a truck so that we would be able to do weekend work, like cutting fence posts or any other work. While we had this truck, it never made a fortune for us but we got into some strife with it.

After working for twelve months we were now due to take our holidays, so we decided to go to Ingham. We packed and loaded the truck with our belongings and tucker and hit the road through Mt Isa, then through to Camooweal where we broke down and stayed two weeks before the truck was fixed. We camped beside a river which had no water and our water was carted from town. It must have been winter because Sam burnt down the tree of knowledge and some of the townspeople got angry at us. It was the only tree on the town side of the bank, and it provided shade for romance. There were quite a few darkies living there and I made friends with them. Sam didn't care much if the whites didn't want to mix with him. He was learning through me about being an outsider and he got on well with the darkies.

At one station we came to, Sam asked the directions to Burke-town. The manager told us which way to go but failed to say there were two roads, one old and a new one, and somehow we took the old one. Sam passed a remark about no tracks on the road we were on, but kept on and thought we might get on the new one. I kept on saying we should turn back and we came to a large river, crossed it and went a few miles. He now decided to turn back, got to the middle of the river and sank. Lucky he had thrown a lot of bags in saying we might need them. He then told me what I had to do and I got angry and screamed at him. "You migaloos have some queer ideas. No blackfella would dream of going over that giving his lubra a piggyback." I had to throw the bags under the wheels, again and again. It was tiring work. I also had to watch the kids from getting too close to the wheels. We were there for a few hours, and it was getting dark, and the kids were hungry and sleepy. We got free about nine o'clock, boiled the billy and had supper. We were tired, dirty and cranky, so we made our bed in the back of the truck and slept very soundly. Early next morning we got back to the station just as the breakfast bell rang. The manager came out to see us and Sam told him we got on the wrong road. The manager said, "Good God. No one's been on that road for over fifty years." We were not invited in for a cuppa. I said to Sam, "Note we were not invited in for breakfast or even for a cuppa," and I said, "You know why." He said, "Stuff 'em. They can go dip their eyes in hot cocky goo for mine." In those days it was station policy to ask any travellers in for a feed.

We travelled all day. Nightfall found us at a waterhole so we camped. Sam shot a turkey and we cooked it for the next day. We all enjoyed a swim. We travelled for a couple of days without a mishap, then suddenly, the truck gave out in the middle of nowhere. Sam tried to fix it, then decided he would walk back to the station we left. The kids and I would have to wait and not move from the truck. I thought this one out and asked, "How far back is the station?" Sam said, "It's about fifty or sixty miles." I said, "Oh no, not on your nelly belly are you going and leaving us in this eerie place." It was very strange that no car or truck came our way although it was a used road. So we camped. Just before I dozed I asked Sam if he felt there was someone around. His answer was, "Go to sleep. You are imagining things". But I did feel a presence and dropped off to sleep feeling safe and happy.

Next morning after breakfast of sorts he tried again, the engine turned over. On the road again, we sang our song, "My Happiness". Next we came to a place, I think a post office and hotel combined, and pulled in to buy some food and drinks. Sam ordered a bottle of beer and a bottle of lemonade so I could make a very light shandy and the rest for the kids. Margaret set up a howl. She wanted beer and to shut her up Sam poured some in her glass. The old man serving was glaring at her and he snatched the glass of beer and said, "Over my dead body she's going to drink beer in my pub." She got her sip of beer in the truck. Next stop Burketown, where we spent a week fishing and resting with Sam's friends and as usual I was a bit reserved until I could sum them up.

The day we arrived in Burketown we wanted to clean ourselves up a bit, so we found a public bathroom. The water was from an artesian bore and was the right temperature: warm. The water was salty but soft. I did some washing and we stayed in soaking for a couple of hours. When we came out there, patiently waiting, were about ten or more people. I was so embarrassed and I apologised and took off. I never did meet any darkies to make friends. We left Burketown and the only fright I got was when we were going down the Palmerston Range. Sam handed me the steering wheel and said, "Here, hold this a minute." I started to scream, "Put it back on you bloody mad migaloo." Later, I had a good laugh.

∾ *Henry Handel Richardson* ∾

To School

Directly the train was clear of the station, she lowered a window and, taking aim at a telegraph post, threw the apple from her with all her might. Then she hung out of the window, as far out as she could, till her hat was nearly carried off. This was the first railway journey she had made by herself, and there was an intoxicating sense of freedom in being locked in, alone, within the narrow compass of the compartment. She was at liberty to do everything that had previously been forbidden her: she walked up and down the carriage, jumped from one seat to another, then lay flat on her back singing to herself, and watching the telegraph poles fly past the windows, and the wires mount and descend. — But now came a station and, though the train did not stop, she sat up, in order that people might see she was travelling alone.

She grew hungry and attacked her lunch, and it turned out that Mother had not provided too much after all. When she had finished, had brushed herself clean of crumbs and handled, till her finger-tips were sore, the pompous half-crown she had found in her pocket, she fell to thinking of them at home, and of what they would now be doing. It was between two and three o'clock: the sun would be full on the flagstones of the back veranda; inch by inch Pin and Leppie would be driven away to find a cooler spot for their afternoon game, while little Frank slept, and Sarah splashed the dinner-dishes in the brick-floored kitchen. Mother sat sewing, and she would still be sitting there, still sewing, when the shadow of the fir tree, which at noon was shrunken like a dwarf, had stretched to giant size, and the children had opened the front gate to play in the shade of the public footpath. — At the thought of these shadows, of all the familiar things she would not see again for months to come, Laura's eyelids began to smart.

They had flashed through several stations; now they stopped; and her mind was diverted by the noise and bustle. As the train swung into motion again, she fell into a pleasanter line of thought. She painted to herself, for the hundredth time, the new life towards which she was journeying, and, as always, in the brightest colours.

She had arrived at school, and in a spacious apartment, which was a kind of glorified Mother's drawing-room, was being introduced to a bevy of girls. They clustered round, urgent to make the acquaintance of the newcomer, who gave her hand to each with an easy grace and an appropriate word. They were too well-bred to cast a glance at her clothes, which, however she might embellish them in fancy, Laura knew were not what they ought to be: her ulster was some years old, and so short that it did not cover the flounce of her dress, and this dress, and her hat with it, were Mother's taste, and consequently, Laura felt sure, nobody else's. But her new companions saw that she wore these clothes with an elegance that made up for their shortcomings; and she heard them whisper: "Isn't she pretty? What black eyes! What lovely curls!" But she was not proud, and by her ladylike manners soon made them feel at home with her, even though they stood agape at her cleverness: none of *them* could claim to have absorbed the knowledge of a whole house. With one of her admirers she had soon formed a friendship that was the wonder of all who saw it: in deep respect the others drew back, forming a kind of allée, down which, with linked arms, the two friends sauntered, blind to everything but themselves. — And having embarked thus upon her sea of dreams, Laura set sail and was speedily borne away.

"Next station you'll be there, little girl."

She sprang up and looked about her, with vacant eyes. This had been the last stoppage, and the train was passing through the flats. In less than two minutes she had collected her belongings, tidied her hair and put on her gloves.

Some time afterwards they steamed in alongside a gravelled platform, among the stones of which a few grass-blades grew. This was Melbourne. At the nearer end of the platform stood two ladies, one stout and elderly in bonnet and mantle, with glasses mounted in a black stick, and shortsighted, peering eyes; the other stout and comely, too, but young, with a fat, laughing face and rosy cheeks. Laura descried them a long way off; and as the carriage swept past them, they also saw her, eager and prominent at her window. Both stared at her, and the younger lady said something, and laughed. Laura instantly connected the remark, and the amusement it caused the speaker, with the showy red lining of her hat, at which she believed their eyes had been directed. She also realised, when it was too late, that her greeting had been childish, unnecessarily effusive; for the ladies had responded only by nods. Here were two thrusts to parry at once, and Laura's cheeks tingled. But she did not cease to smile, and she was still wearing this weak little smile, which did its best to seem easy and unconcerned, when she alighted from the train.

∾ *Ruby Langford* ∾

Uluru

I'd been teaching the sewing class for two years now, and there were twenty-seven of us planning our trip to Ayers Rock. We cooked for the pensioner luncheon each month, made hot meals for the medical service staff, sold cakes, held fêtes, and eventually we had $3000. Then we held a luncheon for the Aboriginal Arts Board and they donated $10,000 to our expenses. After that we approached TAA and they donated two return tickets to the Gold Coast for us to raffle. I'd make a boiler of spaghetti sauce and cook noodles and make three dozen rolls of garlic bread and some times I made chow mein, and it sold like hot cakes; anything to raise funds. Lily Madden banked the money and did all the arranging for the trip. My mother was coming. She'd never been on a plane. I kept telling her it'd be all right. I'd never been on a plane either.

A film crew from the ABC were coming to make a TV doco about us. Twenty-seven urban Aboriginal women seeing Uluru for the first time. We'd said OK, if they contributed towards our expenses. "If you're gonna be shot, get paid for it," Mum said.

Doctor Dianne from the Medical Service came with us. Our plane was to leave at 8.45 a.m. The crew filmed us in the departure lounge while we waited.

It would be the first time I'd ever seen our people in their tribal state. I wanted to see everything. I wanted to feel what it meant to stand near a big rock like that.

I can't describe my first impression of flying, well, very good, but I know I was waiting for that *feeling* of what it would be like to fly. I rushed into the plane so I could be near a window. And as we climbed I thought, this is OK, until the plane stuttered and shook, then it levelled off at 3,000 feet and the captain welcomed us aboard, some muffled voice, and I couldn't look out my window. Next to me was Millie Kemmester who peered around me and Ruby de Santos who lay back and enjoyed it, she'd been on planes to Europe and was a seasoned flyer.

The flight took two and a half hours. When I looked down I thought "big", "rugged", then I remembered reading in the paper that a writer should take to a cliché like a surgeon with a knife, but looking down on that country it seemed big and rugged. We passed over the Birdsville Track and Millie said, "Ruby, what's that big thing sticking out near your window?"

"That's the thing keeping us up, it's the wing."

The plane dipped its right wing for the runway at Alice Springs. Then it dropped like an elevator a few times and we touched ground. I coo-eed loud and Millie hit my arm and said, "Shut up, can't you see you're scaring me?"

We were met by some men with a bus and a couple of cars from the Aboriginal Hostels Ltd. On the road to Alice we stopped at an all-Aboriginal rodeo. The dust flew, they sure could ride those Koori boys. It reminded me of the Khan brothers and the time we had Gwen buckjumping a steer and Aunt Nell cracking the whip.

We drove through Alice to the Melanka Lodge Motel in Todd Street and gathered round Lily for our keys. I teamed up with Aunt Monica and we went to our room for a bath and a rest.

The next day we went out for food. Alice looked full of tourists and souvenirs, I wondered where the Kooris were.

Next morning, the day we were leaving for a half-day tour to Standley Chasm, I got up early and went outside. I could see a lot of tribal people sitting in the shade trees in the Todd riverbed but I didn't go up to them. Then some young ones walked past the Lodge. I talked to some, and said hello, but they turned away. They were so shy.

The bus driver welcomed us aboard and said his name was John. He would point out things on the way. We stopped at Flynn's grave and you could see the colours of the McDonnell Ranges. I took photos, then the driver said this was the country where Namatjira painted. We stopped at the twin ghost gums.

At Standley Chasm there were eight tourist buses already. We paid a toll to enter. There were notices saying DO NOT PAT THE DINGO (MULGA). The chasm was a small oasis in the desert — a cluster of houses, a kiosk, a garden with flowers

blooming, picnic tables. We sat down for morning tea. Mulga
followed us over and lay down not far from me. We took pictures
of him but mine were taken from the back, I thought the clicking
of the camera might disturb him.

On the way back to Alice the driver was making jokes back
and forth with the women. Mum was in the front seat. Every
now and then she'd laugh and hit the rail of the bus with her
cane.

Next morning at seven-thirty the film crew joined us on the
bus to Uluru. Looking out the window I wondered how our an-
cestors survived here. They must have been very strong people
and I was proud to be just a portion of this race.

We pulled into a cattle property called Ebenezer Downs for
morning tea. John said "Here we are, six thousand and seven
hundred square miles, this property is, not acres, square miles."
"Just imagine owning a property that big," I said to Ruby de
Santos.

There was a cafeteria selling food and drinks and Aboriginal
artefacts. "Freshen up, girls, we've got six hours straight travelling now," John said (meaning go to the toilet).

The next property was Curtain Springs, 16,000 square miles,
they were getting bigger, in the meantime the crew were filming
our reactions, and did some interviews with six of us.

It was the first time I'd been interviewed for TV. I was wearing a Land Rights coloured hat, dark glasses and I hope it
showed up good on film. The next property was Erlunda, 26,007
square miles. All these cattle properties and I couldn't see any
grass. It hadn't rained in eighteen months. John said the cattle
fed off bushes and shrubs, saltbush. They looked fat anyhow. We
came to a camel farm, some saltlakes, a big table-shaped rock formation called Mt Connor, then Uluru in the distance.

I sat completely still. It was like a huge animal that was asleep
in the middle of nowhere. We came closer and I could feel the
goosebumps and the skin tightening at the back of my neck. Everyone else was quiet. It made me think of our tribal beginnings,
and this to me was like the beginning of our time and culture.
Time was suddenly shortened to include all of history in the present, and it was also stretched to a way of seeing the earth that was
thousands of years old.

We were going to stay at Yulara village for two days, Yulara
which means "the place where howling dog drinks".

The first day we'd leave after lunch for a tour of the Olgas then come back and see Uluru at sunset. The second day we'd go to Uluru and do the filming.

At Yulara we had a barbecue tea in an enclosure big enough to seat about fifty people. This resort was a goldmine. If you didn't buy food there you'd starve. It put emphasis on how hard it must have been for tribal people to survive.

The Olgas, called Kutajuta in the tribal tongue of that area, were a cluster of rock formations all adjoining. My sense of time was beginning to slow.

Then the bus took us to the sunset viewing place for Uluru, seven kilometres from the rock. There were about thirty cars, vans and buses there, and you had to ignore the other people to enjoy what the rock was doing. It was true that it changed colour at different stages of the sunset. We watched and didn't say anything.

The next morning we were up early. Uluru means "bald", and I was thinking how someone had said it was the magnetic centre and meeting place of all the dreaming tracks. The film crew met us at the bus. First stop was the Ranger's Office to get our permit to film. We had to have two tribal elders on board to show us where we could film and where we couldn't. Only one could speak English and her name was Barbara. They shook hands all round and were made welcome.

We circled the rock three times so the crew could film us coming and going. I stared out at the changing faces of the rock. It was huge. Everything else that you call huge shrinks by comparison. We could see people climbing up and when we stopped some of the women began the climb. There was a notice saying there had been nine deaths from this climb and the last was four months ago, so I didn't attempt it.

We bought some artefacts in a tent and ate some quondong fruit.

Back on the bus we went to the garage and the store called Nginti. It was on their tribal camping area and there were signs saying NO ENTRY AT ALL. I thought the people there were better off than us — they didn't have to pay high rents, or bother about keeping up with the Joneses. But city blacks couldn't survive there, and they couldn't survive in our half black half white world. It was very hard on both sides and for our survival we had to be strong mentally as well as physically. The next day I settled in to sleep for most of the way back to Alice.

Lily organised for us to go to the radio station the next morning: CAAMA which means Central Australian Aboriginal Media Association. First we stopped at the old radio station near the motel, and had freshly cooked damper with jam and syrup and cream. Then we went to CAAMA, which was housed in a nunnery, and was surrounded by grape vines and shrubs. We had a barbecue then the locals asked for two of us to be interviewed. No one volunteered, so Audrey and I said we'd do it.

We spoke about the black movement in Sydney and our involvement with black rights; about the Medical Service and the All Blacks football teams. About four of us joined in giving opinions, and it turned into a good rap session. They videoed it too. Then we were taken back to Melanka Lodge and some of the women made good work of the gambling casino down the street. I dived into bed after a shower and was sound asleep in no time, and so was Aunt Monica.

The next day we packed and rested, and the following day we came back to "civilisation". Coming in from the airport I was writing up my notes for this book, and I wished at that moment I'd been born fullblood instead of the degree of caste that I was. I had a longing for the relaxed tribal sense of time and of looking after the earth, but I knew I enjoyed luxuries like not having to boil the billy for a cup of tea, or having to make a fire to do that — and the hot shower and watching TV. I'd become soft in the modern world.

One time I'd been as tough as I had to be, chopped trees for firewood and carried water buckets on yokes for drinking every day of the year, but that was when I was young and fit and strong as an ox, and had to be to survive with the kids. Now I was middle-aged. Those days were left behind.

At home I lay in bed thinking about the part of the rock that looked like a skull, and like tribal markings. It made me feel very humble and I could sense, even so far away, the spirit of the great rock we call Uluru. I remembered my mother going over with her cane slowly to the rock, laying her hand on it and saying, "Now I can die happy."

～ *Mena Abdullah* ～ and *Ray Mathew*

Because of the Rusilla

The whole day — the trip to town, the nigger word, the singing kettle — was because of the Rusilla. It had flown away.

It was a small bird and of no use to the farm, but it was Lal's and its loss was a tragic thing.

It was Rashida who found it, though, Rashida and I. It was in the grass by the creek, shining red and green and fluttering to get out of the long creek grass. I saw it first and I pointed to it. But Rashida stalked it and caught it. Then we carried it back to Father. That's to say, Rashida carried it. I wanted to and I had the right because I saw it first, but Rashida didn't offer it and I couldn't ask her. She was older than I was and she had the right to decide. And besides, even though we were children on the banks of the Gwydir, we were still Punjabis and Punjabis do not beg. Even a little child like Lal knew that. And so did I. Rashida carried it.

Father looked at the bird. "Young and weak," he said. "Young and weak. It will mostly die."

"Yes," said Rashida in a proud voice, holding herself up to look at life as a Punjabi should. "It will die."

She gave the bird to me then and I took it gladly. I held it tightly, too tightly probably. Its wings flapped at my hands and I could feel, under the wings and the feathers, a wild beating like the noise you hear at night when your ear is on the pillow, and I knew it was the bird's heart beating.

So I held it more gently than before, in a cage of fingers. "What bird?" I said. "What sort of bird? What name?"

Father looked at me and frowned. I was always asking names,

more names than there were words for. I was the dreamy one, the
one he called the Australian.

"Rusilla," he said at last. "It is a bird called Rusilla."

"Rusilla?" I said. "Rusilla." It was a good name and I was
satisfied.

I took it home and showed it to Lal, who was only four. "I
have a Rusilla," I said. "It is a very strange bird, young and
weak, and it will mostly die, but you can help me feed it. Get
grass-seeds and blackberries. Grass-seeds like these."

He pottered away gravely while I put the bird in a chicken-
coop that had been left by some accident in the garden. And from
that day Lal and I hunted the garden, gathering and sorting, to
feed the Rusilla.

The garden was a strange place and lovely. It was our
mother's place, Ama's own place. Outside its lattice walls was
the farmyard with its fowls and goats (Sulieman the rooster and
Yasmin the nanny), and beyond that was Father's place, the
wool-sheds and the yards, and beyond that the hills with their
changing faces and their Australianness. We had never been to
them, and Ama — that was our word for "mother"; *ama* means
love — Ama told us they were very strange. But everything was
strange to Ama, except the garden.

Inside its lattice walls grew the country that she knew. There
were tuberose and jasmine, white violets and the pink Kashmiri
roses whose buds grew clenched, like baby hands. The garden
was cool and sweet and full of rich scent. Even the kitchen smell
of curry and of ghee was lost and had no meaning in that place.
There was Shah-Jehan the white peacock, too. And other birds
came there, free birds of their own will, the magpie day and night
to wake us at morning and to bed us at night, and a shining black
bird that Indians call "kokila" and Australians call "koel". But
these were singing birds that came and went, came and went. For
the Rusilla, the garden was a cage.

It was a cage for Lal, too. He was gentle and small and the
only son because another, an elder one, had merely opened his
eyes to die. Ama and Father were afraid for Lal; they kept him in
the garden. Rashida and I could run mad by the creek, bare feet
and screaming voices, but Lal could not go out without a grown-
up. He had to live in the garden with the baby Jamila, who was
only six months and who spent all her day sucking her fist and
watching the rose-leaves move on the sky or in sleeping and
sleeping. She was not much good for a boy to play with, even a

delicate boy of four. To Lal the Rusilla was a bird, a friend, from heaven.

And it was entirely his. As soon as it was well I lost interest in it and grew sick of the garden. I told him he could have it, that it was no use anyway, and that it would never do anything but walk round in its cage and make whistling noises. Lal didn't care. He loved it and watched it for hours.

And then one morning, just like any other morning, we woke up and it was gone. The door of the cage was open and Salome the cat had disappeared. The magpies went on singing as on any other morning and Lal shook his fist at them as he'd seen Father shake his fist at the sun. And he cried.

How he cried! Tears down his face, and no sound. And all the time he ran round the garden — now quick, now slow — looking, looking. He didn't even speak.

"Ama," said Rashida, "let Lal come to the swamp with us."

"We'll show him the ducks," I said. "Baby ones, Lal. Learning to swim."

But it was no good. Ama told Father it was no good, and Father, smiling a little, nursed Lal for a long time. But the tears were still there and all afternoon Father went round the paddocks with a net trying to find a Rusilla. But the bird from heaven had gone and it seemed that there was no other like it in the world. It was just as Lal had said.

We children slept in the same room and that night Rashida and I lay for a long time listening to Lal, waiting for him to cry himself to sleep. But it was no good. We climbed out of the big bed and went over to him.

"Lal-baba," said Rashida. "Don't cry. Don't cry," she said again, and I saw that there were tears on her cheek and I began to sniffle and to feel my eyes filling.

"Don't cry, don't cry, don't cry," I said. And then I was crying, very loudly, and Rashida, with tears on her face, was disgusted with me, and Ama, as she always was when we needed her, was suddenly there with a lamp. She picked up Lal and held him like a very little baby.

"What noise!" she said. "Go to bed." And when she had seen us safely in, she sat on a chair with Lal and talked to him in her soft Indian voice, so soft that the words were hardly words they seemed so true. And yet we heard them. "My son," she said. "My son, no tears. Allah makes birds to fly. No tears. It is cruel, it is cruel to stay in a cage when you have the wings and the heart to fly. No tears. You cannot hold a bird. You cannot hold things, anything, my son.''

Lal leant against her. I could tell that his face was hot from crying by the way Ama rubbed her cheek on him. Her face was creased and tired, but suddenly she smiled and looked beautiful.

''Tomorrow,'' she said, ''Seyed can take you in the wagon and you can see the town.''

''Me, too, Ama? Me, too?'' Rashida and I jumped up in bed. None of us had ever been to town. Lal stopped crying.

''Yes, sleepers,'' said Ama. ''All of you.'' And she took Lal in her arms into her own room while Rashida and I whispered excitedly about Uncle Seyed, the Rusilla, and the town.

Uncle Seyed came the next day with the wagon. It was always used on town days, but it was very old. It belonged to the time when father first came to Australia. He had nothing but the clothes he wore and the Koran tied in a red handkerchief which he used for a prayer mat. With the money from his first jobs he bought the wagon. Faded, but still proud, the letters on the side said: MUHUMMAD DIN — LICENSED HAWKER.

We'd been in it lots of times, but never to go to town, never to go to town. We hopped about in the back like birds while Seyed worried about us falling out and eventually tried talking to us in an effort to keep us still.

''Good land that,'' he said. He always spoke to us in English, his sort of English. ''Long time ago I want your father to buy it, but no. He want go back home, get marry. I tell him he too young get marry, but no.'' Seyed shook his head and Rashida laughed. She knew that father was forty when he married. Seyed shook his head again. ''Always your father wanting to get marry.''

''When will you get married, Uncle Seyed?'' asked Rashida.

''Plenty time yet,'' said Seyed, who was in his fifties. ''Plenty time yet.''

''I will marry you,'' I said. And then I thought a bit. ''Soon,'' I added, and Rashida laughed.

And so the talking, the good time, went while the sun got big and the paddocks got small and the houses came closer to one another. By the time we drove into the town we had no words to say.

Seyed stopped the wagon in the grass a the side of the road and lifted us down.

"Better you wait in shade," he said. "No run on road. Back in few minutes." He shook a warning finger and left us.

It was only a small town and we looked at it, looked hard.

"What's that?" I said pointing to a high, high, brick building.

"Only a Jesus-house," said Rashida knowledgeably, but she looked at it as curiously as Lal and I.

"Look!" said Lal suddenly. "Rusilla."

We looked. It was a stone rooster near a stone man on the side of the building. It seemed very wonderful to us and we stood staring at it while Lal crowed quietly about Rusilla, the bird from heaven, and how it lived on a house.

It was because of the Rusilla and the stone man that we saw no one approaching. Suddenly they were there, white children — a big boy, a middle-sized girl, and a little boy. We stared at them. They stared at us.

"What y' wearing y' pyjamas in the street f'r?" said the big boy.

"What y' wearin' y' pyjamas in the street f'r?" said the girl.

We stared at them and I kept saying the question over in my head like a song. I didn't know what it meant except that it meant our clothes. We were all dressed alike in the sulwakameez, a sort of loose tunic and baggy cotton trousers caught in at the ankles, serviceable, cheap to buy and easy to make. It was easy to wash, too. And Ama had washed them as white as anything. Why were they pointing, and singing, and saying such sharp pointy words?

"Nigger," sang the big boy. "Nigger, nigger, pull the trigger."

"Nigger, nigger, pull the trigger," said the others. They were all saying it, singing it, like a game.

"Game!" cried Lal. He ran forward. He lived in a world of women, an only son, and here were boys. He ran to meet them.

The big boy caught him around the waist and gave him a throw that sent him backwards to the ground. I saw him there and looked at him sitting up surprised and felt my legs shaking and eyes sore.

"*Sur ka bucha!*" said Rashida. "*Sur ka bucha!*" she screamed and flung herself at the boy, her clenched fists banging at him. I was horrified because that means "son of a pig", and it was a terrible phrase to us, but I followed her, crying, "*Sur! Sur!*" And, jumping at the girl, I grabbed two handfuls of hair.

We were all there fighting — thumping and kicking and

scratching, with Lal sitting amazed on the ground — when Seyed came back.

"*Ai! Ai!*" he cried as he turned the corner and broke into a run. At the sound of his voice and the sight of his turban, the fighting stopped and the strangers ran away. Rashida stood looking after them, still shaking with anger and strength, but I looked towards Seyed wanting him to come to us.

He asked us what had happened and I held up a fist that had some blonde hair in it and started to cry. And, of course, that set Lal off; he couldn't let any of us cry alone. Seyed was distraught, but tried hard to be calm. He picked Lal up and dusted him. He retied the ribbon in my hair, a clumsy bow, but I loved him for it. And he told Rashida, who was being too proud to cry, to wipe her nose.

"Wipe good," he said.

"Take us home," commanded Rashida. "Take us home now."

"Business at bank. No go home yet." Even as he said it he must have seen that Rashida would begin to cry, too, so he hurried us back into the wagon and drove us down the street. We none of us looked out. We crouched in the back.

"Where are we going?" I said, but in a very little voice that Seyed couldn't hear. Rashida sat up and looked.

"We are not going home," she said and her voice trembled. But she stayed sitting up, looking proud, and as I lay there crying into Lal's hair I thought that she looked very like father and wondered if anyone would ever think that about me.

Seyed took us to a cottage on the other side of town where a white lady lived. He told us to stay with her and to give her no trouble because she was a friend, and that if we were good he would come back and take us home soon. Then he went away, into the town, while we stood stock-still in the garden and looked at the ground.

"I don't know your names," said the lady.

Rashida was the eldest. "I am Rashida Bani. This is my sister, Nimmi Kushil. And this is my brother — the only son — Lal Muhummad. We come from Simla Farm."

"I know it," said the lady. "I knew it, and I knew your father before you were thought of." We stared at her with respect; she must be very old. We could not imagine a time when father and Ama had not thought of us, and longed for us.

She took us into the house and like a very wise woman indeed went on with her work and left us alone. We walked round slowly, in sight of one another, and looked at everything. Then we decided.

Rashida stood by the piano. She struck a key. A miracle happened. A note came loud and clear. Then it died away till no matter how carefully you listened it was gone. Only you knew that it would never go because you had it in your mind and in your heart. She struck another one and, after the note started, sang with it. There were two notes then, the same and different, but again the piano note faded away into your mind. Lal laughed and I stood listening and Rashida, sure of herself, sat by the piano and began picking at the keys. High notes some of them were and some were low, and she sang with all of those she could. She was always singing at home and she knew all of Ama's songs.

I sat on the floor near her and turned over the pages of a magazine I'd taken from a big pile of papers. The pages shone and the ink smelt beautifully. There were big pictures, and I put my head close to them to see them and smell them and know them properly.

Lal began talking to a black cat that was sleeping under the table. He talked happily for a long time, but the cat woke up and arched his back and stretched himself and walked off into another room. Lal went after him.

Suddenly there was a whistling noise and a shout from Lal. Such a shout! Rashida and I jumped up and ran after him. He was in the kitchen, standing in front of the stove. On it was a kettle, a kettle that sang. He pointed to it.

"Look," he said. "Listen." We were astounded. We stood wide-eyed as Lal. A kettle that sang, sang high and shrill!

"Like a locust," said Rashida. "Like a bird."

"Magic," said I.

"Rusilla," said Lal.

The lady came in and took the kettle off the stove. "It sings to say that it is boiling," she said. "I saw Seyed coming up the street and put it on to make some tea."

So we all sat down to tea and scones and chattered like relations. We loved the lady now, the kind lady with the piano and the papers, the cat and the kettle. We told her about the farm and the three kangaroos that Ama fed, about the Rusilla and the garden where Lal lived, about Jamila the baby and the long time she was asleep. We told her everything and she listened and laughed and smiled while Seyed drank cups of black tea full of sugar. And when Lal could get a word in, he talked, too. He talked to Seyed and told him, very gravely, about the wonderful kettle that sang like a bird.

Then we all went out to the wagon. We stood for a moment in the garden to say good-bye and the lady, picking a rose from each bush, gave a strong red one to Rashida and a dear pink one to me. "For good girls," she said. Then she looked at Lal and shook her head. "I can't give flowers to a man."

Lal's face fell and we were all afraid he would cry, but he just looked sad and Seyed lifted him into the wagon.

"Don't go," said the lady. "Wait." And she went inside.

We were all in the wagon ready to go when she came out. She was carrying the kettle.

"This is for you," she said and held it towards Lal. "I have two others for myself."

Lal took it, but Seyed was frowning at him and he half held it out for her to take back. Even Lal knew that Punjabi men do not accept gifts easily.

"Let him take it," said the lady. "A friend gives you what is already your own."

Seyed thought about it and then smiled, a huge grin. "You Punjabi lady," he said.

So the kettle was Lal's. All the way home we held on to our presents, even when we fell asleep as we all did. But we woke up near home, not because of any sound or any difference, but only because of the nearness of home. We climbed up on to the seat near Seyed, who worried about us falling off and prayed loudly that we'd stay on until he got us to our father.

The sun was going down as we sighted home. It was the time that Father called the Glory of Allah. The day was burning itself out. The crows cawed and flapped their way towards the trees. There was a night noise of animals, drowsy and faint. There was a smell — growing stronger all the time — of wood-smoke and curry cooking. There was a white gleam down near the cowbail that was Father's turban and there, there in the doorway, with the baby on her arm and a lamp in her hand, was Ama.

"No more," said Seyed Muhummad solemnly and untruthfully as he helped us down from the wagon. "No more as long as Allah let me live will I take these devils in town."

We laughed at him, and we held our roses up for Ama to smell. But Lal pushed between us.

"Look, Ama," he said holding up his kettle. "Rusilla."

∾ *Robyn Davidson* ∾

The Desert

All I remember of that first day alone was a feeling of release; a sustained, buoyant confidence as I strolled along, Bub's nose-line in my sweaty palm, the camels in a well-behaved line behind me and Goliath bringing up the rear. The muffled tinkling of their bells, the soft crunching of my feet in the sand and the faint twittering of the wood-swallows were the only sounds. The desert was otherwise still.

I had decided to follow an abandoned track that would eventually meet up with the main Areyonga road. Now, the definition of a track in Australia is a mark made across the landscape by the repeated passage of a vehicle or, if you are very lucky, initially by a bulldozer. These tracks vary in quality from a corrugated, bull-dust-covered, well-defined and well-used road to something which you can barely discern by climbing a hill and squinting in the general direction you think the said track may go. Sometimes you can see where a track is by the tell-tale blossoms of wildflowers. Those along the track will either be growing more thickly or be of a different type. Sometimes, you may be able to follow the trail by searching for the ridge left aeons ago by a bulldozer. The track may wind around or over hills and ridges and rocky outcroppings, straight into sand-dunes, get swallowed up by sandy creek-beds, get totally lost in stony creek-beds, or fray into a maze of animal pads. Following tracks is most often easy, sometimes frustrating, and occasionally downright terrifying.

When you are in cattle or sheep station country, the following of tracks can be especially puzzling, mainly because one always assumes that a track will lead somewhere. This is not necessarily so since station people just don't think like that. When you are presented with half a dozen tracks all leading off in the general direction you want to go, all used within the last year, and none of them marked on the map, which one do you choose? If you choose the wrong one it may simply stop five miles ahead, so that you have to back-track, having lost half a day's travel. Or it may lead you to an abandoned, waterless windmill and bore, or slap-bang into a new fence-line, which, if followed, will begin leading you in exactly the opposite direction to where you thought you wanted to go, only now you're not quite sure because you've made so many turnings and weavings that you are beginning to lose confidence in your sense of direction. Or it might lead you to a gate made by some jackaroo who thought he was Charles Atlas and which you haven't got a hope in hell of opening, or if you can open it without suffering a rupture, then closing it is impossible without using the camels as a winch, which takes half an hour to do and you're already hot and bothered and dusty and all you really want in life is to get to the next watering place and have an aspirin and a cup of tea and a good lie down.

This is complicated further by the fact that whoever those people are who fly in planes and make maps of the area, they need glasses; or perhaps were drunk at the time; or perhaps just felt like breaking free of departmental rulings and added a few little bits and pieces of imaginative topography, or even, in some cases, rubbed out a few features in a fit of solitary anarchic vice. One expects maps to be always but always 100 per cent correct, and most of the time they are. It's those other times that can set you into a real panic. Make you doubt even your own senses. Make you think that perhaps that sandridge you swore you sat on back there was a mirage. Make you entertain the notion that you are sun-struck. Make you gulp once or twice and titter nervously.

However, that first day held none of these problems. If the track petered out into dust bowls with drinking spots in the middle of them, it was relatively easy to find where it continued on the other side. The camels were going well and behaving like lambs. Life was good. The country I was travelling through held my undivided attention with its diversity. This particular area had had three bumper seasons in succession and was carpeted in green and dotted with white, yellow, red, blue wildflowers. Then I would find myself in a creek-bed where tall gums and delicate acacias cast deep cool shadow. And birds. Everywhere birds. Black cockatoos, sulphur-cresteds, swallows, Major-Mitchells, willy-wagtails, quarrian, kestrels, budgerigar flocks, bronze-wings, finches. And there were kunga-berries and various olanums and mulga apples and eucalyptus manna to eat as I walked along. This searching for and picking wild food is one of the most pleasant, calming pastimes I know. Contrary to popular belief, the desert is bountiful and teeming with life in the good seasons. It is like a vast untended communal garden, the closest thing to earthly paradise I can imagine. Mind you, I wouldn't want to have to survive on bush-tucker during the drought. And even in the good season, I admit I would prefer my diet to be supplemented by the occasional tin of sardines, and a frequent cup of sweet billy tea.

I had learnt about wild foods from Aboriginal friends in Alice Springs, and from Peter Latz, an ethnobotanist whose passion was desert plant-foods. At first, I had not found it easy to remember and recognise plants after they had been pointed out to me, but eventually the scales fell from my eyes. The Solanaceae especially had me confused. These are a huge family, including such well knowns as potatoes, tomatoes, capsicums, datura and nightshades. The most interesting thing about the group is that many of them form a staple diet for Aboriginal people, while others which look almost identical are deadly poisonous. They are tricky little devils. Peter had done some tests of various species and found that one tiny berry contained more vitamin C than an orange. Since these were eaten by the thousands when Aboriginal people were free to travel through their own country, it stands to reason that their modern-day diet, almost totally devoid of vitamin C, is just one more factor contributing to their crippling health problems.

I was a little nervous my first night out. Not because I was frightened of the dark (the desert is benign and beautiful at night, and except for the eight-inch-long, pink millipedes that sleep under the bottom of the swag and may wish to bite you when you roll it up at dawn, or the careless straying of a scorpion under your sleep-twitching hand, or the lonely slithering of a Joe Blake who may want to cuddle up and get warm under the bedclothes then fang you to death when you wake up, there is not too much to worry about) but because I wondered if I would ever see the camels again. I hobbled them out at a dusk, unclogged their bells and tied little Goliath to a tree. Would it work, I asked myself? The answer came back, "She'll be right, mate," the closest thing to a Zen statement to come out of Australia, and one I used frequently in the months ahead.

The process of unloading had been infinitely easier than putting the stuff on. It only took an hour. Then there was wood to be gathered, a fire and lamp to be lit, camels to be checked on, cooking utensils, food and cassette player to be got out, Diggity to be fed, camels to be checked on, food to be cooked and camels to be checked on. They were munching their heads off happily enough. Except Goliath. He was yelling piggishly for his mother, who, thank god, was taking no notice whatsoever.

I think I cooked a freeze-dried dish that night. A vastly over-rated cardboard-like substitute for edible food. The fruit was OK, you could eat that straight like biscuit, but the meat and vegetables dishes were tasteless soggy tack. I fed all my packets to the camels later on, and stuck with what was to be my staple diet: brown rice, lentils, garlic, curry, oil, pancakes made with all manner of cereals and coconut and dried egg, various root vegetables cooked in the coals, cocoa, tea, sugar, honey, powdered milk, and every now and then, the ultimate in luxury, a can of sardines, some pepperoni and Kraft cheese, a tin of fruit, and an orange or lemon. I supplemented this with vitamin pills, various wild foods, and the occasional rabbit. Far from being deficient, this diet had me so healthy, I felt like a cast-iron amazon; cuts and gashes vanished in a day, I could see almost as well at night as I could in sunlight, and I grew muscles on my shit.

After that first lack-lustre meal, I built the fire up, checked again on the camels, and put my Pitjantjara learning tapes into the cassette. *Nyuntu palya nyinanyi. Uwa, palyarna, palu nyuntu,* I mumbled repeatedly at the night sky now thick and gorgeous with billions of stars. There was no moon that night.

I nodded off with Diggity snoring in my arms as usual. And from that first night, I developed a habit of waking once or twice to check on the bells. I would wait until I heard a chime, and if I didn't I would call to them so they turned their heads and chimed, and if that didn't work, I would get up and see where they were. They were usually no more than a hundred yards from camp. I would then fall instantly back to sleep and remember waking up only vaguely in the morning. When I woke well before dawn, one fear at least had diminished. The camels were huddled around my swag, as close as they could get without actually crushing me. They got up at the same time I did, that is, over an hour before sun-up, for their early-morning feed.

My camels were all still young and growing. Zeleika, the oldest, I thought was maybe four and a half or five. Dookie was going on for four and Bub was three — mere puppies, since camels can live until they're fifty. So they needed all the food they could get. My routine was built around their needs and never my own. They were carrying what I would consider a lot of weight for young animals though Sallay would have scoffed at such an idea. He told me how a bull camel had stood up with a ton on its back and that up to half a ton was usually carrying capacity. Getting up and down was the hardest thing for them. Once they were up, carrying the weight was not so difficult. The weight, however, had to be evenly balanced or the saddle would rub, causing discomfort and eventually producing a saddle-sore, so at this stage the process of loading up was fastidiously checked and rechecked. On the second morning I got it down to just under two hours.

I never ate much in the mornings. I would build a cooking fire, boil one or two billies of tea, and fill a small Thermos with what was left. Sometimes I craved sugar and would pile two tablespoons into the billy then wolf down several tablespoons of cocoa or honey. I burnt it up quickly enough.

My main problem now seemed to be whether the gear would hold together, whether the saddles would rub, and how the camels handled the work. I was a little worried over Zeleika. Diggity was doing fine but occasionally got footsore. I felt great, if knock-kneed with exhaustion by the end of a day. I decided to cover approximately twenty miles a day, six days a week. (And on the seventh she rested.) Well, not always. I wanted to keep a fair distance covered in case something went wrong, and I had to sit somewhere for days or weeks. There was a slight pressure on me not to take it as easy as I would have liked. I didn't want to be travelling in summer and I had promised *Geographic* I would be at journey's end before the year was out. That gave me six months of comfortable travel, which I could stretch to eight if needs be.

So, by the time everything was packed away and the fire smothered, the camels would have had a couple of hours of feeding. I would then bring them in nose-line to tail, tie Bub with his halter to the tree and ask them to whoosh down please. The cloths and saddles went on first, front to back, the girths done up, by pushing them underneath the animal and behind the brisket. The nose-lines were taken off the tail and attached to the saddle. Next the loading, first one object, then its equivalent on the other side. It was all checked and checked again, then I asked them to stand up, and the girths were tightened and the holding ropes run through them. All set to go. One more check. Departure. Hey ho.

But wouldn't it be my luck that on the third day, when I was still a puppy, a cub-scout in the ways of the bush, and still believing blindly that all maps were infallible and certainly more reliable than common sense, I found a road that wasn't meant to be there. While the road I wanted to be there was nowhere to be seen.

"You've lost a whole road," I said to myself, incredulously. "Not just a turning or a well or a ridge, but a whole bloody road."

"Take it easy, babe, be calm, she'll be right, mate, settle down settle DOWN."

My little heart felt like a macaw in a canary cage. I could feel the enormity of the desert in my belly and on the back of my neck. I was not in any real danger — I could easily have set a compass course for Areyonga. But I kept thinking, what if this happens when I'm two hundred miles from anywhere? What if, what if. And I felt very small and very alone suddenly in this great emptiness. I could climb a hill and look to where the horizon shimmered blue into the sky and see nothing. Absolutely nothing.

∾ *Eve Langley* ∾

A Woman in Man's Clothes

And reports from Bairnsdale, in the Gippsland district, indicate that Mr Nils Desperandum, of Sarsfield, will have the largest crop of apples, this year, for miles around.

— INTERSTATE WEEKLY.

∾

On a hot Australian morning I read the above advertisement out to June as we sat in the low-roofed kitchen of our old home in Dandenong.

"Well," said I, sitting back in the poet's corner, as my end of the table was called, "here's a chance to get into Gippsland, at last . . .."

Nothing mattered to us except the fact that we were going to Gippsland. At last we should see it through adult eyes. We were eighteen and nineteen years of age at the time. Now that we're going to Gippsland, we said, we must put off our feminine names for ever. As we sat that night around the fire, myself in the poet's corner, little Mia opposite and my sister sitting on a low box between us, playing on her sonorous violin all the Gippsland tunes and old dance melodies that our father had played on the plains of New South Wales, we considered the question of names, and at last . . .

It was decided that my name should be Steve, because the comic literature of the Australian bush has always had a Steve in it and, of course, we had always loved Steve Hart in that bushranging song that Mia sang to us now and again.

Now, come all you young fellows, and listen to me.
If you're wise you will keep out of bad company!

Remember the fate of brothers and friends . . .
Ned and Dan Kelly, Steve Hart and Joe Byrne.

In the corner of the kitchen hung a glistening picture of a hold-up in the early days. Ah, what grand colour in it! Against the silver and blue trunks of the eucalyptus-trees the bushranger's chestnut mare strained, as her rider levelled his revolver, his face hidden by his hat and a brilliant red handkerchief around his neck. The blue and sultry Australian sky seemed to ring with the words we had heard as children, while the elders talked at evening in the bush. Out from their quiet conversation, the brazen-sounding words had come suddenly and fiercely, " 'Bail-up!' said Kelly." Or at other times it was Ben Hall, or Thunderbolt or Morgan.

So I am Steve. We spoke of this new person as a long, crooked-moustached fellow who didn't care much for women and was sure to end up living alone, a hatter, in the scrub, through which he would ride wildly and with passionate sorrow on mournful wet nights.

By at the gallop he goes and then,
By at the gallop comes back again.
Late in the night when the fires are out,
Why does he gallop and gallop about?

They said to me, "That'll be you, Steve."

"But cripes," I answered, "I can't ride."

"Well, now we know why you gallop and gallop about. You can't ride, you don't know how to stop the horse, you see."

"But what about a name for you?" I said to my sister, staring at her short handsome figure clothed in old fawn riding breeches, with a khaki-shirt over her breast and a red handkerchief around her neck.

She crossed her legs and said she didn't care what she was called.

"What about Jim?" I suggested: "You know how Lawson says that 'There are a lot of good old mates named Jim, working around in the bush.' But I've always had a feeling that we might pick up a mate named Jim, so I won't take the right of priority from him."

And we had just agreed on that when there was a hollow tumbril-like sound from up the street and a deep uncanny rumble rang through the black night.

"Whoa, there!" howled an agonised voice and heavy hooves scuffled on the rough country road.

Then someone burst in through our back gate, stumbled over the drain and, falling across the clothes line, was flung by it head-first into the wire-netting around the wood shed and, with his head in a mass of snails and nasturtiums, we heard him gasp despairingly, "Where the — hell am I?"

A voice yelled encouragingly from the cart, "To your left, Blue . . . Back-trapdoor!"

Stepping bravely forward now with his burden, he found his object. There was a heavy scraping sound. One was removed, and one inserted, then the laden Blue thumped heavily but contentedly over our onions, on his way out to the tumbril. As it rolled hollowly with a clanking accompaniment down the road in the late hours of the night, I said, "I think the name is Blue."

"Yes," replied Blue, putting the violin under her soft white chin. "That'll do me, Steve."

∽

The day came, *"Der tag"*, we said, airing one of our four German phrases. "Well, Mia, we're off. By-by, we're off to the Doubles! Look after Priestly and the Twenty Trained V-Frawgs while we're away . . ." and in our wide-legged trousers, silk shirts and sweaters, we made off down the dusty Australian road to the dingy station and the palpitating train.

Our chief glory was our sweaters. Not that you need sweaters in Australia, which is a sweater itself, manufactured by the sun . . . But the fine cardinal, gold and royal blue of those sweaters against our tawny faces (with our imaginary black whiskers of the eighties, which we stroked as we waited for the train to come) gave us the air which seemed to be necessary to enter Gippsland.

Our grandfather had come to it by bullock dray from Ballarat, wearing a scarlet and gold cummerbund, a bright Spanish hat, yellow moleskins, an embroidered vest with brilliant buttons, and rings of pure gold from his own mine hot on his fingers.

We looked at each other and felt that we hadn't let him down.

Under the dark interest of the travellers around us, we got aboard the train.

"Dandenong! . . . Gippsland line train . . . stopping at all stations!" the porter cried musically.

Outward it shuffled, deeply sighing and picking up speed, fled grinding through the short green grass, and in its singing, lilting, grumbling, bumbling, knocking, rocking theatre we flew forth to Gippsland.

At some part of the journey, my hereditary Gippsland mind awoke. It was a totally different apparatus to my Dandenongian mind. A sweet shower had fallen in the country through which we were travelling in the fair morning, and I saw on my left a hill-side divided into fields of such depth and colour . . . such blue earths, mauve earths, brown soils (to change my tune), red grounds, yellow clays, black malm and grey clods that I felt disappointed because the ploughman standing on the edge of his boots and ploughing therein, did not, with his horse, change into a chameleon.

I looked at Blue who sat on the end of the rocking seat playing her violin, from which not a sound came, because we were passing through hills that roared as wildly as the train. But I was comforted by the look of her, and if, as I believe, every fine memory petrifies into immortality that part of the brain into which it was entered, then there is a millionth part of an inch of mine that will never die . . . for Blue's big handsome head looked, that morning, just like the head of our father.

At every station men and women got into the train. The women carrying big bunches of pink, white and red heath, and the men carrying their coats over their shoulders, with the air of men come from the hills. This is the indisputable sign of the true Gippslander, especially those around the shire of Warragul, the country of the Wild Dog. This shire, through which we rushed, was like miles of patched quilts left out in the weather, and wherever the quilt had been torn a beautiful body showed through, silver and rapid in its movements. This was the rain. It was the rain married and settled down into rivers; willows round about attempted a few repairs with their green threads, where the fences were broken down.

The sight of the wild dogs (warrigals) flying across this country, is given only to children and poets. What a swarming of tails and males, of teeth and tongues, black and brindle, white and red, yellow and sallow, as the wild dogs of all time follow the train to the refreshment rooms at Warragul. They looked up, showing the whites of their eyes, as they rushed along with the train. Sometimes, they turned into tall men leaning on shovels, yelling, "Pape . . . pape!"

"Whee!" they turned into white gates.

"Whoosh!" into the first houses outside the town; and then,

with a million snarls and clashes of teeth and frizzling, steaming and puffing of their whiskers, they became the station and the rattle of cups in the refreshment rooms — in which was secreted a most potent drug which was dropped into the tea and coffee.

We went into the railway refreshment rooms and were intoxicated. But then, how little it takes to intoxicate those who travel through Gippsland. How could we help ourselves, landing as we did on the Warragul platform, exalted by the effluvia coming from the celebrated blue clay, the streaked yellowish and red clay, the red ferruginous earth and gravel, quartz pebbles of moderate size, large quartz pebbles and boulders, blue and white clay, and pipe-clay?

Exalted, I repeat, by these exhaltations, we added it to a pinch of that opiate which dwelt in clashing white cups, the individual coffee, the flying spoons and the starch in the caps of the waitresses, and staggered out to catch the train again, drugged into joviality.

The guard with the bell in his hand, the whistle in his mouth and flag in his eye, sent us sighing and panting farther still into the country of Gippsland.

At last, in the dry afternoon, we came to the town of Moe, which is Gippsland's outermost door. Ah, now we near our Promised Land, that country which we saw lying like a bubble on the hills one morning as we went down into the red and purple paddocks of Wandin Yallock.

Up from the dust rose the station and on the coppery gravel platform stood an old Gippslander, tall, thin and long whiskered; around his hat was a snake-skin, the small metallic scales gleaming and the snake's eyes staring towards the low hills far in the distance.

Near the gate stood a beautiful woman with bare arms and much black hair which appeared to have been lying for miles on the road, but had been abruptly chopped off just as we came along. She looked at everything but the train. This meeting of trains and looking beyond them is a custom of Gippsland females, religious in its punctuality and intensity. It is a form of worship among the young and unmarried, and consists of exposing the body to glances that exalt it, while the eyes are veiled from what is known to be there.

At Moe many passengers alighted and others joined us. These were wept over by women in black net veils which had thick furry insects lying on nose and cheek, and when the mourners had gone these new travellers sat in the hottest parts of the carriage, staring at their new dusty boots and disturbed and alarmed by the look of their wild hands against the new cloth in their trousers.

The fire buckets along the station wall turned into a man lying naked in a crimson coffin, as the great bell of the border of Gippsland walked along the train, ringing itself and crying . . .

"O, go to the country of Gippsland then! For it is all ended, and your youth is over. O, be crushed utterly in the country of Gippsland, for love is not there. Labour is not sweet there, nor is time to be recaptured. Nor shall any die there. Yet all is ended!"

The whistle ran about with the whiskers of the stationmaster hanging to it like a sporran and piped the song of the country of Gippsland, and the flag dripped blood and flew about on shoulders like a harpy, crying that we should never return as flesh from the country of Gippsland.

Mysteriously then, the train moved backward along the route we had come. It slid aside from that route and was raised and winged, and began to run with us swiftly into Gippsland. The angry sun of the late afternoon filtered in tiger shadows through the wooden slats of the window shades. Sliding apart the doors edged with green velvet, we walked back and forth like a concertina. Over it lay a mat of twisted fibre to hide the instrument from our sight, but yet we heard the song which made us hold to each other's hands and laugh and weep.

> The strong sob of the chafing stream
> That seaward fights its way
> Down crags of glitter, dells of gleam,
> Is in the hills today.

Listening to this song, we saw hanging in a frame on the trembling wall of the train a map of Gippsland drawn on the hide of a still-born native bear and, largely on it, "Bairnsdale".

"The dale of bairns," I said, and my heart opened up and gave our life and blood to the dreams that name aroused in me . . .

There, I thought, the children would laugh as those who are beginning life laugh, and they should weep as those who are beginning life weep.

"Here's Fernbank that Mia told us about," I said to Blue, looking out on a plain of green reeds.

"But the fern . . . where is she?" wondered Blue.

On the dusty white road between the rough railway gates, an old teamster, his snowy beard lying on his chest, halted beside the long line of musing bullocks he drove, and halted, in me forever.

Lindenow, the last station before the dale of bairns, sounded German, and should have had a green tree somewhere around. An old man limped out of the blue gums with a box strung around his neck by a dark oiled strap. He had a wooden leg and a black patch over his eye, and in the box lay many poisons wrapped about with red and yellow papers. These, he implored us not to buy, saying that the gods had sent him out into Gippsland to slay those who came looking for old days.

"But what about Bairnsdale?" we said. "What's it like?"

"She's a good big place," answered the old Gippslander. The wind blew among his rigging and his mast leant forward and carried him away, crying from a flute hidden in his beard, "Chocerlits! Pea-nuts!"

The train burnt its way through acres of grey maize, sawed through a fence and past a blue hotel outside which stood some Gippslanders holding bridles in their hands. Then came a bare desolate tangle of yards where cattle stood casting their wet mouths upward and rolling their eyes towards their ears, or backward, where death was waiting, just between the horns.

"Perhaps these are the bairns . . ." I said.

The station came to us in that first unfamiliar line of light which is poetry, and I see it even now as a dark smudge in a darker place, outside which lay bright yellow sand. It was all veiled, then, in the excitement of being imperial, for ever young, for ever handsome and for ever unloved.

Catching Bairnsdale's one black cab, in which our mother had ridden years ago behind the same driver, now old, we drove along the main street, with black oilskin arms waving on either side and black buttons boring deeply into the seats on which we sat.

I felt afraid as we entered the gate of Mr Nils Desperandum, the orchardist, for on this journey into Gippsland I noticed that Blue had grown taller, lovelier, wiser and more powerful than myself. I felt weak and lost . . . dependent on those about me to decide what I should be. Sadness overcame me. Had not the bell at Moe foretold it? Had not the flag and whistle cried it? My only reason for living at that moment was the remembrance of,

Autumn bold
With universal tinge of sober gold.

Who else among the Gippslanders knew this? I had brought a small book of Keats's birthday quotations with me, imagining that his entire works lay in it, and I turned to it whenever I was judged.

The dry garden behind the yellow fence was full of cosmos, those flowers I had stolen long ago in childhood and been whipped for stealing. I was afraid of them at once.

And when the door opened out came my punishment again.

Mr Nils Desperandum was a Gippslander of purpose. The map of his flesh was short and broad, and on it was drawn a keen harsh mind, kind to those it had studied and understood, and impatient of those who evaded it, not through any fault of his, but through some implacable twist in the character of the evader.

He saw at once that I was one of these.

When we had introduced ourselves, he marvelled, looking from one to the other, "that you two could be sisters".

The twilight in which we stood grew darker then, for me, and I laid myself aside until those who would come, in the future, should understand and love me.

Yet I respected the man, for he, like my father, began with a large head that terminated in a small rather crumpled body.

The sadness that came about me, when I knew that he rejected me, is, and shall be, about me forever. I regarded him as a collection of days and experiences in this loved country of mine, and with sorrow I saw that these things scorned me, and in the scorning almost denied themselves being.

For I had brought to the country of Gippsland a great marking power which held and judged all that I saw there, and any overturning or dismissing of that power by those I found saddened me, for it meant that they stayed outside my strength.

At the moment, however I was only a woman in man's clothes asking for work on an orchard.

❦ *Mrs Aeneas Gunn* ❦

Keeping Cool

There was no sign of rain; and as bushmen only pitch a tent when a deluge is expected, our camp was very simple: just camp sleeping mosquito-nets, with calico tops and cheese net for curtains — hanging by cords between stout stakes driven into the ground. "Mosquito pegs" the bushmen call these stakes.

Jackeroo, the unpoetical, was even then sound asleep in his net; and in ten minutes everything was "fixed up". In another ten minutes we had also "turned in", and soon after I was sound asleep, rolled up in a "bluey", and had to be wakened at dawn.

"The river's still rising," Mac announced by way of good morning. "We'll have to bustle up and get across, or the water'll be over the wire, and then we'll be done for."

Bustle as we would, however, "getting across" was a tedious business. It took nearly an hour's hustling and urging and galloping before the horses could be persuaded to attempt the swim, and then only after old Roper had been partly dragged and partly hauled through the backwash by the amphibious Jackeroo.

Another half-hour slipped by in sending the horses' hobbles across on the pulley that ran on the wire, and in the hobbling out of the horses. Then, with Jackeroo on one side of the river, and the Maluka and Mac on the other, swags, saddles, pack-bags, and camp baggage went over one by one; and it was well past midday before all was finished.

Then my turn came. A surcingle — one of the long thick straps that keep all firm on a pack-horse — was buckled through the pulley, and the Maluka crossed first, just to test its safety. It was safe enough; but as he was dragged through the water most of the way, the pleasantness of "getting across" on the wire proved a myth.

Mac shortened the strap, and then sat me in it, like a child in a swing. "Your lighter weight will run clear of the water," he said, with his usual optimism. "It's only a matter of holding on and keeping cool"; and as the Maluka began to haul he added final instructions. "Hang on like grim death, and keep cool, whatever happens," he said.

I promised to obey, and all went well until I reached mid-stream. Then, the wire beginning to sag threateningly towards the water, Mac flung his whole weight on to his end of it, and, to his horror, I shot up into the air like a sky-rocket.

"Hang on! Keep cool!" Mac yelled, in a frenzy of apprehension, as he swung on his end of the wire. Jackeroo became convulsed with laughter; but the Maluka pulled hard, and I was soon on the right side of the river, declaring that I preferred experiences when they were over. Later on, Mac accounted for his terror with another unconscious flash of humour. "You never can count on a woman keeping cool when the unexpected happens," he said.

∾ *Lorna Grantham* ∾

Every Rockhole a Story

And they go out camping longway to the rockholes and after that I been going with them to another rock hole, not far from Malpuma and I been see emu tracks on the stone, (Dreaming story), seen the emu, all the little emus tracks gone hard on top of the rock.

Rockhole everywhere. One man been killed a big snake — big carpet snake — going along they been telling me about the yarn (Dreaming story) long time ago. Old people been going along, along, along — sleeping there — cooking big carpet snake and been went to sleep then and after that the sandhill all white. "What this one here? Sandhill white?" Told me then — one man been cooking big carpet snake — big snake — mundu they call it — big carpet snake. "They been killed this one here and they been run back and sleeping over there and burned that sandhill white."

Every rockhole they been telling me names and all. You know, every rockhole got a name — they got blackfellas's names — another rockhole — another name. Another place called Italyu, another one called Mapa. That's blackfella's names. Rockholes everywhere. I been going along — I see the one, two, three holes and I was standing there, green, green, rainwater over there in the middle. Rainwater there in the middle on the side, another one that's green.

Every rockhole a story — old people — nice — when they tell stories.

They take a lot of sugar, tea leafs when they go out, rock hole, rock hole and they digging big maku, digging around makus, they dig 'em out. Billy can full and sort of leafs like this one here (indicating bushy acacia tree) you see the sugar (lerps) and you hold the leaf — all white and you pull the leaf out and fill the big billy can and they go back and do like this, like that, like this, like that, they put one leaf here, one leaf there and get the wool and tie 'em around then. Outside dry but nice and sweet inside — sweet. And when you go along you hear birds — oh — all sort of birds sing out when you go along — nice — in the trees — flying around — and you know where the sugar is and you come along and you see it all white on the leaves. This line here — Ooldea way — Immarna to Barton — you see nice ones again — like a banana — but the banana's a round one. This one here a little straight one — nice — you feel them — get the nice ones and cook 'em in the ashes. (Called *Mayaaka* in some places).

Sometimes you dig out roots — sometimes you see like a nice flat one — you cut them and sit down dig them then and when you cook them in the fire — hot ashes — you taste 'em like a potato. Audrey been eating them. We always cook 'em in the ashes. Another one they get real hot — little one like a onion — seen 'em — take all the little leaves off — all white inside.

And you see wild one — little small animal (marsupial mole) — small one. These all go under the sand — stand watching them — got to be quick — we digging them — they go through the little hole and come out there and we all standing in middle and go that-a-way, that-a-way — all the little kids — that way, that way — stand and watch 'em — he come out then another hole — ah we killed him — he must be dead — put 'em back again — all go under the sand. Little lizard — we always get that one there and go back. Put chewing tobacco (pitjuri — a mild narcotic) in mouth. Use 'em long time back and we all see that lizard going like this — like drunk — and we all laugh. Oh terrible long time we laugh — little lizards!

Tarcoola way, you know, Wynbring, Barton, Immarna, Ooldea — we always go back to Ooldea, always jump on the train, go to Watson and one girl again's been sick — Ooldea Home there — been die now — I been taking 'em — was very sick. I been jump on the train — we not pay nothing — jump on the tray — I been take 'em right to Cook Hospital — put 'em in there and I been come back then.

Mrs Dix was on the line then working. They was stopping at tank first when Beverley was little and after that shift into the railway house then — working on the railway. My uncle knew 'em. Mum's cousin too, he been come back and tell me "Eh, good lady over there". "Where?" "Ooldea — Christian woman — she give me water and all, and she have a little baby girl". After that we been going over and have a look and playing with her kids — lot of kids went — got photos and all there.

Before, my old granny told me they always go out no blankets, no mattresses, no billycan — only take water and put 'em on the head in container and thing underneath like I make (indicating a protective hair ring — like a cushion) — like that — big one — put them on head and go like that. Put the little babies on back — that's what they do — no blankets — but they make a nice (shelter), strong tree, you know cutting up when it's raining — put a nice strong one — another one there, another one there, another one there, another one there and after that put the leaves — like that one there (acacia) — like tent when it's up — and you know prickly one — take 'em from underneath — flatten them with the stick — rain won't come through, nothing. That's what they do long time ago and we have big fire — sleep anyway — no blankets.

No tea then, no sugar, nothing — they only go and shoot with the spear — come back with kuka — that's how they do — long time. They tell me everything — my granny — I been asking them lot of questions — old granny told to me you know. "How you fellas do no billy can, no sugar?" "No we have water, meat, no sugar, nothing, no coffees, just water, drink water that's all and meat". Wild tuckers they get off the trees, that's all — long time ago — that's how they do it long time ago.

Ooldea — we come this way and dig sand — water — we digging — what happens — wait — water comes — pannikin been full. Lake Dey Dey, Fregon — same water again — same water there — dig 'em out — sit down and get rain water. Ooldea soakage still there — they got that right up. Got green water, trees, lawn, trees.

We carry them (in a sling), I'll show you. I'll make one. I want to give to Audrey. Cut little piece of rag and I make 'em and put a bit of string on and make nice little soft thing and put the baby down there and you can put 'em on back or on here (front) and tie the little seat on it. Long time ago when they having baby out that-a-way — no houses — they carry baby like that (in a large wooden dish) like they carry water. That's a long time ago — no blankets. When they get a little bit bigger, they put 'em on the back then so that how they go for walk. Mine I always tie 'em with the blankets to me.

We always walk around. Go on the camels, just on the camels. When Gloria was little — jump on the camels. When the camels get up say "Give me that tjitji" — kid you know. "Want tjitji". When the camel start up they give me Gloria on the lap and get started then — go along. Gloria sitting up — big camel saddles — water and everything on them. I can ride on the camels. We always travel, travel, travel, travel to other places. We leave the camels, have a spell, help the camels up, let go the camels, have a spell, help the camels up, let go the camels, you know, the bell ringing. Go and get them. About six or seven camels we had. Lot of camels. Take a lot of blankets and all, everything, water. There was my old man, my uncle and auntie, big mob, lot of them. Some walk. When feel tired you can jump on the camel.

We go around to (pastoral) stations. Work on the stations. Everyone travel around. Old man was working — fencing. We travel around with the old people. Old people all finished. We go around to another station, another station, they give the ration out. No money was that time there. No pension was that time then. No social service or nothing. They give ration out when we ask 'em. They give 'em. That's how they do.

Ration day we always go clean. Big lump of sugar. Standing there, big lump of sugar. "That's for lollies" they say. We always put 'em in the bag. Sugar for tea. We been on Tarcoola when they been giving rations out.

We been stopping there and they reckon they can see that big cave there. Big cave with the women singing that song (Dreaming story). That one there that two sisters. That's a story about two sisters going back from here. Remember that hill. You know the women dancing, singing. Those women, going along, going along, stop there, another one sister was standing and the youngest one was crying then, crying, crying, crying. Cave there, side of Tarcoola. Other side, man's cave.

∾ *Margaret Coombs* ∾

Regards to the Czar

We were arriving in Sydney like refugees, my mother said,
just about everything we owned crammed with us in the
car, not an inch to spare. All our furniture had been sold with the
house, except for my parents' walnut bedroom suite which was
coming down with the Beard Watson's men and going into stor-
age. I wondered if there really was a person called Beard Watson.
There really was a person called David Jones. My mother didn't
approve of beards, said she always suspected a man with a beard
but didn't say of what. Christ had had a beard, my father said,
not to mention numerous others. He went ahead and mentioned
numerous others. My mother said she didn't care, things must
have been different then, there was something funny about all the
men with beards *she'd* met. All the same, she didn't seem to mind
Beard Watson's. She said she thought it a reputable firm.

My own name was Helen. *Not Pix*, my mother sometimes in-
effectually insisted. My mother had really wanted to call me Esther, but my father had laughed and said *Why not Polly Esther?* —
which was funny in a different way from men with beards — and
that there were enough Biblical names in the family already,
thanks very much. My father was called Isaac Solomon Diamond, my mother Jessica Emily Louise Diamond, nee Croft. *Nee
Croft* meant that Croft had been her name before she got married,
and was Nan's name. It was my father whose names were the
Biblical ones. And Spot. As a joke, my father had called our dog
Spot Hezekiah Poonce. *Out damned Spot!* he would say in his voice
for quotations, and laugh, very pleased with himself. But Spot itself was Shakespearian, he said. It was the Hezekiah that was
Biblical. I wasn't sure about the Poonce. Nan often said what a

card Isaac was to give a dog names like that. My mother played cards, or had done in Narramundi. I didn't know what she'd do now.

Narramundi was the place we'd just left, the place where I'd been born, where I'd lived all my life. It was also an Aboriginal word meaning Crow's Nest in the Hills: I'd learnt that at school. When I'd told my brothers that, they'd said I was wrong, and sniggered, and pretended that what Narramundi really meant was Bloody Flat Arsehole at the End of the Earth. My brothers were old. They lived at college now, at the University of Sydney. I'd looked forward to moving to Sydney, which was a proper English name, not Aboriginal or Biblical or a joke.

Before we'd left, we'd given Spot Hezekiah Poonce away to the Lewises, Pussy to the Hammetts. The poultry had been bequeathed to the new owners, but my father had decided on a last minute impulse to bring three day-old chicks to Sydney with us in the car. He enjoyed doing things like this to prove he wasn't dull and conventional. What he said was that *I* had insisted on it. I pretended I had. At first my mother had said they couldn't be brought as there wasn't room, but when my father had proved there *was* room, she'd had to relent. My mother was always saying things like *There isn't room* when she just meant *No*, and my father was always proving her wrong so she'd have to relent. If ever she did say *No, full stop!*, he'd mock her for thinking *It can't be done* or *It isn't the done thing* or for caring dreadfully *What People Might Think*. Sometimes I felt my mother might have other reasons for saying *No, full stop!* that she couldn't put words to, but my father never seemed to consider this.

The chicks were in a shoe-box rammed in amongst the suitcases and cartons and coats and other paraphernalia packed in the back. They smelt. Every time we went over a bump, their water spilt and we had to stop and fill their dish. Then we had to put newspaper in the bottom of their box to stop the suitcase underneath them getting wet. *Those wretched chickens*, my mother called them. Those wretched chickens slowed us down quite a lot, held us up quite a bit. My mother kept saying those wretched chickens were a plurry nuisance, but kindly really. She was in a hopeful frame of mind. My father was elated. He sang:

"Young man," quoth Abdul, "has life grown so dull
   That you wish to end your career?
For, vile infidel, know you have trod on the toe
   Of Abdul A-Bulbul Emir."

"Oh, take your last look at sunshine and brook,
  And send your regards to the Czar,
For by this I imply you are going to die
  Mr Ivan Skavinsky-Skavar."

When my mother said she was sick of the sound of that non-sense, couldn't he sing something else, he began to recite *The Pobble Who Has No Toes*. He said it was cognate with *Abdul*, an-other *toe* poem, and laughed. My mother told him to look up the way to Auntie Elsie's in the Gregory's. We'd have to call in there to ask her to mind the chicks for the time being. You could hardly expect to keep chickens in a flat.

Even with the aid of the Gregory's, we got lost. All the streets out this way looked the same to us. There were no real landmarks anywhere, there was hardly even a tree in sight. It was a laby-rinth, a maze. We just didn't know what possessed Else and Bert to bury themselves out here, how they could stand it. The monot-ony of the place would have got us down in no time, would have driven us right around the bend. It was such a dump. It was so dead. All that was visible for miles around was a sea of identical little brick and fibro bungalows with red tiled roofs, we agreed. My father referred to the houses as *kennels* and *boxes*, and then went on to discuss *the suburban sprawl*. He said that people would be better off living in the country proper than here, and my mother confirmed that Narramundi was a haven of delight com-pared. She said she just hoped we'd done the right thing in leav-ing, Isaac, and my father replied ellubiently that of course we had, Jess.

By the time we arrived at Auntie Elsie's it was starting to get dark. We wouldn't stay long, my mother told her. We were anx-ious to get to the flat and settle in. *We'll just have a quick cuppa and be off, if you don't mind, Else*, she said. She was quite sure we wouldn't stop to tea.

We had to keep our voices down as Uncle Bert was having a sleep. He'd have to be getting up later on, to go to work, it was a curse. He was working on the night shift, would be until Easter, preferred to work it long stretches, six months on, then six months off. Auntie Elsie said she'd had just about enough of it. In Narramundi there were no such things as night shifts that I knew of. They scared me. They scared my mother too. I was glad when my father upset his ashtray onto the floor and changed the subject. Auntie Elsie bustled out to get the dustpan and broom.

When she came back, the story of the chickens was told.

Auntie Elsie said, *Oh for goodness sake*, and that she couldn't get over it, and then said *Isn't someone spoilt?* meaning me. She said she'd be glad to mind them for us until we got a house and that Bert would build a coop for them out the back. My mother said she'd be happy to pay, of course, and Auntie Elsie said lamely, *No need of that, Jess,* and my mother said she wouldn't hear of not paying and that settled it, and it did. All the time I was very quiet and Auntie Elsie said so, and said what a pity it was that Nev and Trish weren't there to play with me. Auntie Elsie told my mother where they were and why. Then she asked if I wanted to spend a penny. My mother answered at once that I must. I had to concede that I did.

That was an ordeal. They still hadn't been connected, as Auntie Elsie put it. They were expecting to be connected any day, and had been for some years. There was no proper lavatory at all, just a tin can with a wooden seat on it situated in a little fibro shed up the yard. The can didn't flush. What everybody did into it just collected there putrefying until it became almost full. It stank from miles off. The stink of the contents mingled with the stink of the eucalyptus disinfectant and almost put me right off gum trees for life. I tried hard to distract myself by staring at the fly-spattered, decorated motto on the wall. It was cryptic. *Our aim is cleanliness,* it said. *Your aim will help.* The illustration, however, explained what it meant. I knew my mother would have died rather than have a sign like that in our bathroom, and so it only made me feel even more ill at ease.

Auntie Elsie fetched guest towels out of the linen press for our hands. My mother said, *These are nice, Else.* Auntie Elsie said they were made in China and my mother said she would never have guessed they were from the East. Auntie Elsie said she had to confess they'd been cheap. My mother said that nevertheless the embroidery was beautifully done and Auntie Elsie said she thought so too, to tell you the truth. She said she'd got them at a sale at the shop up at the Junction and my mother said *Did you really?* and wasn't that the kettle she heard? Auntie Elsie had a kettle which you heated on top of the stove and which whistled when it boiled. My mother had a Hotpoint electric jug.

Over afternoon tea, my mother and Auntie Elsie discussed how late it was to be having afternoon tea. Then they discussed the china, which was the cups, saucers and plates. The china had not come from China but from England. The point about it, though, was that it had not come from Japan. My Uncle Bert had been in the War, had fought against the Japs in New Guinea, wouldn't have any Jap stuff in the house. My mother considered the Jap stuff inferior anyway and wouldn't buy anything but English herself. She said she thought you could always tell the good stuff. She turned her saucer upside down and studied it sagely, then praised the elegance of Elsie's cups. My mother and Auntie Elsie agreed that you had to be very careful when buying as the Japs were a cunning lot, named the blocks of land where their factories were things like *Derby* and *Staffordshire* and *England*, and then stamped *Made in England* (or whatever it was) on the china, bold as brass, adding *Japan* in smaller letters in a less conspicuous place. They cited various instances of this sort of thing that they'd heard of or read about. My father sat and smoked and munched. He munched one slice of tea cake after another, and made no comment except for an occasional sceptical grunt. He'd been in the War too, but regarded it as having been against Hitler, a German. I knew this though he never talked about it and somehow let you know that he scorned anyone who did. In private he often pointed out to my mother that Bert's name was German. Uncle Bert was as Australian as they come, but his surname was Haupt.

When my father had finished the tea cake, he began on the lamington bar. My mother at last chose to notice him, said *Not another slice, Isaac, you'll burst!* She picked up her handbag and gloves from beside her chair and said, *Anyway, we really must be off*, and that she'd just pop into the bedroom and put on some lippy and her coat. Auntie Elsie noticed, *Oh, Isaac, you haven't drunk your tea!* My father swallowed it down at once in several noisy gulps. He said he really preferred it cold, didn't he, Jessy-Bell. My mother said *Oh Isaac!* and shook her head, looking cross. Auntie Elsie simply wasn't permitted to make him another cup.

Just as we were stepping out the front door, my mother remembered the chicks. *Oh those wretched chickens!* she said. As I was lifting them out of the car, the bottom fell out of their box. My mother cursed the mess. About twenty minutes later, we actually left. It was dark.

I felt subdued now. It was strange to think we didn't have a home any more. For the time being we were going to live in *a furnished flat* at a place called Kings Cross. This was only a temporary measure, I was to understand — just so we could get our bearings and look around for a practice and a house. It was strange to think I might never see Narramundi again. Appletree Flats was near

Narramundi, but it was just a flat place. There were no buildings there at all. Nor appletrees. Just gum trees and wattle and stuff like everywhere else. I wondered what a furnished flat would be like. I was very tired.

"Oh, take your last look at sunshine and brook,
    And send your regards to the Czar,
For by this I imply you are going to die
Mr Ivan Skavinsky-Skavar,"

my father sang. But by now his voice had lost its punch.

NOTES ON THE AUTHORS

MENA ABDULLAH (1930-) is a New South Wales-born writer of Punjabi background. Her early years were spent in the country where her grandfather ran a property. The family later moved to Sydney for the children's schooling. She has recently retired from the Commonwealth Public Service.

JESSICA ANDERSON (1916-) was born in Brisbane but has spent most of her life in Sydney. She began writing as a child, "doggerel verses and plays in which I took no part because I stammered". She later travelled to London to join the lover who became her first husband, where to earn her living she wrote plays and radio adaptations. Her second marriage provided a degree of financial security and she began writing novels.

DORA BIRTLES (1903-) studied Oriental History at the University of Sydney, where she met her husband, journalist and travel writer Bert Birtles. After their marriage Dora took off without Bert on the voyage described in *North-West by North*. She continued on to England and after three years' separation was reunited with Bert in Greece, where they lived for a time.

STELLA BOWEN (1894-1946) was taught art as a teenager by Margaret Preston. After her mother's death, she went to London to pursue an artistic career and studied with Sickert. For many years she lived with Ford Madox Ford (much of the time in France), with whom she had a daughter, Julie. After separating from Ford, she returned with Julie to England and worked there during World War II as an official artist for the Australian War Memorial Board.

joanne burns (1945-) has worked as a teacher of creative writing since graduating from the University of Sydney. She has lived in London and has travelled in Asia, India, Greece and Portugal. She toured America in 1985 with the Four Australian Poets tour.

ADA CAMBRIDGE (1844-1926) was born in Norfolk and emigrated to Australia with her clergyman husband in 1870. She began writing after a carriage accident left her a semi-invalid. Her second book of poetry, published anonymously and immediately suppressed, was notable for poems displaying religious doubt, frank sexuality and concern for the disadvantaged.

ROSA CAPPIELLO (1942-) was born in Italy and emigrated to Australia in 1971. Her semi-autobiographical novel *Paese Fortunata*, with its feminist and working class focus, was first published in Italy and later translated into English as *Oh Lucky Country*.

EMMA CICCOTOSTO (1926-) was born in the Abruzzi in Italy, where travel meant a journey of a few kilometres. She arrived in Australia in 1939 and spent her youth on the family farm south of Perth. She married in 1943 and has lived most of her adult life in Fremantle, where she raised four children and worked for thirty-two years in a biscuit factory.

MRS CHARLES (ELLEN) CLACY (c.1830-?), an Englishwoman, visited Australia for a year in 1852-53 and published a fascinating and lively account of her visit to the Victorian goldfields.

CHARMIAN CLIFT (1923-1969) worked as a journalist on the Melbourne *Argus* where she met George Johnston. After years away living in London and Greece, they returned to Australia in 1964 with their three Greek-speaking children. Clift resumed her journalistic career in Australia, becoming an immensely popular columnist for the *Sydney Morning Herald*.

JOAN COLEBROOK grew up in Queensland's Atherton Tableland in the 1920s. She spent the years 1937-40 in London and now lives in Truro, Massachusetts.

MARGARET COOMBS was born in country New South Wales and studied philosophy and government at the University of Sydney before travelling to London. Her fiction has appeared in various journals and anthologies and she has published a collection of short stories and a novel.

BLANCHE D'ALPUGET (1944-) was born in Sydney. After working as a journalist in Sydney, she spent nine years living abroad, mostly in Southeast Asia. Her first two novels, *Monkeys in the Dark* and *Turtle Beach*, focus on Australian women journalists in Asia.

ROBYN DAVIDSON (1950-) was born on a cattle station in Queensland. After studying biology and music at Queensland and Sydney universities she moved to Alice Springs. From there she made her 1977 journey across the desert to the Western Australian coast, accompanied by her dog and the camels she had only recently learned to handle. Her book about that journey, *Tracks*, was published in 1980.

DULCIE DEAMER (1890-1972) was born in New Zealand, and travelled with an acting company in Asia, Europe and the USA before settling in Sydney where she began to write. During the 1920s and 1930s, she was known as "the Queen of Bohemia" in Sydney's literary and artistic circles.

JEAN DEVANNY (1894-1962) came to Australia from New Zealand in 1929 with her miner husband and three children. She wrote to help support her family but her stronger commitment was to the Communist Party. Most of her Australian years were spent in north Queensland, where she was a prominent party agitator and orator.

MABEL EDMUND (1930-), with South Sea Island, Aboriginal and European forebears, was born in Rockhampton. At fourteen, she went to work on remote sheep stations and by sixteen she was married with a young family. After moving back to Rockhampton from the bush, she became a shire councillor, founded a black legal service and began a new career as an artist, and more recently as a writer.

MARIAN ELDRIDGE (1936-) grew up on a farm in Victoria and was educated by correspondence before attending the University of Melbourne. Eldridge has travelled in Africa, the United States, South America and Europe. She now lives and works in Canberra where she is a book reviewer and fiction writer.

MILES FRANKLIN (1879-1954) left her home in the wild uplands southwest of Canberra to live in Sydney. In 1905 she went to Chicago, where she managed the office of the Women's Trade Union League and edited their journal. During World War I she went to England and joined the Scottish Women's Hospital Unit and served as an orderly in Serbia. Franklin resettled permanently in Australia in 1933.

MARY GAUNT (1861-1942) was one of the first two women students at the University of Melbourne. After her husband's death in 1900 she lived in London, where most of her novels and travel writings were published. She travelled extensively through the West Indies, Africa and China, taking and developing her own photographs. Her later years were spent in Italy, and she died in France.

YASMINE GOONERATNE (1935-) was born in Sri Lanka, and came to Australia in 1972. She is a professor of literature and the foundation director of the Post Colonial Literatures and Languages Research centre at Macquarie University. *A Change of Skies* is her first novel, but she has also published various critical studies and a history of her own family, the Bandaranaikes.

LORNA GRANTHAM grew up at Ooldea when Daisy Bates was living there, the daughter of a Kookatha woman and a European railway worker. After she married, she and her husband travelled from property to property, living a semi-traditional life and working as casual labourers. She still speaks her traditional language as well as English.

KATE GRENVILLE (1950-) attended the University of Sydney and the University of Colorado where she received an MA. She has worked as a film editor, teacher, subtitles editor and journalist. She now writes full time.

MRS AENEAS (JEANNIE) GUNN (1870-1961) graduated from the University of Melbourne and ran a private school with her sister. In 1901 she married Aeneas Gunn and went to live on the remote Elsey Station in the Northern Territory. After her husband's death she returned to Melbourne to write her best-seller on life in the Territory.

MARION HALLIGAN (1940-) was born in Newcastle, New South Wales. She lived for several years in France, to which she often returns, drawn by its gastronomy and language. She is now a full-time writer and lives in Canberra.

BARBARA HANRAHAN (1939-1991) eventually settled in her birthplace Adelaide after some years travelling between London and Australia. An internationally recognised painter and printmaker, she began to write when her grandmother's death triggered powerful memories of a childhood in an all-female household.

SHIRLEY HAZZARD (1931-) was educated in Sydney and later worked for the United Nations in New York for ten years. She has been guest lecturer at New York, Columbia and Princeton universities and divides her time between New York and Capri.

RACHEL HENNING (1826-1914) was born in Bristol and came to Australia in 1854 to join her brother and sister. Homesick, she returned to England declaring "all parts of Australia are alike". In 1869 she determined to give Australia another try, and this time she stayed. Her lively letters, most of them to her sisters, tell of her adventures and travels in her new country.

AGNES HODGSON (1906-1984) was sent to Scotland for a year when she was orphaned at fourteen, but completed her schooling in Melbourne, where she was born. Trained as a nurse, she went to Europe to work and travel, finding jobs in Rome, Budapest, Spain and North Africa. She returned to Australia in 1933, only to leave again in 1936 as a volunteer in an

Australian medical aid unit nursing the Republican wounded in the Spanish Civil War. She later revisited Spain and Italy several times before her death.

LEANNE HOLLINGSWORTH was born in Cairns and studied at James Cook University in the Aboriginal and Islander Teacher Education Program. She lives in Townsville.

JANETTE TURNER HOSPITAL (1942-) was born in Melbourne but grew up in Brisbane. She left Australia for the United States in 1965 and is now based in Canada after living in India, London, Boston and Los Angeles. Her highly acclaimed writing is often permeated by a strong sense of place.

LOLO HOUBEIN (1934-) was born in the Netherlands and educated at universities in Australia and Papua New Guinea. She has worked as a teacher of English as a second language, in various posts in social services and tertiary institutions, and as a herb farmer and importer of Tibetan handcrafts.

KATE JENNINGS (1948-) was born in country New South Wales. In 1975 she caused a stir with the feminist poetry anthology which she edited, *Mother I'm Rooted*. Jennings now lives in the USA where she writes short stories, social commentary and reviews.

ELIZABETH JOLLEY (1923-) was born in England, and educated there and in Paris, Strasbourg and Hamburg. She trained as a nurse in London and Birmingham, and served as a nursing sister during World War II. She came to Australia in 1959. A highly regarded novelist, she teaches creative writing and escapes to her small orchard and goose farm outside Perth for solitude.

MARGARET JONES (1923-) was a foreign correspondent with the *Sydney Morning Herald*, with postings to London and the USA as well as to China during the Cultural Revolution. Later she was foreign editor, then literary editor, of the same newspaper. An enthusiastic and knowledgeable traveller, she is based in Sydney but is usually away travelling.

VASSO KALAMARIS was born in Greece where she studied fine arts, language and drama. She arrived in Western Australia in 1951, and worked a tobacco farm with her husband. After further study in Perth, she taught sculpture and has also exhibited her paintings. She always writes in Greek and later translates the work into English. She is a lecturer in Modern Greek at Perth Technical College.

NANCY KEESING (1923-) was born in Sydney where she attended the University of Sydney. Her writing has involved her in various publications, most particularly in the editorship of collections and anthologies. She is active in many writers' groups, and recently founded, in memory of her parents, a studio in Paris for the use of Australian writers.

MARNIE KENNEDY (1919-1985) was born on the banks of Coppermine Creek in western Queensland. She grew up on Palm Island where her people were taken under the notorious Aborigines Protection Act. She later worked on cattle stations throughout northern Queensland.

RUBY LANGFORD (1934-) left the north coast of New South Wales when she was fifteen to work as a clothing machinist in Sydney. Two years later her first child was born. Her life has alternated between spells in the bush near Coonabarabran and periods in Koori areas of Sydney. She is active in Aboriginal politics and works at Redfern's Aboriginal Medical Service.

EVE LANGLEY (1908-1974) was born in New South Wales, and followed her family around that state and to various Victorian towns before heading for New Zealand in 1930. After her marriage there she returned to Australia, mixing with the Sydney literati for a short time. She later became a recluse living in a bush shack near Katoomba, dressing in masculine clothes, and claiming Oscar Wilde as an alter ego.

LOUISE MACK (1874-1935) was born in Hobart, and as a child lived in Adelaide and Sydney. At Sydney Girls' High she edited the school magazine, and later wrote for the *Bulletin* before leaving for London in 1901. She lived for some time in Italy, editing a newspaper for the English residents of Florence, and was in Belgium when World War I was declared. Best known for her children's books, she also published several novels for adults and wrote about her experiences in London, Antwerp and Brussels.

OLGA MASTERS (1919-1986) was born on the south coast of New South Wales and worked for many years on suburban and country newspapers. After raising seven children she began publishing fiction when she was in her fifties. She travelled extensively within Australia on tours related to her writing and in 1985 went to Russia as part of a writers' delegation from the Literature Board of the Australia Council.

GILLIAN MEARS (1964-) spent her childhood on the north coast of New South Wales and studied Communications at the New South Wales Institute of Technology. Her one novel and two short story collections have all been prize-winners. Mears has recently lived in Africa and has been a resident of the Keesing studio, Paris.

DRUSILLA MODJESKA (1946-) was born in London and educated in England. She lived in New Guinea for three years before coming to Australia in 1971. Her doctoral thesis on Australian women writers of the early twentieth century was published in 1981, and she is a frequent reviewer. Modjeska has lectured in writing and textual studies and is also a book editor.

NETTIE PALMER (1885-1964) graduated from the University of Melbourne in 1912, and spent some years travelling and studying in London, Marburg and Paris. Her marriage to Vance Palmer in 1914 began a remarkable literary and travelling partnership. She fostered the development of many Australian women writers, worked for socialism, and her literary journalism, poetry, memoirs, letters and journals and critical studies were widely published.

HENRY HANDEL RICHARDSON (Ethel Robertson; 1870-1946) was born in Melbourne where her father was a physician. After his death in 1879, she lived in country towns in Victoria where her mother worked as a postmistress. She went to boarding school in Melbourne, and then travelled to Europe with her mother and sister to continue an already impressive musical career. Studying in Leipzig, she married a Scottish doctoral student and discovered the stimulating world of European letters, ultimately abandoning music for writing.

BETTY ROLAND (1903-) left school at seventeen to become a journalist. Her first play, *A Touch of Silk*, was performed by the Melbourne Repertory Company in 1929. After the failure of her first marriage, Roland went to Russia with her lover, where she worked as a translator and journalist. Returning to Australia, she joined the Communist Party, and wrote political plays and sketches. For a time she was involved in Justus Jorgensen's attempt to create an artistic community at Eltham, outside Melbourne, although her independent nature doomed her involvement to certain failure.

GEORGIA SAVAGE was born in Tasmania. In the late 1950s she moved to Victoria and worked on grape-growing properties. She travelled to Queensland in 1980 where she spent four years on the Gold Coast, and now writes full-time in Melbourne.

CHRISTINA STEAD (1902-1983) spent most of her life in Europe and the USA, although she was born and educated in Australia and returned in 1974. Leaving her childhood home at Watson's Bay in 1928, she headed for London. After her marriage to Marxist banker and writer William Blake, she worked for five years in Paris. The couple then lived in the United States, where Stead taught in New York.